Level 1

PAINTING & DECORATING

NVQ/SVQ & DIPLOMA

carillion

www.pearsonschoolsandfecolleges.co.uk

✓ Free online support
✓ Useful weblinks
✓ 24 hour online ordering

0845 630 44 44

Heinemann

Part of Pearson

Heinemann is an imprint of Pearson Education Limited, Edinburgh Gate, Harlow, Essex, CM20 2JE.

www.pearsonschoolsandfecolleges.co.uk

Heinemann is a registered trademark of Pearson Education Limited

Text © Carillion Construction Ltd 2011
Typeset by Brian Melville
Original illustrations © Pearson Education Ltd
Illustrated by Oxford Designers and Illustrators/Pearson
Copyright 2011
Cover design by Wooden Ark

First published 2011

14 13 12 11
10 9 8 7 6 5 4 3 2

British Library Cataloguing in Publication Data
A catalogue record for this book is available from the British Library

ISBN 978 0 435 04833 4

Printed and bound in Spain by Grafos

Websites
There are links to relevant websites in this book. In order to ensure that the links are up-to-date, that the links work, and that the sites are not inadvertently linked to sites that could be considered offensive, we have made the links available on our website at www.pearsonhotlinks.co.uk. Search for Diploma Painting and Decorating Candidate Handbook or 9780435048334.

Acknowledgements

The publisher would like to thank the following for their kind permission to reproduce their photographs:

(Key: b-bottom; c-centre; l-left; r-right; t-top)

Alamy Images: B E Eyley Construction Images 143b, BuildPix 158t, Dan Atkin 142c, David J Green 46, Gabe Palmer 164/3, Geoff du Feu 64, Image Source Pink 22t, Justin Kase 27, 101b, Nic Hamilton 3, Photolibrary Wales 23, Red Cover 156, Ted Foxx 205, Westend61 GmbH 142tl; **Construction Photography:** BuildPix 15, 101t, Chris Henderson 7, 92, Cultura 85, David Potter 99, 108, David Stewart-Smith 100, Ken Price 45r, Ray Hardinge 125, Sally-Ann Norman 45l, Xavier de Canto 12, 105, 142tr, Xavier de Canto 12, 105, 142tr; **Corbis:** 107c; **CSCS:** 14; **Doug Bardwell:** 187/6; **Getty Images:** PhotoDisc 107t; **Graham Hare:** 157t; **Pearson Education Ltd:** Chris Honeywell 49/1, David Sanderson 50t, 50b, 52/2, 52/3, 52/4, 52b, Gareth Boden 21, 31tl, 31tr, 31bl, 31bc, 31br, 36t, 36c, 36b, 41, 42, 43, 52/1, 93, 96, 128/1, 128/4, 129/1, 129/2, 129/3, 129/4, 129/5, 129/6, 130/2, 130/3, 130/4, 131, 133t, 133b, 135/1, 135/2, 135/3, 135/4, 136, 137, 146, 158b, 161, 163t, 163c, 163b, 164/1, 164/2, 164/5, 164/6, 164/7, 165t, 165c, 165b, 166t, 166c, 166b, 169b, 179, 186t, 186c, 186bl, 186br, 187/3, 187/4, 187/5, 187/7, 188/1, 188/2, 188/3, 188/4, 188/5, 190, 207, 209, 210t, 210bl, 210br, 212/4, 212/5, Jules Selmes 132, 149t, 149c, 149b, Naki Photography 19, 130/1, 130/5, 147l, 147c, 147r, 164/4, 169t, 169c, 170, 171t, 171b, 187/2, 193, 199, 212/1, 212/3, 213; **Photolibrary.com:** Age Fotostock 153; **Robert Clare:** 142b, 212/2; **Science Photo Library Ltd:** Gerry Weston 28t, Paul Rapson 157b, Scott Camazine 22b; **Shutterstock.com:** Abramov Dmytro 185, Alex Kosev 48, Andrey Bayda 28c, Chiran Vlad Page design/1, Chiran Vlad Page design/1, design65 49/2, Edd Westmacott 49/5, 128/3, Frances A. Miller 44, Guy Erwood 107b, IOFoto 49/3, Joachim Wendler 187/1, mast3r 24, Megumi Ito 1, picamaniac Page design/2, Rob Byron 49/4, Sebastian Duda 57, stevanovic.igor 128/2, StillFX 49/6, Yabidaba 28b, Yuri Arcurs 14 (inset); **Will Burwell:** 143t; **www.imagesource.com:** 89

Cover images: Front: **Getty Images**: Photographer's Choice

All other images © Pearson Education

Picture Research by: Chrissie Martin

Every effort has been made to trace the copyright holders and we apologise in advance for any unintentional omissions. We would be pleased to insert the appropriate acknowledgement in any subsequent edition of this publication.

Contents

Introduction

Welcome to NVQ/SVQ CAA Diploma Level 1 Painting and Decorating!

Painting and Decorating combines many different practical and visual skills with a knowledge of specialised materials and techniques. This book will introduce you to the construction trade and covers the knowledge you will need to begin work at height, prepare surfaces, complete specialist decorative effects and work with surface coverings such as paint and paper.

About this book

This book has been produced to help you build a sound knowledge and understanding of all aspects of the Diploma and NVQ requirements associated with painting and decorating.

The information in this book covers what you will need to attain your Level 1 qualification in Painting and Decorating. Each chapter of the book relates to a particular unit of the CAA Diploma and provides the information needed to form the required knowledge and understanding of that area. The book is also designed to support those undertaking the NVQ at Level 1.

This book has been written based on a concept used with Carillion Training Centres for many years. The concept is about providing learners with the necessary information they need to support their studies and at the same time ensuring the information is presented in a style that is both manageable and relevant.

This book will also be a useful reference tool for you in your professional life once you have gained your qualifications and are a practising painter and decorator.

This introduction will introduce the construction industry and the qualifications you can find in it, alongside the qualifications available.

About the construction industry

Construction means creating buildings and services. These might be houses, hospitals, schools, offices, roads, bridges, museums, prisons, train stations, airports, monuments – and anything else you can think of that needs designing and building! What about an Olympic stadium? The 2012 London games will bring a wealth of construction opportunity to the UK and so it is an exciting time to be getting involved.

In the UK, 2.2 million people work in the construction industry – more than in any other – and it is constantly expanding and developing. There are more choices and opportunities than ever before. Your career doesn't have to end in the UK either – what about taking the skills and experience you are developing abroad? Construction is a career you can take with you wherever you go. There's always going to be something that needs building!

The construction industry is made up of countless companies and businesses which all provide different services and materials. An easy way to divide these companies into categories is according to their size.

- A small company is defined as having between 1 and 49 members of staff.
- A medium company consists of between 50 and 249 members of staff.
- A large company has 250 or more people working for it.

A business might even consist of only a single member of staff (a sole trader).

Different types of construction work

There are four main types of construction work:

new work – this refers to a building that is about to be or has just been built

maintenance work – this is when an existing building is kept up to an acceptable standard by fixing anything that is damaged so that it does not fall into disrepair

refurbishment/renovation work – this generally refers to an existing building that has fallen into a state of disrepair and is then brought up to standard by repair work being carried out. It also refers to an existing building that is to be used for a different purpose, for example changing an old bank into a pub

restoration work – this refers to an existing building that has fallen into a state of disrepair and is then brought back to its original condition or use.

These four types of work can fall into one of two categories depending upon who is paying for the work:

- **public** – work that is paid for by the government, as is the case with most schools and hospitals, etc.
- **private** – work that is paid for by a private client and can range from extensions on existing houses to new houses or buildings.

Jobs and careers

Jobs and careers in the construction industry fall mainly into one of four categories:

- **building** – the physical construction (making) of a structure. It also involves the maintenance, restoration and refurbishment of structures

- **civil engineering** – the construction and maintenance of work such as roads, railways, bridges etc.
- **electrical engineering** – the installation and maintenance of electrical systems and devices such as lights, power sockets and electrical appliances etc.
- **mechanical engineering** – the installation and maintenance of things such as heating, ventilation and lifts.

The category that is the most relevant to your course is building.

What is a building?

There are of course lots of very different types of building, but the main types are:

- **residential** – houses, flats etc.
- **commercial** – shops, supermarkets etc.
- **industrial** – warehouses, factories etc.

These types of building can be further broken down by the height or number of storeys that they have (one storey being the level from floor to ceiling):

- **low-rise** – a building with one to three storeys
- **medium-rise** – a building with four to seven storeys
- **high-rise** – a building with seven storeys or more.

Buildings can also be categorised according to the number of other buildings they are attached to:

- **detached** – a building that stands alone and is not connected to any other building
- **semi-detached** – a building that is joined to one other building and shares a dividing wall, called a party wall
- **terraced** – a row of three or more buildings that are joined together, of which the inner buildings share two party walls.

Building requirements

Every building must meet the minimum requirements of the building reulations. The purpose of building regulations is to ensure that safe and healthy buildings are constructed for the public and that conservation (the preservation of the environment and the wildlife) is taken into account when they are being constructed. Building regulations enforce a minimum standard of building work and ensure that the materials used are of a good standard and fit for purpose.

What makes a good building?

When a building is designed, there are certain things that need to be taken into consideration, such as:

- security
- warmth
- safety

- light
- privacy
- ventilation.

A well-designed building will meet the minimum standards for all of the considerations above and will also be built in line with building regulations.

Qualifications for the construction industry

There are many ways of entering the construction industry, but the most common method is as an apprentice.

Apprenticeships

You can become an apprentice by being employed:

- directly by a construction company which will send you to college
- by a training provider, such as Carillion, which combines construction training with practical work experience.

ConstructionSkills is the national training organisation for construction in the UK and is responsible for setting training standards.

The framework of an apprenticeship is based around an NVQ (or SVQ in Scotland). These qualifications are developed and approved by industry experts and will measure your practical skills and job knowledge on-site.

You will also need to achieve:

- a technical certificate
- the ConstructionSkills health and safety test
- the appropriate level of functional skills assessment
- an Employers' Rights and Responsibilities briefing.

You will also need to achieve the right qualifications to get on a construction site, including qualifying for the CSCS card scheme (see page 14).

CAA Diploma

The Construction Awards Alliance (CAA) Diploma was launched on 1 August 2008 to replace Construction Awards. They aim to make you:

- more skilled and knowledgeable
- more confident with moving across projects, contracts and employers.

The CAA Diploma is a common testing strategy with knowledge tests for each unit, a practical assignment and the Global Online Assessment (GOLA) test.

The CAA Diploma meets the requirements of the new Qualifications and Credit Framework (QCF) which bases a qualification on the number of credits (with ten learning hours gaining one credit):

- Award (1 to 12 credits)
- Certificate (13 to 36 credits)
- Diploma (37+ credits)

As part of the CAA Diploma you will gain the skills needed for the NVQ as well as the functional skills knowledge you will need to complete your qualification.

National Vocational Qualifications (NVQs)

NVQs are available to anyone, with no restrictions on age, length or type of training, although learners below a certain age can only perform certain tasks. There are different levels of NVQ (for example 1, 2, 3), which in turn are broken down into units of competence. NVQs are not like traditional examinations in which someone sits an exam paper. An NVQ is a 'doing' qualification, which means it lets the industry know that you have the knowledge, skills and ability to actually 'do' something.

NVQs are made up of both mandatory and optional units and the number of units that you need to complete for an NVQ depends on the level and the occupation.

NVQs are assessed in the workplace, and several types of evidence are used:

- witness testimony provided by individuals who have first-hand knowledge of your work and performance relating to the NVQ
- your performance can be observed a number of times in the workplace
- historical evidence means that you can use evidence from past achievements or experience, if it is directly related to the NVQ
- assignments or projects can be used to assess your knowledge and understanding
- photographic evidence showing you performing various tasks in the workplace can be used, providing it is authenticated by your supervisor.

Functional Skills

Throughout this book you will find references to Functional Skills.

Functional skills are processes of representing, analysing and interpreting information. They are the skills needed to work independently in everyday life and are transferable to any given context. We will focus on the mathematics and English skills specifically in a construction context, so that you can identify and practise them by working through the units of the book. The references are headed **FM** for mathematics and **FE** for English. You will also use speaking and listening skills in your learning, which will support you through the programme. If you have any questions on how the skills fit into your learning, please speak to your tutor(s).

Carillion would like to thank Stephen Olsen and Kevin Jarvis for their hard work and dedication in preparing the content of this book. Carillion would like to thank John McLaughlin Harvie for preparing Functional Skills references.

Pearson Education Limited would like to thank Brian Bibby and Nicole Simpson of Furness College and John Spalding of Fareham College for the excellent technical feedback.

Introduction

Functional skills

This feature is designed to support you with your functional skills, by identifying opportunities in your work where you will be able to practise your functional skills.

Features of this book

This book has been fully illustrated with artworks and photographs. These will help to give you more information about a concept or a procedure, as well as helping you to follow a step-by-step procedure or identify a tool or material.

This book also contains a number of different features to help your learning and development.

Remember

This highlights key facts or concepts, sometimes from earlier in the text, to remind you of important things you will need to think about

Did you know?

This feature gives you interesting facts about the building trade

Safety tip

This feature gives you guidance for working safely on the tasks in this book

Find out

These are short activities and research opportunities, designed to help you gain further information about, and understanding of, a topic area

Key term

These are new or difficult words. They are picked out in **bold** in the text and then defined in the margin

Working life

This feature gives you a chance to read about and debate a real-life work scenario or problem. Why has the situation occurred? What would you do?

FAQ

These are frequently asked questions appearing at the end of each unit to answer your questions with informative answers from the experts

Check it out

A series of questions at the end of each unit to check your understanding. Some of these questions may support the collecting of evidence for the NVQ

Getting ready for assessment

This feature provides guidance for preparing for the practical assessment. It will give you advice on using the theory you have learned about in a practical way

Check your knowledge

This is a series of multiple choice questions in the style of the GOLA end of unit tests at the end of each unit.

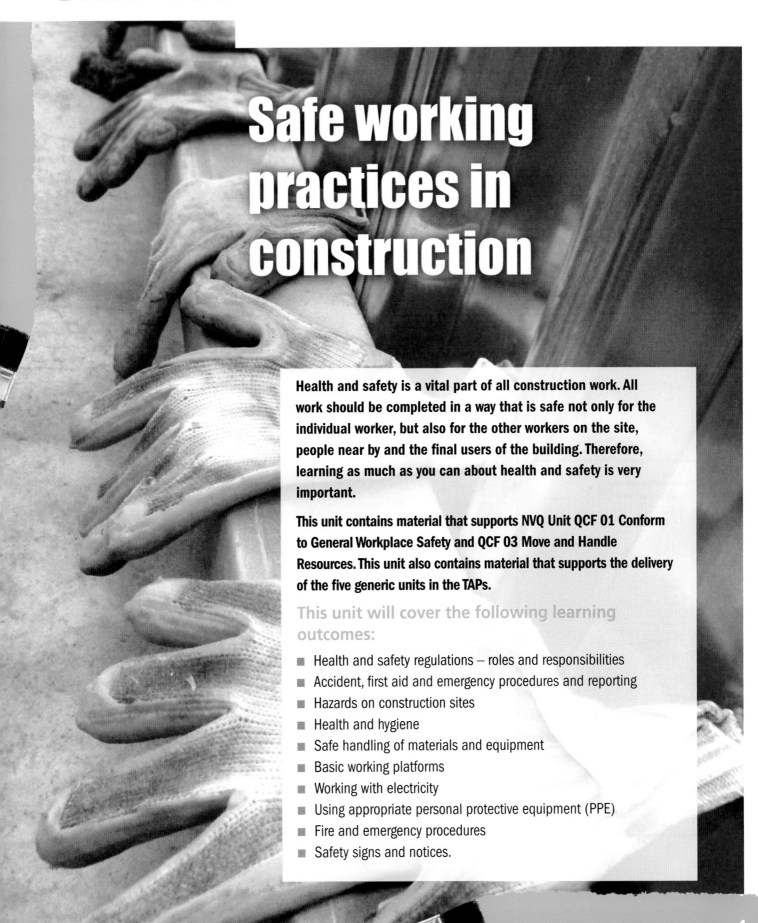

UNIT 1001

Safe working practices in construction

Health and safety is a vital part of all construction work. All work should be completed in a way that is safe not only for the individual worker, but also for the other workers on the site, people near by and the final users of the building. Therefore, learning as much as you can about health and safety is very important.

This unit contains material that supports NVQ Unit QCF 01 Conform to General Workplace Safety and QCF 03 Move and Handle Resources. This unit also contains material that supports the delivery of the five generic units in the TAPs.

This unit will cover the following learning outcomes:

- Health and safety regulations – roles and responsibilities
- Accident, first aid and emergency procedures and reporting
- Hazards on construction sites
- Health and hygiene
- Safe handling of materials and equipment
- Basic working platforms
- Working with electricity
- Using appropriate personal protective equipment (PPE)
- Fire and emergency procedures
- Safety signs and notices.

Key terms

Legislation – a law or set of laws passed by Parliament, often called an Act

Hazardous – something or a situation that is dangerous or unsafe

Employer – the person or company you work for

Employee – the worker

Key terms

Proactive – acting in advance, before something happens (such as an accident)

Reactive – acting after something happens, in response to it

Functional skills

When reading and understanding the text in this unit, you are practising several functional skills:

FE 1.2.1 – Identifying how the main points and ideas are organised in different texts

FE 1.2.2 – Understanding different texts in detail

FE 1.2.3 – Read different texts and take appropriate action, e.g. respond to advice/ instructions

If there are any words or phrases you do not understand, use a dictionary, look them up using the Internet or discuss with your tutor.

K1. Health and safety regulations – roles and responsibilities

While at work, whatever your location or the type of work you are doing, there is important **legislation** you must comply with. Health and safety legislation is there not just to protect you – it also states what you must and must not do to ensure that no workers are placed in a situation **hazardous** to themselves or others.

There are hundreds of Acts covering all manner of work from hairdressing to construction. Each Act states the duties of the **employer** and **employee** – you should be aware of both. If an employer or employee does something they shouldn't – or doesn't do something they should – they can end up in court and be fined or even imprisoned.

Approved code of practice, guidance notes and safety policies

As well as Acts, there are two sorts of codes of practice and guidance notes: those produced by the Health and Safety Executive (HSE; see page 5), and those created by companies themselves. Most large construction companies – and many smaller ones – have their own guidance notes, which go further than health and safety law. For example, the law states that everyone must wear safety boots in a hazardous area, but a company's code may state that everyone must wear safety boots at all times. This is called taking a **proactive** approach, rather than a **reactive** one.

Most companies have some form of safety policy outlining the company's commitment and stating what they plan to do to ensure that all work is carried out as safely as possible. As an employee, you should make sure you understand the company's safety policy as well as its codes of practice. If you don't follow company policy you may not be prosecuted in court, but you could still be disciplined by the company or even fired.

Health and safety legislation

There are some 20 pieces of legislation you will need to be aware of, each of which sets out requirements for employers and often for employees.

We will now look at the regulations that will affect you most.

The Health and Safety at Work Act 1974 (HASAWA)

HASAWA applies to all types and places of work and to employers, employees, self-employed people, **subcontractors** and even **suppliers**. The Act is there to protect not only the people at work, but also the general public, who may be affected in some way by the work that has been or will be carried out.

Figure 1.1 Legislation is there to protect employees and the public alike

The main objectives of the Health and Safety at Work Act are to:

- ensure the health, safety and welfare of all persons at work
- protect the general public from all work activities
- control the use, handling, storage and transportation of explosives and highly **flammable** substances
- control the release of noxious or offensive substances into the atmosphere.

To ensure that these objectives are met there are duties for all employers, employees and suppliers.

The employer's duties

Employers must:

- provide safe **access** and **egress** to and within the work area
- provide a safe place to work
- provide and maintain plant and machinery that is safe and without risks to health
- provide information, instruction, training and supervision to ensure the health and safety at work of all employees

Key terms

Subcontractors – workers who have been hired by the main contractor to carry out works, usually specialist works, e.g. a general builder may hire a plumber as a subcontractor as none of their staff can do plumbing work

Supplier – a company that supplies goods, materials or services

Did you know?

One phrase that often comes up in the legislation is 'so far as is reasonably practicable'. This means that health and safety must be adhered to at all times, but must take a common-sense, practical approach.
The Health and Safety at Work Act 1974 states that an employer must 'so far as is reasonably practicable' ensure that a safe place of work is provided. Yet employers are not expected to do everything they can to protect their staff from lightning strikes, as there is only a 1 in 800,000 chance of this occurring – this would not be reasonable!

Key terms

Flammable – something that is easily lit and burns rapidly

Access – entrance, a way in

Egress – exit, a way out

Key terms

Risk assessment – this means measuring the dangers of an activity against the likelihood of accidents taking place

PPE – personal protective equipment such as gloves, a safety harness or goggles

Omission – something that has not been done or has been missed out

Obligation – something you have a duty or a responsibility to do

- ensure safety and the absence of risks to health in connection with the handling, storage and transportation of articles and substances
- have a written safety policy that must be revised and updated regularly, and ensure all employees are aware of it
- involve trade union safety representatives, where appointed, in all matters relating to health and safety
- carry out **risk assessments** (see page 23) and provide supervision where necessary
- provide and not charge for personal protective equipment (**PPE**; see pages 48–50).

The employee's duties

Employees must:

- take reasonable care for their own health and safety
- take reasonable care for the health and safety of anyone who may be affected by their acts or **omissions**
- co-operate with their employer or any other person to ensure legal **obligations** are met
- not misuse or interfere with anything provided for their health and safety
- report hazards and accidents (see pages 15–18)
- use any equipment and safeguards provided by their employer.

Employers can't charge their employees for anything that has been done or provided for them to ensure that legal requirements on health and safety are met. Self-employed people and subcontractors have the same duties as employees. If they have employees of their own, they must also obey the duties set down for employers.

The supplier's duties

Persons designing, manufacturing, importing or supplying articles or substances for use at work must ensure that:

- articles are designed and constructed so that they will be safe and without risk to health at all times while they are being used or constructed
- substances will be safe and without risk to health at all times when being used, handled, transported and stored
- tests on articles and substances are carried out as necessary
- adequate information is provided about the use, handling, transporting and storing of articles or substances.

Health and Safety Executive (HSE)

HASAWA, like most of the other Acts mentioned, is enforced by the HSE.

The HSE is the government body responsible for the encouragement, regulation and enforcement of health, safety and welfare in the workplace in the UK. It also has responsibility for research into occupational risks in England, Wales and Scotland. In Northern Ireland the responsibility lies with the Health and Safety Executive for Northern Ireland.

The HSE's duties are to:

- assist and encourage anyone who has any dealings with the objectives of HASAWA
- produce and encourage research, publications, training and information on health and safety at work
- ensure that employers, employees, suppliers and other people are provided with an information and advisory service, and are kept informed and advised on any health and safety matters
- propose regulations
- enforce HASAWA.

To aid in theses duties the HSE has several resources, including a laboratory used for, among other things, research, development and **forensic** investigation into the causes of accidents. The enforcement of HASAWA is usually delegated to local government bodies such as county or district councils or an **enforcing authority**.

An enforcing authority may appoint **inspectors**, who, under the authority, have the power to:

- enter any premises which she or he has reason to believe it is necessary to enter to enforce the Act, at any reasonable time, or in a dangerous situation
- bring a police officer if there is reasonable cause to fear any serious obstruction in carrying out their duty
- bring any other person authorised by the enforcing authority, and any equipment or materials required
- examine and investigate any circumstance that is necessary for the purpose of enforcing the Act
- give orders that the premises, any part of them or anything therein, shall be left undisturbed for so long as is needed for the purpose of any examination or investigation

Did you know?

The HSE now also includes the Health and Safety Commission (HSC), which was merged with it in 2008

Key terms

Forensics – a branch of science that looks at how accidents/incidents happen

Enforcing authorities – organisations or people who have the authority to enforce certain laws or Acts, as well as providing guidance or advice

Inspector – someone who is appointed or employed to inspect/examine something in order to judge its quality or compliance with any laws

- take measurements, photographs and make any recordings considered necessary for the purpose of examination or investigation
- take samples of any articles or substances found and of the atmosphere in or in the vicinity of the premises
- have an article or substance which appears to be a danger to health or safety dismantled, tested or even destroyed if necessary
- take possession of a hazardous article and retain it for so long as is necessary in order to examine it and ensure that it is not tampered with and that it is available for use as evidence in any **prosecution**
- interview any person believed to have information, ask any questions the inspector thinks fit to ask and ensure all statements are signed as a declaration of the truth of the answers
- require the production of, inspect and take copies of any entry in any book or document necessary for the purposes of any examination or investigation
- any other power which is necessary to enforce the Act.

Key term

Prosecution – accusing someone of committing a crime, which usually results in the accused being taken to court and, if found guilty, being punished

Contacting the Health and Safety Executive

Employers, self-employed people or someone in control of work premises have legal duties to record and report to the HSE some work-related accidents. Incidents that must be reported are:

- **Death** – where someone is killed as a result of an accident related to work. This includes deaths resulting from physical violence.
- **Major injury** – this includes fractures, amputations, loss of sight and loss of consciousness.
- **Dangerous occurrence** – this is an event that may not have caused injury, but clearly could have done so. For example, some kinds of fire or explosion, collapse of buildings or scaffolding.
- **Over-three-day injury** – this is where someone suffers an injury at work that results in them being away from work or unable to do their full duties for more than three consecutive days.
- **Disease** – this is where a doctor notifies the person that they are suffering from some work-related disease.

Reporting of Injuries, Diseases and Dangerous Occurrences Regulations 1995 (RIDDOR)

Under RIDDOR, employers have a duty to report accidents, diseases or dangerous occurrences. The HSE uses this information to identify where and how risk arises and to investigate serious accidents.

Control of Substances Hazardous to Health Regulations 2002 (COSHH)

These regulations state how employees and employers should work with, handle, store, transport and dispose of potentially hazardous substances (substances that might adversely affect your health) including:

- substances used directly in work activities (e.g. adhesives or paints)
- substances generated during work activities (e.g. dust from sanding wood)
- naturally occurring substances (e.g. sand dust)
- biological agents (e.g. germs such as bacteria).

These substances can be found in nearly all work environments.

The Control of Noise at Work Regulations 2005

At some point in your career in construction, you are likely to work in a noisy working environment. These regulations help protect you against the consequences of being exposed to high levels of noise. High levels of noise can lead to permanent hearing damage. These regulations state that the employer must:

- assess the risks to the employee from noise at work
- take action to reduce the noise exposure that produces these risks
- provide employees with hearing protection or, if this is impossible, reduce the risk by other methods
- make sure the legal limits on noise exposure are not exceeded
- provide employees with information, instruction and training
- carry out **health surveillance** where there is a risk to health.

> **Remember**
>
> All hazardous substances are covered by COSHH regulations, except asbestos and lead paint, which have their own regulations

Figure 1.2 Noise at work

> **Key term**
>
> **Health surveillance** – where a company will assess the risks of tasks that are to be done and see if these task will create risks to health

The Electricity at Work Regulations 1989

These regulations cover any work involving the use of electricity or electrical equipment. An employer has the duty to ensure that the electrical systems their employees come into contact with are safe and regularly maintained. They must also have done everything the law states to reduce the risk of their employees coming into contact with live electrical currents.

Construction (Design and Management) Regulations 2007

The Construction (Design and Management) Regulations 2007, often referred to as CDM, are important regulations in the construction industry. They were introduced by the HSE's Construction Division. The regulations deal mainly with the construction industry and aim to improve safety.

The duties for employers under the regulations are to:

- plan, manage and monitor own work and that of workers
- check competence of all their appointees and workers
- train their employees
- provide information to their workers
- comply with the specific requirements in Part 4 of the regulations, which deals with lighting, excavations, traffic routes, etc.
- ensure there are adequate welfare facilities for their workers.

The duties for employees are to:

- check their own competence
- co-operate with others and co-ordinate work so as to ensure the health and safety of construction workers and others who may be affected by the work
- report obvious risks.

The CDM also requires certain duties from the clients (with the exception of domestic clients). These duties are to:

- check competence and resources of all appointees
- ensure there are suitable management arrangements for the project welfare facilities
- allow sufficient time and resources for all stages
- provide pre-construction information to designers and contractors.

There is a general expectation by the HSE that all parties involved in a project will co-operate and co-ordinate with each other.

Remember

On large projects, a person is appointed as the CDM co-ordinator. This person has overall responsibility for compliance with CDM

Provision and Use of Work Equipment Regulations 1998 (PUWER)

These regulations cover all new or existing work equipment – leased, hired or second-hand. They apply in most working environments where the HASAWA applies, including all industrial, offshore and service operations.

PUWER covers starting, stopping, regular use, transport, repair, modification, servicing and cleaning.

The general duties of the Act require equipment to be:

- suitable for its intended purpose and only to be used in suitable conditions
- maintained in an efficient state and maintenance records kept
- used, repaired and maintained only by a suitably trained person, when that equipment poses a particular risk
- able to be isolated from all its sources of energy
- constructed or adapted to ensure that maintenance can be carried out without risks to health and safety
- fitted with warnings or warning devices as appropriate.

In addition, the Act requires:

- all those who use, supervise or manage work equipment to be suitably trained
- access to any dangerous parts of the machinery to be prevented or controlled
- injury to be prevented from any work equipment that may have a very high or low temperature
- suitable controls to be provided for starting and stopping the work equipment
- suitable emergency stopping systems and braking systems to be fitted to ensure the work equipment is brought to a safe condition as soon as reasonably practicable
- suitable and sufficient lighting to be provided for operating the work equipment.

Manual Handling Operations Regulations 1992

These regulations cover all work activities in which a person rather than a machine does the lifting. The regulations state that, wherever possible, manual handling should be avoided, but where this is unavoidable, a risk assessment should be done.

> **Did you know?**
>
> 'Work equipment' includes any machinery, appliance, apparatus or tool, and any assembly of components that are used in non-domestic premises. Dumper trucks, circular saws, ladders, overhead projectors and chisels would all be included, but substances, private cars and structural items fall outside this definition

Unit 1001

Safe working practices in construction

In a risk assessment, there are four considerations:

- **Load** – is it heavy, sharp-edged, difficult to hold?
- **Individual** – is the individual small, pregnant, in need of training?
- **Task** – does the task require holding goods away from the body, or repetitive twisting?
- **Environment** – is the floor uneven, are there stairs, is it raining?

After the assessment, the situation must be monitored constantly and updated or changed if necessary.

Personal Protective Equipment at Work Regulations 1992 (PPER)

These regulations cover all types of PPE, from gloves to breathing apparatus. After doing a risk assessment and once the potential hazards are known, suitable types of PPE can be selected. PPE should be checked prior to issue by a trained and competent person and in line with the manufacturer's instructions. Where required, the employer must provide PPE free of charge along with a suitable and secure place to store it.

The employer must ensure that the employee knows:

- the risks the PPE will avoid or reduce
- its purpose and use
- how to maintain and look after it
- its limitations.

The employee must:

- ensure that they are trained in the use of the PPE prior to use
- use it in line with the employer's instructions
- return it to storage after use
- take care of it, and report any loss or defect to their employer.

Work at Height Regulations 2005

Construction workers often work high off the ground, on scaffolding, ladders or roofs. These regulations make sure that employers do all that they can to reduce the risk of injury or death from working at height.

The employer has a duty to:

- avoid work at height where possible
- use any equipment or safeguards that will prevent falls
- use equipment and any other methods that will minimise the distance and consequences of a fall.

As an employee, you must follow any training given to you, report any hazards to your supervisor and use any safety equipment provided to you.

Other Acts to be aware of

You should also be aware of the following pieces of legislation:

- The Fire Precautions (Workplace) Regulations 1997
- The Fire Precautions Act 1991
- The Highly Flammable Liquids and Liquid Petroleum Gases Regulations 1972
- The Lifting Operations and Lifting Equipment Regulations 1998
- The Construction (Health, Safety and Welfare) Regulations 1996
- The Environmental Protection Act 1990
- The Confined Spaces Regulations 1997
- The Working Time Regulations 1998
- The Health and Safety (First Aid) Regulations 1981.

You can find out more at the library or online.

Sources of health and safety information

Health and safety is a large and varied subject that changes regularly. The introduction of new regulations or updates to current legislation means it's often hard to remember or keep up to date. Your tutor will be able to give you information on current legislation.

Your employer should also keep you updated on any changes to legislation that will affect you. You can also access other sources of information to keep you informed.

Health and Safety Executive

The HSE has a wide range of information ranging from the actual legislation documents to helpful guides to working safely. Videos, leaflets and documents are available to download free from its website. Specific sections of the website are dedicated to different industries ranging from agriculture to hairdressing. The specific construction website address is www.hse.gov.uk/construction.

ConstructionSkills

ConstructionSkills mainly offers advice on qualifications in construction. However, it also has advice on health and

Find out

Look into the other regulations listed here via the HSE website. A link to this website has been made available at www. pearsonhotlinks.co.uk

Remember

Legislation can change or be updated. New legislation can be created as well – this could even supersede all pieces of legislation safety matters and on sitting the CSCS (Construction Skills Certification Scheme) health and safety test as well as providing a way of booking the test. A link to the website has been made available at www.pearsonhotlinks.co.uk.

Royal Society for the Prevention of Accidents (RoSPA)

RoSPA provides information, advice, resources and training. RoSPA is actively involved in the promotion of safety and the prevention of accidents in all areas of life – at work, in the home, on the roads, in schools, at leisure and on (or near) water. A link to the website has been made available at www. pearsonhotlinks.co.uk.

Royal Society for the Promotion of Health (RSPH)

The Royal Society for the Promotion of Health aims to promote and protect health and well-being. It uses **advocacy**, mediation, knowledge and practice to advise on policy development. It also provides education and training services, encourages research, communicates information and provides certification to products, training centres and processes.

RSPH's main focus is people working in healthcare, for example doctors. It publishes two monthly newsletters:

- Public health
- Perspectives on Public Health

Site inductions

Site **induction** is the process that an individual undergoes in order to accelerate their awareness of the potential health and safety hazards and risks they may face in their working environment. Site induction doesn't include job-related skills training.

Different site inductions will include different topics, depending on the work that is being carried out. The basic information that should be included in inductions will cover:

- the scope of operations carried out at the site, project, etc.
- the activities that have health and safety hazards and risks
- the control measures in place
- emergency arrangements
- local organisation and management structure

> **Key terms**
>
> **Advocacy** – actively supporting or arguing for
>
> **Induction** – a formal introduction you will receive when you start any new job, where you will be shown around, shown where the toilets and canteen etc. are, and told what to do if there is a fire

Figure 1.3 A site induction talk

- consultation procedures
- the resource for health and safety advice
- the welfare arrangements
- a zero tolerance approach to health and safety risks at work
- the process for reporting near misses (see page 17).

Inductions are also vital for informing all people working on the site of amenities, restricted areas, dress code (PPE) and even evacuation procedures. Inductions must be carried out by a competent person. Records of all inductions must be kept to ensure that all workers have received an induction. Some sites will even hand out cards to those who have been inducted and people without cards will not be admitted to the site.

Visitors to the site who may not be actually doing any work should still receive an induction of sorts as they also need to be aware of amenities, restricted areas and procedures etc.

Toolbox talks

Toolbox talks are used by management, supervisors and employees to deliver basic training and/or to inform all workers of any updates to policy, hazardous activities/areas or any other information.

Toolbox talk topics should be relevant to the people they are being delivered to (there is no point delivering a talk on plumbing systems to bricklayers unless it directly affects them!). The topics can vary from being informative, such as letting everyone know a reclassification of a PPE area, to basic training on the use of a certain tool.

They should be delivered by a competent person and a record of all attendees should be kept.

> **Remember**
>
> A site induction must take place *before* you start work on that site

> **Working life**
>
> Alex and Molly have been asked to attend a toolbox talk on scaffolding safety. They had both attended a toolbox talk on the same subject just over a week ago. Molly thinks they should attend this talk too as it could be important. However, Alex thinks it's a mistake and that it will be the same as the last one. Molly agrees that they are very busy and that if they don't attend they can get the job they are doing finished on time; but she is concerned about missing the talk.
>
> - Why could Alex and Molly be asked to attend if they had a similar titled toolbox talk recently?
> - What could the outcome be if they do/don't attend?
> - What things could be discussed in a toolbox talk on scaffolding?

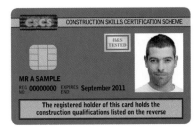

Figure 1.4 A CSCS card

> **Remember**
>
> The key legislation that controls the reporting of accidents is RIDDOR

Construction Skills Certification Scheme (CSCS)

The Construction Skills Certification Scheme was introduced to help improve the quality of work and to reduce accidents. It requires all workers to obtain a CSCS card before they are allowed to carry out work on a building site. There are various levels of card, which indicate your competence and skill background. This ensures that only skilled and safe tradespeople can carry out the required work on site.

To get a CSCS card all applicants must sit a health and safety test. The aim of the test is to examine knowledge across a wide range of topics to improve safety and productivity on site. You usually take the test as a PC-based touch screen test, either at a mobile testing unit or an accredited test centre. The type of card you apply for will determine the level of test that you need to take.

As a trainee, once you pass the health and safety test you will qualify for a trainee card. Once you have achieved a Level 2 qualification you can then upgrade your card to an experienced worker card. Achieving a Level 3 qualification allows you to apply for a gold card. People who make regular visits to sites can apply for a visitor card.

K2. Accident, first aid and emergency procedures and reporting

Major types of emergency

There are several types of major emergency that could occur on site. These include not only accidents but also:

- fires
- security alerts
- bomb scares.

At your site induction, it should be made perfectly clear to you what you should do in an emergency. You should also be aware of any sirens or warning noises that accompany each and every type of emergency, such as bomb scares or fire alarms. Some sites may have different variations on sirens or emergency procedures, so it is vital that you pay attention and listen to all the instructions. If you are unsure always ask.

Health and welfare in the construction industry

Jobs in the construction industry have one of the highest injury and accident rates. As a worker you will be at constant risk unless you adopt a good health and safety attitude. By following the rules and regulations set out to protect you and by taking reasonable care of yourself and others, you will become a safe worker and thus reduce the chance of any injuries or accidents.

Accidents

We often hear the saying 'accidents will happen', but when working in the construction industry, we should not accept that accidents just happen sometimes. When we think of an accident, we quite often think about it as being no one's fault and something that could not have been avoided. The truth is that most accidents are caused by human error, which means someone has done something they shouldn't have done or, just as importantly, not done something they should have done.

Accidents often happen when someone:

- is hurrying
- is not paying enough attention to what they are doing
- has not received the correct training.

Reporting accidents

When an accident occurs, there are certain things that must be done. All accidents need to be reported and recorded in the accident book. The injured person must report to a trained first aider to receive treatment. Serious accidents must be reported under RIDDOR.

Accidents and emergencies must be reported to the relevant authorised persons. These can be:

- **First aiders** – all accidents need to be reported to a first aider. If you are unsure who the first aiders are or have no direct way of contacting them, you must report it to your supervisor.
- **Supervisors** – you must inform your supervisor of any accident as it is vital that they can act immediately to inform the relevant first aider or their manager, and stop the work if necessary to prevent any further accidents.
- **Safety officers** – your supervisor or the site manager will alert the safety officer, who will assess the area to check if it is safe, investigate what may have caused the accident and prepare reports for the HSE (if needed).

Remember

Health and safety laws are there to protect you and other people. If you take shortcuts or ignore the rules, you are placing yourself and others at serious risk

Figure 1.5 Accidents can happen if your work area is untidy

Safe working practices in construction **Unit 1001**

Remember

An accident that falls under RIDDOR should be reported by the safety officer or site manager. It can be reported to the HSE by phone (0845 3009923) or via the RIDDOR website. A link to this website has been made available at www.pearsonhotlinks.co.uk

Safety tip

The emergency services would rather be called twice than not at all

Find out

Visit the NHS Choices website to find out more about these diseases, and other conditions that can be caused by the workplace. A link to this website has been made available at www. pearsonhotlinks.co.uk

- **HSE** – if death or major injury occurs to a member of staff or a member of the public is killed or taken to hospital the accident must be reported to the HSE immediately, and followed up by a written report within ten days. The written report is made on form F2508. If an employee suffers an 'over-three-day' injury it must be reported on the F2508 form within 10 days.
- **Managers** – managers should be informed by either the supervisor or safety officer as they may need to report to head office. They may also be the one tasked with contacting the HSE.
- **Emergency services** – the emergency services should be called as soon as possible. Usually the first aiders will call the ambulance and the supervisors will call the fire brigade, but if in doubt you should also call.

Under RIDDOR your employer must report to the HSE any accident that results in:

- death
- major injury
- an injury that means the injured person is not at work for more than three consecutive days
- disease.

Diseases that can be caused in the workplace include:

- certain poisonings
- some skin diseases – such as occupational dermatitis, skin cancer, chrome ulcer, oil folliculitis/acne
- lung diseases – including occupational asthma, farmer's lung, pneumoconiosis, asbestosis, mesothelioma
- infections – such as leptospirosis (see page 29), hepatitis, tuberculosis, anthrax, legionellosis and tetanus
- other conditions – such as occupational cancer, certain musculoskeletal disorders, decompression illness and hand–arm vibration syndrome (see page 29).

The nature and seriousness of the accident will determine who it needs to be reported to. There are several types of documentation used to record accidents and emergencies.

The accident book

The accident book is completed by the person who had the accident or, if this is not possible, someone who is representing the injured person. The accident book will ask for some basic details about the accident, including:

- who was involved
- what happened

- where it happened
- the day and time of the accident
- any witnesses to the accident
- the address of the injured person
- what PPE was being worn
- what first aid treatment was given.

Major and minor accidents

If an accident happens, you or the person it happened to may be lucky and will not be injured. More often, an accident will result in an injury which may be minor (e.g. a cut or a bruise) or possibly major (e.g. loss of a limb). Accidents can also be fatal. The most common causes of fatal accidents in the construction industry are:

- falling from scaffolding
- being hit by falling objects and materials
- falling through fragile roofs
- being hit by forklifts or lorries
- cuts
- infections
- burns
- electrocution.

Near misses

As well as reporting accidents, 'near misses' must also be reported. A 'near miss' is when an accident nearly happened but did not actually occur. Reporting near misses might identify a problem and can prevent accidents from happening in the future. This allows a company to be proactive rather than reactive.

Safety tip

Near misses must be recorded because they are often the accidents of the future

Work-related injuries in the construction industry

Construction has the largest number of fatal injuries of all the main industry groups. In 2007–2008 there were 72 fatal injuries. This gave a rate of 3.4 people injured per 100 000 workers. The rate of fatal injuries in construction over the past decade has shown a downward trend; however, the rate has shown little change in the most recent years.

- From 1999–2000 to 2006–2007 the rate of reported major injuries in construction fell. It is unclear whether the rise in 2007–2008 means an end to this trend. Despite this falling trend, the rate of major injury in construction is the highest of any main industry group (599.2 per 100 000 employees in 2007–2008).

- A higher proportion of the reported injuries in construction were caused by falls from height, falling objects and contact with moving machinery.
- The THOR-GP surveillance scheme data (2006–2007) indicates a higher rate of work-related illness in construction than across all industries. The rate of self-reported work-related ill health in construction is similar to other industries.

The cost of accidents

As well as the tragedy, pain and suffering that accidents cause, they can also have a negative financial and business impact.

Small accidents will affect profits as sick pay may need to be paid. Production may also slow down or stop if the injured person is a specialist. Replacement or temporary workers may need to be used to keep the job going. This can cost small companies with a handful of employees hundreds of pounds for every day that an injured person can't work. Larger companies with many employees may have several people off work at once, which can cost thousands of pounds per day.

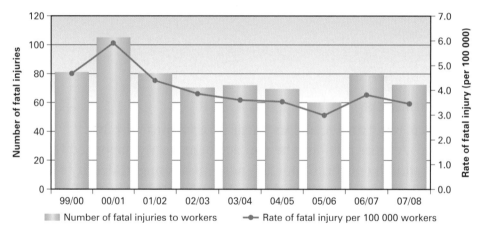

Figure 1.6 Number and rate of fatal injury to workers, 1999–2000 to 2007–2008

More serious accidents will see the financial loss rise as the injured person will be off work for longer. This can cause jobs to fall seriously behind and, in extreme cases, may even cause the contractor to lose the job and possibly have to close the site.

Companies that have a lot of accidents will have a poor company image for health and safety. They will also find it increasingly difficult to gain future contracts. Unsafe companies with lots of accidents will also see injured people claiming against their insurance, which will see their premiums rise. This will eventually make them uninsurable, meaning they will not get any work.

Remember

Clients don't want to hire companies that are not deemed safe

First aid

In the unfortunate event of an accident on site, first aid may have to be administered. If there are more than five people on a site, then a qualified first aider must be present at all times. On large building sites there must be several first aiders. During your site induction you will be made aware of who the first aiders are and where the first aid points are situated. A first aid point must have the relevant first aid equipment to deal with the types of injury that are likely to occur. However, first aid is only the first step and, in the case of major injuries, the emergency services should be called.

A good first aid box should have plasters, bandages, disposable gloves, eye patches, slings, wound dressings and safety pins. Other equipment, such as eye wash stations, must also be available if the work being carried out requires it.

Figure 1.7 A first aid box provides the supplies to deal with minor injuries

Actions for an unsafe area

On discovering an accident the first thing to do is to ensure that the victim is in no further danger. This will require you to do tasks such as switching off the electrical supply. Tasks like this must only be done if there is no danger to yourself.

Turning off the electricity is just one possible example. There will be specific safety issues for individual jobs the injured person may have been working on.

You must next contact the first aider. Unless you have been trained in first aid you must not attempt to move the injured person as you may cause more damage. If necessary, the first aider will then call the emergency services.

> **Remember**
>
> Health and safety is everyone's duty. If you receive first aid treatment and notice that there are only two plasters left, you should report it to your line manager

K3. Hazards on construction sites

A major part of health and safety at work is being able to identify hazards and to help prevent them in the first place, therefore avoiding the risk of injury.

Housekeeping

Housekeeping is the simple term used for cleaning up after you to ensure your work area is clear and tidy. Good housekeeping is vital on a construction site, as an unclean work area is dangerous.

To maintain good housekeeping it is important that you:

- work tidily to reduce the chances of anyone getting hurt
- don't overfill skips as they can lead to fire hazards

> **Safety tip**
>
> After an accident, always make sure the area is safe before you continue work – otherwise you could become a casualty as well

- ensure fire exits and emergency escape routes are clear
- correctly dispose of food waste as this can attract cockroaches, rats and other vermin
- only get as many nails and screws as you need – loose nails and screws can puncture tyres and even cause injury to feet
- clean and sweep up at the end of each day
- avoid blocking exits and walkways
- be aware while you are working – how might your mess affect you or others?

Storing combustibles and chemicals

It is vital to store **combustibles** and chemicals on site correctly.

Chemicals

Certain chemicals such as brick cleaner or some types of adhesive are classified as dangerous chemicals. All chemicals should be stored in a locked area to prevent misuse or cross-contamination.

Highly flammable liquids

Liquefied petroleum gas (LPG), petrol, cellulose thinners, methylated spirits, chlorinated rubber paint and white spirit are all highly flammable liquids. These materials require special storage.

- Containers should only be kept in a special storeroom built of concrete, brick or some other fireproof material.
- The floor should also be made of concrete and should slope away from the storage area. This is to prevent leaked materials from collecting under the containers.
- The roof should be made from an easily shattered material to minimise the effect of any explosion.
- Doors should be at least 50 mm thick and open outwards.
- Any glass used in the structure should be wired and not less than 6 mm thick.
- The standing area should have a sill surrounding it that is deep enough for the largest container stored.
- Containers should always be stored upright.
- The area should not be heated.
- Electric lights should be safe.
- Light switches should be flameproof and should be on the outside of the store.
- The building should be ventilated at high and low levels and have at least two exits.

Remember

Learning to work tidily is part of your apprenticeship

Key term

Combustibles – substances that burn or can be burnt

Find out

Check out the storage details for any chemicals that you come across – look at the manufacturer's instructions or the COSHH regulations

Safety tip

- Never expose materials such as LPG, white spirit, methylated spirit and turps to a naked flame (including cigarettes) – they are highly flammable
- Make sure when working with potentially hazardous materials that you take the appropriate precautions, for example wear gloves and eye protection, work in a ventilated area etc.

- Naked flames and spark producing materials should be prohibited, including smoking.
- The storeroom should be clearly marked with red and white squares and 'Highly Flammable' signage.

In addition to these requirements, there are storage regulations specifically for LPG.

- It must be stored in the open, usually in a locked cage.
- It should be stored off the floor, protected from direct sunlight and frost or snow.
- The storage of LPG is governed by the Highly Flammable Liquids and Liquefied Petroleum Gases Regulations. These regulations apply when 50 or more litres are stored, and permission must be obtained from the District Inspector of Factories.

Figure 1.8 Storage of highly flammable liquids

Glass

Glass should be stored vertically in racks. The conditions for glass storage should be:

- clean – storing glass in dirty or dusty locations can cause discolouration
- dry – if moisture is allowed between the sheets of glass it can make them stick together, which may make them difficult to handle and more likely to break.

If only a small number of sheets of glass are to be stored, they can be leant against a stable surface, as shown in Figure 1.9.

Figure 1.9 Storage of glass

Hazards on the building site

The building industry can be a very dangerous place to work, and there are certain hazards that all workers need to be aware of. The main types of hazard that you will face are:

- falling from height
- tripping
- chemical spills
- burns
- electricity
- fires.

Falling from height

When working in the construction industry a lot of the work that you do will be at height. The main hazard of working at height is falling. A fall from a scaffold, even if it is at low level, can cause serious injuries such as broken bones.

> **Remember**
>
> Always wear appropriate PPE when handling glass

> **Did you know?**
>
> 'Inflammable' means the same thing as flammable, that is it is easily lit and capable of burning rapidly

Safe working practices in construction **Unit 1001**

A worker may also suffer permanent damage from the fall. This could leave them as a wheelchair user for life or even kill them.

Tripping

The main cause of tripping is poor housekeeping. Whether working on scaffolding or on ground level, an untidy workplace is an accident waiting to happen. All workplaces should be kept tidy and free of debris. All off-cuts should be put either in a wheelbarrow (if you aren't near a skip) or straight into the skip.

Chemical spills

Chemical spillages can range from minor inconvenience to major disaster. Most spillages are small and create minimal or no risk. If the material involved is not hazardous, it simply can be cleaned up by normal operations such as brushing or mopping up the spill. Occasionally, the spill may be on a larger scale and may involve a hazardous material. It is important to know what to do before the spillage happens so that remedial action can be prompt and harmful effects minimised. Of course, when a hazardous substance is being used a COSHH or risk assessment will have been made, and it should include a plan for dealing with a spillage. This in turn should mean that the materials required for dealing with the spillage should be readily available.

Burns

Burns can occur not only from the obvious source of fire and heat but also from materials containing chemicals such as cement or painter's solvents. Even electricity can cause burns. It is vital when working with materials that you are aware of the hazards they may present and take the necessary precautions.

Electricity

Electricity is a killer. Around 30 workers a year die from electricity-related accidents, with over 1000 more being seriously injured (source: HSE). One of the main problems with electricity is that it is invisible. You don't even have to be working with an electric tool to be electrocuted. Working too close to live overhead cables, plastering a wall with electric sockets, carrying out maintenance work on a floor, or drilling into a wall can all lead to an electric shock.

Electric shocks may not always be fatal; electricity can also cause burns, muscular problems and cardiac (heart) problems.

Figure 1.10 An untidy work site can present many trip hazards

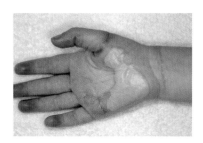

Figure 1.11 Fire, heat, chemicals and electricity can cause burns

Fires

The obvious main risk from fires is burns, but during fires, the actual flames are often not the cause of injury or death. Smoke inhalation is a very serious hazard and this is what mainly causes death. Fires will be covered in greater depth later in this unit (pages 51–53).

Risk assessments

Most of the legislation we have looked at requires risk assessments to be carried out. The Management of Health and Safety at Work Regulations 1999 requires every employer to make suitable and sufficient assessment of:

- the risks to the health and safety of their employees to which the employees are exposed while at work
- the risks to the health and safety of persons not in their employment, arising out of or in connection with their work activities.

It is vital that you know how to carry out a risk assessment. Often you may be in a position where you are given direct responsibility for this, and the care and attention you take over it may have a direct impact on the safety of others. You must be aware of the dangers or hazards of any task, and know what can be done to prevent or reduce the risk.

There are five steps in a risk assessment – here we use cutting the grass as an example.

- **Step 1** – Identify the hazards

When cutting the grass the main hazards are from the blades or cutting the wire, electrocution and any stones that may be thrown up.

- **Step 2** – Identify who will be at risk

The main person at risk is the user, but passers-by may be struck by flying debris.

- **Step 3** – Calculate the risk from the hazard against the likelihood of an accident taking place

The risks from the hazard are quite high: the blade or wire can remove a finger, electrocution can kill and the flying debris can blind or even kill. The likelihood of an accident happening is medium: you are unlikely to cut yourself on the blades, but the chance of cutting through the cable is medium, and the chance of hitting a stone high.

> **Remember**
>
> Good housekeeping will not only prevent trip hazards, but it will also prevent costly clean-up operations at the end of the job and will promote a good professional image

Figure 1.12 Even an everyday task like cutting the grass has its own dangers

Key term

RCD – residual current device, a device that will shut the power down on a piece of electrical equipment if it detects a change in the current, thus preventing electrocution

Working life

Ralph and Vijay are working on the second level of some scaffolding, clearing debris. Ralph suggests that, to speed up the task, they should throw the debris over the edge of the scaffolding into a skip below. The building Ralph and Vijay are working on is on a main road and the skip is not in a closed-off area.

What do you think of Ralph's idea? What are your reasons for this answer?

Remember

Some health problems do not show symptoms straight away and what you do now can affect you much later in life

Figure 1.13 Always wash your hands to prevent ingesting hazardous substances

- **Step 4** – Introduce measures to reduce the risk

Training can reduce the risks of cutting yourself. Training and the use of an **RCD** can reduce the risk of electrocution. Raking the lawn first can reduce the risk of sending up stones.

- **Step 5** – Monitor the risk

Constantly changing factors mean any risk assessment may have to be modified or even changed completely. In our example, one such factor could be rain.

Method statements

Method statements are key safety documents that take the information about significant risks from your risk assessment and combine them with the job specification to produce a practical and safe working method for the workers to follow on site.

Method statements should be specific and relevant to the job in hand and should detail what work is to be done, how the work should be done and what safety precautions need to be taken.

Hazard books

The hazard book is a tool used on some sites to identify hazards within certain tasks. It can also help to produce risk assessments. The book will list tasks and what hazards are associated with those tasks. Different working environments can create different types of hazard so risk assessments must always look at the specific task separately.

K4. Health and hygiene

As well as keeping an eye out for hazards, you must also make sure that you look after yourself and stay healthy. This is a responsibility that lies with both the employer and the employee.

Staying healthy

One of the easiest ways to stay healthy is to wash your hands regularly. By washing your hands you are preventing hazardous substances from entering your body through ingestion (swallowing). You should always wash your hands after going to the toilet and before eating or drinking. Personal hygiene is vital to ensure good health.

Welfare facilities

Welfare facilities are things such as toilets, which must be provided by your employer to ensure a safe and healthy workplace.

There are several things that your employer must provide to meet welfare standards.

- **Toilets** – the number of toilets provided depends on the number of people who are intended to use them. Males and females can use the same toilets provided there is a lock on the inside of the door. Toilets should be flushable with water or, if this is not possible, with chemicals.

- **Washing facilities** – employers must provide a basin large enough to allow people to wash their hands, face and forearms. Washing facilities must have hot and cold running water as well as soap and a means of drying your hands. Showers may be needed if the work is very dirty or if workers are exposed to **corrosive** and **toxic** substances.

- **Drinking water** – there should be a supply of clean drinking water available, either from a tap connected to the mains or from bottled water. Taps connected to the mains need to be clearly labelled as drinking water, and bottled drinking water must be stored in a separate area to prevent **contamination**.

- **Storage or dry room** – every building site must have an area where workers can store the clothes that they do not wear on site, such as coats and motorcycle helmets. If this area is to be used as a drying room then adequate heating must also be provided in order to allow clothes to dry.

- **Lunch area** – every site must have facilities that can be used for taking breaks and lunch well away from the work area. These facilities must provide shelter from the wind and rain and be heated as required. There should be access to tables and chairs, a kettle or urn for boiling water and a means of heating food, such as a microwave.

Substance abuse

Substance abuse is a general term that mainly covers things such as drinking alcohol and taking drugs.

Taking drugs or inhaling solvents at work is not only illegal, but is also highly dangerous to you and everyone around you. These acts result in reduced concentration problems and can lead to accidents. Drinking alcohol is also dangerous at work; going to the pub for lunch and having just one drink can slow down your reactions and have an adverse effect on your concentration.

Although not a form of abuse as such, drugs prescribed by a doctor as well as over-the-counter drugs can be dangerous.

Key terms

Corrosive – a substance that can damage things it comes into contact with (e.g. material, skin)

Toxic – poisonous

Contamination – when harmful chemicals or substances pollute something (e.g. water)

Safety tips

When placing clothes in a drying room, do not put them directly on heaters as this can lead to fire.

When working in an occupied house, you might be able to make arrangements with the client to use the facilities in their house

> **Did you know?**
>
> Substance abuse on a worksite doesn't just endanger yourself. It puts everyone you are working with in danger as well

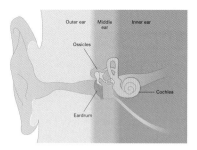

Figure 1.14 Inner workings of the human ear

> **Did you know?**
>
> Noise is measured in decibels (dB). The average person may not notice a rise of 3 dB, but with every 3 dB rise, the noise is doubled. What may seem like a small rise is actually very significant

> **Remember**
>
> Hearing loss affects the young as well as the old

Many medicines carry warnings such as 'may cause drowsiness' or 'do not operate heavy machinery'. Always follow any instructions on prescriptions and, if you feel drowsy or unsteady, then stop work immediately.

Health effects of noise

Hearing can be damaged by a range of causes, from ear infections to loud noises. Hearing loss can result from one very loud noise lasting only a few seconds, or from relatively loud noise lasting for hours, such as a drill.

To appreciate the damage caused by noise, it helps to first understand how the human ear works.

- When the hairs contained within the ear vibrate they move like grass blowing in the wind. Very loud noises have the same effect on the hairs that a hurricane would have on a field.
- The hairs get blown away and can NEVER be replaced.
- The fewer of these hairs you have, the worse is your hearing. This is called 'noise induced hearing loss'.

The damage to hearing can be caused by one of two things.

- **Intensity of the noise** – your hearing can be hurt in an instant from an explosive or very loud noise that can burst your ear drum.
- **Duration of the noise** – noise doesn't have to be deafening to harm you; a quieter noise over a long period, e.g. a 12-hour shift, can also damage your hearing.

Reducing the risks

This can be done in a number of ways:

- **Remove** – get rid of whatever is creating the noise.
- **Move** – locate the noisy equipment away from people.
- **Enclose** – surround noisy equipment, e.g. with sound-proof material.
- **Isolation** – move the workers to protected areas.

Even after all of these are considered, PPE may still be required. The two most common types of hearing protection aids are ear-plugs and ear defenders. See page 49 for more details.

Hazardous substances

Hazardous substances need to be handled, stored, transported and disposed of in very specific ways. To comply with COSHH regulations, eight steps must be followed by the employer:

- Step 1 – assess the risks to health from hazardous substances used or created by employees' activities.
- Step 2 – decide what precautions are needed.
- Step 3 – prevent employees from being exposed to any hazardous substances. If prevention is impossible, the risk must be adequately controlled.
- Step 4 – ensure control methods are used and maintained properly.
- Step 5 – monitor the exposure of employees to hazardous substances.
- Step 6 – carry out health surveillance to ascertain if any health problems are occurring.
- Step 7 – prepare plans and procedures to deal with accidents such as spillages.
- Step 8 – ensure all employees are properly informed, trained and supervised.

Identifying a substance that may fall under the COSHH regulations is not always easy, but you can ask the supplier or manufacturer for a COSHH data sheet, outlining the risks involved with a substance. Most substance containers carry a warning sign stating whether the contents are corrosive, harmful, toxic or bad for the environment.

Waste

Many different types of waste material are produced in construction work. It is your responsibility to identify the type of waste you have created and the best way of disposing of it.

There are several pieces of legislation that dictate the disposal of waste materials. They include:

- Environmental Production Act 1990
- Controlled Waste Regulations 1992
- Waste Management Licensing Regulations 1994.

Several different types of waste are defined by these regulations:

- household waste – normal household rubbish
- commercial waste – for example, from shops or offices
- industrial waste – from factories and industrial sites.

All waste must be handled properly and disposed of safely. Only those authorised to do so may dispose of waste and a record must be kept of all waste disposal.

Figure 1.15 Hazardous substances

Figure 1.16 Common safety signs for corrosive, toxic and explosive materials

Remember

If you leave material on site when your work is completed you may be discarding them. You are still responsible for this waste material!

Safety tip

Not all substances are labelled, and sometimes the label may not match the contents. If you are in any doubt, don't use or touch the substance

Key terms

Symptom – a sign of illness or disease (e.g. difficulty breathing, a sore hand or a lump under the skin)

Leptospirosis – an infectious disease that affects humans and animals. The human form is commonly called Weil's disease. The disease can cause fever, muscle pain and jaundice. In severe cases it can affect the liver and kidneys. Leptospirosis is a germ that is spread by the urine of the infected person. It can often be caught from contaminated soil or water that has been urinated on

Dermatitis – a skin condition where the affected area is red, itchy and sore

Vibration white finger – a condition that can be caused by using vibrating machinery (usually for very long periods of time). The blood supply to the fingers is reduced, which causes pain, tingling and sometimes spasms (shaking)

Hazardous waste

Some types of waste, such as chemicals or material that is toxic or explosive, are too dangerous for normal disposal and must be disposed of with special care. The Hazardous Waste (England and Wales) Regulations cover this disposal. Examples include:

- asbestos
- used engine oils and filters
- solvents
- pesticides
- lead-based batteries
- oily sludges
- chemical waste
- fluorescent tubes.

If hazardous material is inside a container, the container must be clearly marked and a consignment note completed for its disposal.

Health risks in the workplace

While working in the construction industry, you will be exposed to substances or situations that may be harmful to your health. Some of these health risks may not be noticeable straight away. It may take years for **symptoms** to be noticed and recognised.

Ill health can result from:

- exposure to dust (such as asbestos), which can cause eye injuries, breathing problems and cancer
- exposure to solvents or chemicals, which can cause **leptospirosis**, **dermatitis** and other skin problems
- lifting heavy or difficult loads, which can cause back injury and pulled muscles
- exposure to loud noise, which can cause hearing problems and deafness
- exposure to sunlight, which can cause skin cancer
- using vibrating tools, which can cause **vibration white finger** and other problems with the hands
- head injuries, which can lead to blackouts and epilepsy
- cuts, which if infected can lead to disease.

Everyone has a responsibility for health and safety in the construction industry but accidents and health problems still happen too often. Make sure you do what you can to prevent them.

K5. Safe handling of materials and equipment

Manual handling

Manual handling means lifting and moving equipment or material from one place to another without using machinery. Lifting and moving loads by hand is one of the most common causes of injury at work.

Most injuries caused by manual handling result from years of lifting items that are too heavy, are awkward shapes or sizes, or from using the wrong technique. However, it is also possible to cause a lifetime of back pain with just one single lift.

Poor manual handling can cause injuries such as muscle strain, pulled ligaments and hernias. The most common injury by far is spinal injury. Spinal injuries are very serious because there is very little that doctors can do to correct them and, in extreme cases, workers have been left paralysed.

What you can do to avoid injury

The first and most important thing you can do to avoid injury from lifting is to receive proper manual handling training. **Kinetic lifting** is a way of lifting objects that reduces the chance of injury and is covered in more detail in the next section.

Before you lift anything ask yourself some simple questions:

- Does the object need to be moved?
- Can I use something to help me lift the object? A mechanical aid such as a forklift or crane or a manual aid such as a wheelbarrow may be more appropriate than a person.
- Can I reduce the weight by breaking down the load? Breaking down a load into smaller and more manageable weights may mean that more journeys are needed, but it will also reduce the risk of injury.
- Do I need help? Asking for help to lift a load is not a sign of weakness and team lifting will greatly reduce the risk of injury.
- How much can I lift safely? The recommended maximum weight a person can lift is 25 kg but this is only an average weight and each person is different. The amount that a person can lift will depend on their physique, age and experience.
- Where is the object going? Make sure that any obstacles in your path are out of the way before you lift. You also need to make sure there is somewhere to put the object when you get there.
- Am I trained to lift? The quickest way to receive a manual handling injury is to use the wrong lifting technique.

> **Remember**
>
> Always read the manufacturer's label and remember to wear the relevant safety equipment when dealing with hazardous substances

> **Remember**
>
> The Manual Handling Operations Regulations 1992 is the key piece of legislation related to manual handling

> **Key term**
>
> **Kinetic lifting** – a way of lifting objects that reduces the risk of injury to the lifter

> **Remember**
>
> Even light loads can cause back problems so when lifting anything, always take care to avoid twisting or stretching

Kinetic lifting

When lifting any load it is important to keep the correct posture and to use the correct technique:

- feet should be shoulder width apart with one foot slightly in front of the other
- knees should be bent
- back must be straight
- arms should be as close to the body as possible
- grip firmly using the whole hand and not just the fingertips.

When lowering a load, you must also adopt the correct posture and technique:

- bend at the knees, not the back
- adjust the load to avoid trapping fingers
- release the load.

Safe handling

When handling any materials or equipment, always think about the health and safety issues involved and remember the manual handling practices explained to you during your induction.

You aren't expected to remember everything but basic common sense will help you to work safely.

- Always wear your safety helmet and boots at work.
- Wear gloves and ear defenders when necessary.
- Keep your work areas free from debris and materials, tools and equipment not being used.
- Wash your hands before eating.
- Use barrier cream before starting work.
- Always use correct lifting techniques.

Ensure you follow instructions given to you at all times when moving any materials or equipment. The main points to remember are:

- Always try to avoid manual handling (or use mechanical means to aid the process).
- Always assess the situation first to decide on the best method of handling the load.
- Always reduce any risks as much as possible (e.g. split a very heavy load, move obstacles from your path before lifting).
- Tell others around you what you are doing.
- If you need help with a load, get it. Don't try to lift something beyond what you can manage.

Remember

Activities on site can also damage your body. You could have eye damage, head injury and burns along with other physical wounds

Correct lifting procedure

Step 1: Approach the load squarely facing the direction of travel.

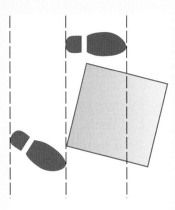

Step 2: Adopt the correct posture.

Step 3: Place your hands under the load and pull the load close to your body.

Step 4: Lift the load using your legs and not your back.

Step 5: Move smoothly with the load.

Step 6: Adopt the correct posture and technique when lowering.

Working life

Ahmed and Glynn are unloading bags of plaster from a wheelbarrow. While handling a bag of plaster. Glynn gets a sudden sharp pain in his back and drops the bag. Ahmed goes and tells their supervisor, who comes over to where Glynn is sitting in a great deal of pain.

What do you think should happen next? Glynn will not want to continue working and possibly doing further damage to his back. What should his supervisor do straight away to look after Glynn's well-being?

Could the accident be prevented? Glynn may not have been working in a safe manner, and there are several important health and safety issues that both Ahmed and Glynn should be made aware of before they carry out another lifting task.

What should their supervisor do in the long term to stop this happening again? The supervisor will want to make sure that they prevent another accident happening across the whole site. What risk assessments and hazard checks will they need to carry out?

Basic health and safety for tools

All tools are potentially dangerous. You, as an operator of tools, must make sure that all health and safety requirements relating to the tools are always carried out. This will help ensure that you do not cause injury to yourself, and, equally important, to others who may be working around you and to the general public. Make sure you follow any instructions and demonstrations you are given on the use of tools, as well as any manufacturer's instructions provided with purchase of the tools.

Basic rules for handling tools:

- Always make sure you use the correct PPE required to use the tool and do the job you are carrying out.
- Never 'make do' with tools. Using the wrong tool for the job usually breaks health and safety laws.
- Never play or mess around with a tool regardless of the type, whether it is a hand tool or power tool.
- Never use a tool you have not been trained to use, especially a power tool.

Power tools

Always treat power tools with respect: they have the potential to cause harm either to the person using them or to others around. All power tools used on site should be regularly tested (PAT tested) by a qualified person. There are several health and safety regulations governing the use of power tools. Make sure that you wear suitable PPE all times and that power tools are operated safely. In some cases, you must be qualified to use them. Refer to PUWER (Provision and Use of Work Equipment Regulations) 1998 if needed.

On-site transformers are used to reduce the mains voltage from 230 volts to 110 volts. All power tools used should be designed for 110 volts.

As well as the traditional powered tools there are also tools powered by gas or compressed air. Gas powered tools, such as nail guns, also require batteries to operate them. They must be handled carefully similar to other power tools.

Compressed air powered tools such as spray paint systems require an electric powered compressor to operate them. Care must be taken when dealing with these tools. As well as electrical hazards there is the additional danger of working with compressed air. If the air supply is held against the skin it can create air bubbles in your blood stream. This can lead to death.

Special care should be taken with electrical tools.

ALWAYS:

- check plugs and connections (make sure you have the correct fuse rating in the plug)
- inspect all leads to ensure no damage
- check that the power is off when connecting leads
- unwind extension leads completely from the reel to prevent the cable from overheating.

NEVER:

- use a tool in a way not recommended by the manufacturer
- use a tool with loose, damaged or makeshift parts
- lay a driver down while it is still switched on
- use a drill unless the chuck (the part in which the drill bit is held) is tight
- throw the tool onto the ground
- pass the tool down by its lead
- use a drill where it is difficult to see what you are doing or hold the tool tightly
- allow leads to trail in water.

Safe storage and handling of tools, equipment and materials

Hand tools

Hand tools need to be stored safely and securely. Tools such as chisels, saws, craft knifes etc. must be stored either in a roll or with a cover over the blade. This is because accidents could happen when people put their hands into tool bags to get something and cut their fingers on a sharp edge.

All tools must be stored in a suitable bag/box that will protect the tools from the elements. With a lot of tools being made from metal components, rust will affect them.

When not in use tools should be securely locked away – theft of tools can occur. It is your responsibility to look after your tools.

Power tools

Power tools should be handled with care. The manufacturer's guidance in the tool's manual will explain the safe handling and storage of the tool. You must follow this guidance.

Generally power tools should be carried by the handle and not the cable. When not in use, the tool should be stored away safely.

Did you know?

PAT stands for 'portable appliance testing'

Safety tip

When using power tools, always read the manufacturer's instructions and safety guidelines before use. This will ensure that they are being operated correctly and for the correct purpose

Remember

Follow the basic health and safety rules regarding the use of tools and you (and others) will be safe. Tools are expensive and very important for work so they need to be looked after

Key terms

Pneumatic – powered by compressed air

Hydraulic – powered by a liquid, e.g. oil

Safety tips

NEVER:

- store equipment, cables and plugs in wet areas/outdoors
- store equipment where leads may be damaged (near blades etc.)
- store equipment at height where it may fall on someone

ALWAYS:

- store power tools away from children
- allow hot equipment to cool before storing
- unplug and coil leads before storing

Most power tools come in a plastic carry case. They should be kept in this case when not in use and stored in a safe location to protect from damage and theft. Power tools that have gas powered cartridges must be stored in an area that is safe and away from sources of ignition to prevent explosion. Used cartridges must be disposed of safely. **Pneumatic** and **hydraulic** tools must also be carried correctly and stored in a way that prevents damage.

Power tools include pressurised painting vessels and equipment and compressed air and hydraulic powered equipment.

Wheelbarrows

Wheelbarrows are generally used where large amounts of material need to be transported over a distance. The best type is one specially designed to go through narrow openings.

Always clean the wheelbarrow out after use. Do not hit the body of the wheelbarrow with a heavy object. Keep types inflated to allow ease of movement. Check that all metal stays are in place.

Do not overload the wheelbarrow as it will put strain on your back and arms. Approach the barrow between the lifting arms and hold the arms at the end, bend your knees and lift. The weight of the material should be over the wheel.

Bricks

Most bricks delivered to sites are now pre-packed and banded using either plastic or metal bands to stop the bricks from separating until ready for use. The edges are also protected by plastic strips to help stop damage during moving, usually by forklift or crane. They are then usually covered in shrink-wrapped plastic to protect them from the elements.

On arrival to site bricks should be stored on level ground and stacked no more than two packs high. This is done to prevent over-reaching or collapse, which could result in injury to workers. The bricks should be stored close to where they are required so further movement is kept to a minimum. On large sites they may be stored further away and moved by telescopic lifting vehicles to the position required for use.

Safety tip

Take care and stand well clear of a crane used for offloading bricks on delivery

If bricks are unloaded by hand they should be stacked on edge in rows, on firm, level and well-drained ground. The ends of the stacks should be bonded and no higher than 1.8 m. To protect the bricks from rain and frost, all stacks should be covered with a tarpaulin or polythene sheets.

Using bricks

Great care should be taken when using the bricks from the packs. Once the banding is cut, the bricks can collapse, which can damage the bricks, especially on uneven ground.

Bricks should be taken from a minimum of three packs and mixed to stop changes in colour. This is because the positioning of the bricks in the kiln can cause slight colour differences:

● the nearer the centre of the kiln, the lighter the colour
● the nearer the edge of the kiln, the darker the colour as the heat is stronger.

If the bricks are not mixed, you could get sections of brickwork in slightly different shades. This is called banding, and this can be clearly made out even by people not working in construction.

Blocks

Blocks are made from concrete, which may be dense or lightweight. Lightweight blocks could be made from a fine aggregate that contains lots of air bubbles. The storage of blocks is the same as for bricks.

Paving slabs

Paving slabs are made from concrete or stone and are available in a variety of sizes, shapes and colours. They are used for pavements and patios, with some slabs given a textured top to improve appearance.

Paving slabs are normally delivered to sites by lorry and crane offloaded, some in wooden crates covered with shrink-wrapped plastic, or banded and covered on pallets. They should not be stacked more than two packs high for safety reasons and to prevent damage to the slabs due to weight pressure.

Paving slabs unloaded by hand are stored outside and stacked on edge to prevent the lower ones, if stored flat, from being damaged by the weight of the stack. The stack is started by laying about ten to 12 slabs flat with the others leaning against these. If only a small number of slabs are to be stored, they can be stored flat (since the weight will be less).

Slabs should be stored on firm, level ground with timber bearers below to prevent the edges from getting damaged. This can happen if the slabs are placed on a solid surface.

Figure 1.17 Paving slabs stacked flat

Figure 1.18 Paving slabs on a pallet

Kerbs

Kerbs are concrete units laid at the edges of roads and footpaths to give straight lines or curves and retain the finished surfaces. The size of a common kerb is 100 mm wide, 300 mm high and 600 mm long. Path edgings are 50 mm wide, 150 mm high and 600 mm long.

Kerbs should be stacked on timber bearers or with overhanging ends, which provides a space for hands or lifting slings if machine lifting is to be used. When they are stacked on top of each other, the stack must not be more than three kerbs high.

To protect the kerbs from rain and frost it is advisable to cover them with a tarpaulin or sheet.

Figure 1.19 Stacked kerbs

Roofing tiles

Roofing tiles are made from either clay or concrete. They may be machine-made or handmade and are available in a variety of shapes and colours. Many roofing tiles are able to interlock to prevent rain from entering the building. Ridge tiles are usually half round but sometimes they may be angled.

Half round ridge tile

Angled ridge tile

Figure 1.20 Roofing tiles

Storage of roofing tiles

Roofing tiles are stacked on edge to protect their 'nibs', and in rows on level, firm, well-drained ground. See Figure 1.21. They should not be stacked any higher than six rows. The stack should be tapered to prevent toppling. The tiles at the end of the rows should be stacked flat to provide support for the rows.

Ridge tiles may be stacked on top of each other, but no higher than ten tiles.

To protect roofing tiles from rain and frost before use, they should be covered with a tarpaulin or plastic sheeting.

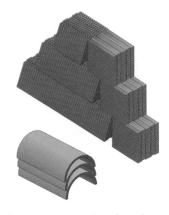

Figure 1.21 Stacks of roofing tiles

Rolled materials

Rolled materials, for example damp proof course or roofing felt, should be stored in a shed on a level, dry surface. Narrower rolls may be best stored on shelves but in all cases they should be stacked on end to prevent them from rolling and to reduce the possibility of damage by compression. See Figure 1.22. In the case of bitumen (see page 93), the layers can melt together under pressure.

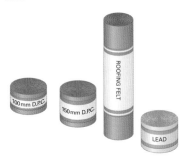

Figure 1.22 Rolled materials stored on end

Aggregates

Aggregates are granules or particles that are mixed with cement and water to make mortar and concrete. Aggregates should be hard and durable.

They should not contain any form of plant life or anything that can be dissolved in water.

Aggregates are classed in two groups:

- Fine aggregates are granules that pass through a 5-mm sieve.
- Coarse aggregates are particles that are retained by a 5-mm sieve.

Sand and mortar

The most commonly used fine aggregate is sand. Sand may be dug from pits and riverbeds, or dredged from the sea. The most common fine aggregate for making mortar is 'soft' or 'building' sand. It should be well graded, which means having an equal quantity of fine, medium and large grains which are more rounded (see Figures 1.23 and 1.24.

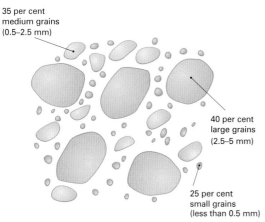

35 per cent medium grains (0.5–2.5 mm)

40 per cent large grains (2.5–5 mm)

25 per cent small grains (less than 0.5 mm)

Figure 1.23 Sand particles

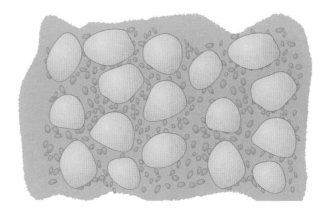

Figure 1.24 Mortar particles

Concrete

Concrete requires both fine and coarse aggregates. The most common fine aggregate is 'sharp' sand, which is more angular and has a coarser feel than soft sand.

The most common coarse aggregate is limestone chippings, which are quarried and crushed to graded sizes, 10 mm, 20 mm or even larger. See figure 1.25

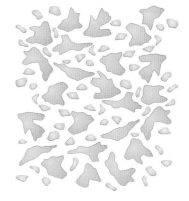

Figure 1.25 Concrete particles

Storage of aggregates

Aggregates are usually delivered in tipper lorries, although nowadays 1-tonne bags are available and may be crane handled. The aggregates should be stored on a concrete base, with a fall to allow for any water to drain away.

To protect aggregates from becoming contaminated with leaves and litter it is a good idea to situate stores away from trees and cover aggregates with a tarpaulin or plastic sheets.

Did you know?

Sea sand contains salts, which may affect the quality of a mix. It should not be used unless it has been washed and supplied by a reputable company

Safety tip

It is good practice to put an intermediate flat stack in long rows to prevent rows from toppling

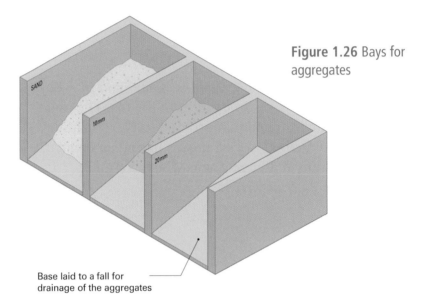

SAND
10mm
20mm

Base laid to a fall for drainage of the aggregates

Figure 1.26 Bays for aggregates

Remember

The different sizes of aggregate should be stored separately to prevent the different aggregates getting mixed together.
Aggregates can be supplied as bagged materials, as can cement and plaster.
Poorly graded sands, with single-size particles, contain a greater volume of air and require cement to fill the spaces

Did you know?

On larger sites some companies use a machine spray system to cover large areas with plaster quickly, using many plasterers to complete the work

Plaster

Plaster is made from gypsum, water and cement or lime. Aggregates can also be added depending on the finish desired. Plaster provides a joint-less, smooth, easily decorated surface for internal walls and ceilings.

- **Gypsum plaster** is for internal use and contains different grades of gypsum, depending on the background finish. Gypsum is a very soft mineral. When gypsum powder is mixed with water it becomes rock hard. Browning is usually used as an undercoat on brickwork, but in most cases, a one-coat plaster is used, and on plasterboard, board finish is used.
- **Cement-sand plaster** is used for external rendering, internal undercoats and waterproofing finishing coats.
- **Lime-sand plaster** is mostly used as an undercoat, but may sometimes be used as a finishing coat.

Storage of cement and plaster

Both cement and plaster are usually available in 25-kg bags. The bags are made from multi-wall layers of paper with a polythene liner. Care must be taken not to puncture the bags before use. Each bag, if offloaded manually, should be stored in a ventilated, waterproof shed, on a dry floor on pallets. If offloaded by crane, the bags should be transferred to the shed and the same storage method used.

The bags should be kept clear of the walls, and piled no higher than five bags. It is most important that the bags are used in the same order as they were delivered. This minimises the length of time that the bags are in storage, preventing the contents from setting in the bags, which would require extra materials and cause added cost to the company.

Plasterboard

Plasterboard is a sheet material that comes in various sizes. Some of the larger size sheets can be very awkward to carry. Special care must be taken when there is a strong wind as this can catch hold of the sheet and make the handling difficult and dangerous. Ideally two people should be used to transport larger sheets.

Plasterboard is a gypsum-based product, so it must be stored in a waterproof area. As it is a sheet material it must also be stored flat and not leant up against a wall, which will cause the sheet to bow.

Wood and sheet materials

Various types of wood and sheet materials are available. The most common are described below.

Carcassing timber

Carcassing timber is wood used for non-load-bearing jobs such as ceiling and floorboard supports, stud wall partitions and other types of framework. It should normally be stored outside under a covered framework. It should be placed on timber bearers clear of the ground. The ground should be free of vegetation and ideally covered over with concrete. This reduces the risk of absorption of ground moisture, which can damage the timber and cause wet rot.

Piling sticks or cross-bearers should be placed between each layer of timber, about 600 mm apart, to provide support and allow air circulation. Tarpaulins or plastic covers can be used to protect the timber from the elements, however care must be taken to allow air to flow freely through the stack. See Figure 1.28.

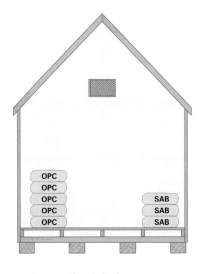

- Dry, ventilated shed
- Stock must be rotated so that old stock is used before new
- Not more than five bags high
- Clear of walls
- Off floor

Figure 1.27 Storage of cement and plaster bags in a shed

Remember

The storage racks used to store wood must take account of the weight of the load. Access to the materials being stored is another important consideration

Unit 1001 Safe working practices in construction

Safety tip

Due to the size, shape and weight of sheet materials, always get help to transport them. If possible, use a purpose-made plywood trolley. Always wear the correct PPE

Find out

What are the PPE requirements when moving sheet materials?

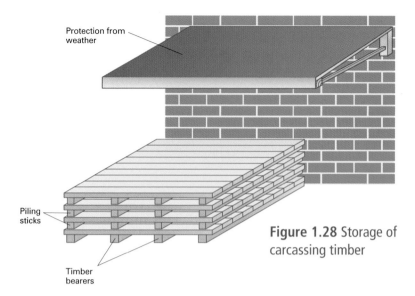

Figure 1.28 Storage of carcassing timber

Joinery grade and hardwoods

These timbers should be stored under full cover wherever possible, preferably in a storage shed. Good ventilation is needed to avoid build-up of moisture through absorption. This type of timber should also be stored on bearers on a well-prepared base.

Plywood and other sheet materials

All sheet materials should be stored in a dry, well-ventilated environment. Specialised covers are readily available to give added protection for most sheet materials. This helps prevent condensation that is caused when non-specialised types of sheeting are used.

Figure 1.29 Storage of sheet materials

Sheet materials should be stacked flat on timber cross-bearers, spaced close enough together to prevent sagging. Alternatively, where space is limited, sheet materials can be stored on edge in purpose-made racks that allow the sheets to rest against the backboard. There should be sufficient space around the plywood for easy loading and removal. The rack should be designed to allow sheets to be removed from either the front or the ends.

Leaning sheets against walls is not recommended, as this makes them bow. This is then difficult to correct.

For sheet materials with faces or decorative sides, the face sides should be placed against each other. This is done to minimise the risk of damage due to friction when they are moved. Different sizes, grades and qualities of sheet materials should be kept separate with off-cuts stacked separately from the main stack.

Joinery components

Joinery components, such as doors or kitchen units, must be stored safely and securely to prevent damage. Doors, windows, frames, etc. should ideally be stored flat on timber bearers under cover, to protect them from exposure to the weather. Where space is limited, they can be stored upright using a rack system (similar to sheet materials). However, they must never be leant against a wall. This will bow the door/frame and make it very hard to fit.

Wall and floor units – whether kitchen, bedroom or bathroom units – must be stacked on a flat surface, and no more than two units high. Units can be made from porous materials such as chipboard. Therefore, it is vital they are stored inside, preferably in the room where they are to be fitted, to avoid double handling. Protective sheeting should be used to cover units to prevent damage or staining from paints, etc.

Ideally all components and timber products such as architrave should be stored in the room where they are to be fitted. This will allow them to acclimatise to the room and prevent shrinkage or distortion after fitting. This is known as 'second seasoning'.

Figure 1.30 Doors should be stacked on a flat surface

> ### Did you know?
> - Wood and wood-based materials are susceptible to rot if the moisture content is too high, to insect attack and to many other defects such as bowing or warping
> - Proper seasoning and chemical sprays can prevent defects

Unit 1001 Safe working practices in construction

Figure 1.31 Store adhesives according to the manufacturer's instructions

Key terms

Shelf life – how long something will remain fit for its purpose

Inverted – tipped and turned upside down

Skinning – formation of a skin on the product when the top layer dries out

Figure 1.32 Correct storage of paints

Adhesives

Adhesives are substances used to bond (stick) surfaces together. Because of their chemical nature, there are potentially serious risks connected with adhesives if they are not stored, used and handled correctly.

All adhesives should be stored and used in line with the manufacturer's instructions. This usually involves storing them on shelving, with labels facing outwards, in a safe, secure area (preferably a lockable store room).

The level of risk when using an adhesive depends on the type of adhesive being used. Some of the risks include:

- explosion
- poisoning
- skin irritation
- disease.

As explained on page 20, these types of material are closely controlled by COSHH, which aims to minimise the risks involved with their storage and use.

All adhesives have a recommended **shelf life**. This must be taken into account when storing adhesives to ensure the oldest stock is stored at the front and used first. Remember to check the manufacturer's guidelines as to how long the adhesive will remain fit for purpose once opened. Poor storage can affect the quality of the adhesives, such as loss in adhesive strength and prolongation of the setting time.

Paint and decorating equipment

Oil-based products

Oil-based products such as gloss and varnish should be stored on clearly marked shelves, with their labels turned to the front. They should always be used in date order with new stock at the back and old stock at the front.

Oil-based products should be **inverted** at regular intervals to stop settlement and separation of the ingredients. They must also be kept in tightly sealed containers to stop the product **skinning**. Storage at a constant temperature will ensure the product retains its desired consistency.

Water-based products

Water-based products, such as emulsions and acrylics, should also be stored on shelves with labels to the front and in date order.

Some water-based products have a very limited shelf life and must be used before their use-by date. As with oil-based products, water-based products keep best if stored at a constant temperature. It is also important to protect them from frost to prevent the water component of the product from freezing.

Powdered materials

Powdered materials a decorator might use include adhesives, fillers, paste and sugar soap.

Large items such as heavy bags should be stored at ground or platform level. Smaller items can be stored on shelves. Sealed containers, such as a bin, are ideal for loose materials.

Powdered materials can have a limited shelf life and can set in high **humidity** conditions. They must also be protected from frost and exposure to any moisture, including condensation. These types of materials must not be stored in the open air.

Substances hazardous to health

Some substances the decorator will work with are potentially hazardous to health, as they can be **volatile** and highly flammable. COSHH Regulations apply to such materials and describe how they must be stored and handled. See page 27 for general information about COSHH.

Some larger bags of powdered materials are heavier than they first appear. Make sure you use the correct manual handling techniques (see pages 30–33).

Decorating materials that might be hazardous to health include spirits (i.e. methylated and white), turpentine (turps), paint thinners and varnish removers. These should be stored out of the way on shelves, preferably in a suitable locker or similar room that meets the requirements of COSHH. The temperature must be kept below 15°C. A warmer environment may cause storage containers to expand and blow up.

The storage of LPG and other highly flammable liquids is covered on pages 20–21.

Key terms

Humidity – dampness or moisture in the air

Volatile – a substance that is quick to evaporate (turn into a gas)

Remember

Don't leave emulsions in a garage or shed over the winter. They are water based and will freeze, and when they thaw it will affect the finish

Remember

Heavy materials should be stored at low levels to aid manual handling and should never be stacked more than two levels high

Unit 1001

Safe working practices in construction

K6. Basic working platforms

Working at height

We will look at working at height in greater depth in Unit 1007, pages 105–24. In this section, we will look at some of the issues connected with safety when working at height.

General safety considerations

You should be able to identify potential hazards associated with working at height, as well as hazards associated with equipment. It is essential that access equipment is well maintained and checked regularly for any deterioration or faults. These could compromise the safety of someone using the equipment and anyone else in the work area.

Although obviously not as important as people, equipment can also be damaged by the use of faulty access equipment. When maintenance checks are carried out they should be properly recorded. This provides very important information that helps to prevent accidents.

Fall protection

With any task that involves working at height, the main danger to workers is falling. Although scaffolding, etc. should have edge protection to prevent falls, there are certain tasks where edge protection or scaffolding simply can't be used. In these instances some form of fall protection must be in place to:

- prevent the worker falling
- keep the fall distance to a minimum
- ensure the landing point is cushioned.

A variety of fall protection devices are available. The most commonly used ones are:

- harness and **lanyard**
- safety netting
- airbags.

Harness and lanyard

Harness and lanyard is a type of **fall-arrest system**. The system works with a harness that is attached to the worker and a lanyard attached to a secure beam/eyebolt. If the worker slips, they will only fall as far as the length of the lanyard and will be left hanging, rather than falling to the ground.

Figure 1.33 A harness and lanyard can prevent a worker from falling to the ground

> **Key terms**
>
> **Lanyard** – a rope that is used to support a weight
>
> **Fall-arrest system** – this means that in the event of a slip or fall, the worker will only fall a few feet at most

Figure 1.34 Safety netting is used when working at the highest point

Figure 1.35 Safety netting can be used under fragile roofs

Safety netting

Safety netting is used mainly on the top floor where there is no higher point to attach a lanyard. Safety nets are primarily used when decking roofing. They are attached to the joists/beams and catch any worker who slips or falls. Safety netting is also used on completed buildings where there is a fragile roof.

Airbags

An airbag safety system is a form of soft fall-arrest. It consists of interlinked modular air mattresses. The modules are connected by push connectors and/or flexible couplings and are inflated by a pump-driven fan, which can be electric, petrol, or butane gas powered. As the individual airbags fill with low-pressure air, they expand to form a continuous protective safety surface, giving a cushioned soft fall and preventing serious injury.

The system must be kept inflated. If it is run on petrol or gas, it should be checked regularly to ensure that it is still functioning. This system is ideal for short fall jobs, but should not be used where a large fall could occur.

K7. Working with electricity

Electricity is a killer. One of the main problems with electricity is that it is invisible. You don't even have to be working with an electric tool to be electrocuted. You can get an electric shock:

- working too close to live overhead cables
- plastering a wall with electric sockets
- carrying out maintenance work on a floor
- drilling into a wall.

Did you know?

Around 30 workers a year die from electricity-related accidents, with over 1000 more being seriously injured (source: HSE)

However, not all electric shocks are fatal – they can also cause injuries such as burns and problems with your muscles and heart.

A common error is to think that the level of voltage is directly related to the level of injury or danger of death. However, a small shock from static electricity may contain thousands of volts but has very little current behind it.

Voltages

There are two main types of voltage in use in the UK: 230 V and 110 V. The standard UK power supply is 230 V and this is what all the sockets in your house are. On construction sites, 230 V has been deemed as unsafe and 110 V must be used here. The 110 V is identified by a yellow cable and different style plug. It works from a transformer which converts the 230 V to 110 V. When working within domestic dwellings, ideally a portable transformer should be used to reduce the voltage to 110V. If this is not possible then residual current devices (RCDs) should be used, which are designed to disconnect the power very quickly as an extra safety precaution.

Contained within the wiring there should be three wires: the live and neutral, which carry the alternating current, and the earth wire, which acts as a safety device. The three wires are colour-coded so that all electrical installations are standardised and any person needing to do work can identify which wire is which easily.

Current coding complies with European colours as follows:

- live – brown
- neutral – blue
- earth – yellow and green.

Some older properties will have the following older colour-coding:

- live – red
- neutral – black
- earth – yellow and green.

Precautions to take to prevent electric shocks

NEVER:

- carry electrical equipment by the cable
- remove plugs by pulling on the lead
- allow tools to get wet. If they do, get them checked before use.

ALWAYS:

- check equipment, leads and plugs before use. If you find a fault don't use the equipment and tell your supervisor immediately
- keep cable off the ground where possible to avoid damage/trips

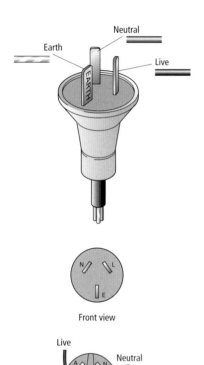

Figure 1.36 Colour coding of the wires in a 230 V plug

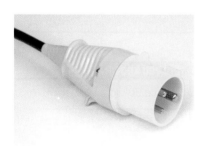

Figure 1.37 A 110 V plug

- avoid damage to the cable by keeping it away from sharp edges
- keep the equipment locked away and labelled to prevent it being used by accident
- use cordless tools where possible
- follow instructions on extension leads.

Dealing with electric shocks

In helping the victim of an electric shock, the first thing you must do is disconnect the power supply – if it is safe to do and will not take long to find. Touching the power source may put you in danger.

- If the victim is in contact with something portable, such as a drill, attempt to move it away using a non-conductive object such as a wooden broom.
- Time is precious and separating the victim from the source can prove an effective way to speed the process.
- Don't attempt to touch the affected person until they are free and clear of the supplied power. Be especially careful in wet areas, such as bathrooms – most water will conduct electricity and electrocuting yourself is also possible.

People 'hung up' in a live current flow may think they are calling out for help but most likely no sound will be heard from them. When the muscles contract under household current (most electrocutions happen from house current at home), the person affected will appear in a 'locked-up' state, unable to move or react to you.

- Using a wooden object, swiftly and strongly knock the person free, trying not to injure them, and land them clear of the source.
- The source may also be lifted or removed, if possible, with the same wooden item. This is not recommended on voltages that exceed 500 V.

First aid procedures for an electric shock victim

- Check to see if you are alone. If there are other people around, instruct them to call an ambulance immediately.
- Check for a response and breathing.
- If the area is safe for you to be in, and you have removed the object or have cut off its power supply, shout to the person to see if they are conscious. At this stage, do not touch the victim.
- Check once again to see if the area is safe. If you are satisfied that it is safe, start resuscitating the victim. If you have no first aid knowledge, call 999 for an ambulance.

Safety tip

Make sure the electricity supply has been turned off before going near a victim of electric shock. Do not approach anyone who you think has received an electric shock until the supply has been isolated

Working life

Tyrone and Macy are knocking down a small wall in an old block of flats. The wall has an electric socket in it. Tyrone says that they should switch off the power at the mains, disconnect the socket and put some tape over the wires. Macy isn't sure, but they find the mains switch in the flat and switch off the power. Tyrone removes the socket cover and suddenly there is a bang. Tyrone is thrown backwards.

- What do you think has happened?
- How could this have happened?
- What should have been done?
- What should Macy do now?

K8. Using appropriate personal protective equipment (PPE)

Personal protective equipment is the name for clothes and other wearable items that form a line of defence against accidents or injury. It should be used with all the other methods of staying healthy and safe in the workplace (equipment, training, regulations and laws etc.).

Maintaining and storing PPE

The effectiveness of the protection it offers will be affected if the PPE is damaged in any way. Maintenance may include:

- cleaning
- examination
- replacement
- repair and testing.

The wearer may be able to carry out simple maintenance (such as cleaning), but more intricate repairs must only be carried out by a competent person. The costs associated with the maintenance of PPE are the responsibility of the employer.

Where PPE is provided, adequate storage facilities must also be provided for when it is not in use, unless the employee may take PPE away from the workplace (e.g. footwear or clothing). Storage should be adequate to protect the PPE from contamination, loss, damage, damp or sunlight.

PPE should be 'CE' marked. This will indicate that it meets EU (European) safety, health and environmental requirements and complies with the requirements of the Personal Protective Equipment Regulations. In some cases it may have been tested and certified by an independent body.

Types of PPE

Head protection

Figure 1.38 A safety helmet

There are several different types of head protection; the one most commonly used in construction is the safety helmet (or hard hat). This is used to protect the head from falling objects and knocks and has an adjustable strap to ensure a snug fit. Some safety helmets come with attachments for ear defenders or eye protection. Safety helmets are meant to be worn directly on the head and must not be worn over any other type of hat.

Eye protection

Eye protection is used to protect the eyes from dust and flying debris. The three main types are:

- **Safety goggles** – made of a durable plastic and used when there is a danger of dust getting into the eyes or a chance of impact injury.
- **Safety spectacles** – these are also made from a durable plastic but give less protection than goggles. This is because they don't fully enclose the eyes and so only protect from flying debris.
- **Face masks** – again made of durable plastic, face masks protect the entire face from flying debris. They do not, however, protect the eyes from dust.

Figure 1.39 Safety goggles

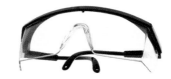

Figure 1.40 Safety spectacles

Foot protection

Safety boots or shoes are used to protect the feet from falling objects and also from sharp objects such as nails. Safety boots should have a steel toe-cap and steel mid-sole.

Figure 1.41 Safety boots

Hearing protection

Hearing protection is used to prevent damage to the ears caused by very loud noise. There are several types of hearing protection available, but the two most common types are ear-plugs and ear defenders.

- **Ear-plugs** – these are small fibre plugs that are inserted into the ear and used when the noise is not too severe. Before inserting ear-plugs, make sure that you have clean hands. Never use plugs that have been used by somebody else.
- **Ear defenders** – these are worn to cover the entire ear and are connected to a band that fits over the top of the head. They are used when there is excessive noise and must be cleaned regularly.

Figure 1.42 Ear-plugs

Figure 1.43 Ear defenders

Respiratory protection

Respiratory protection is used to prevent the worker from breathing in any dust or fumes that may be hazardous. The main type of respiratory protection is the dust mask. Dust masks are used when working in a dusty environment and are lightweight, comfortable and easy to fit. They should be worn by only one person and must be disposed of at the end of the working day. There are several different types and an employer should provide the correct mask to be used when working with a specific dust problem.

Figure 1.44 A respiratory system

Hand protection

There are several types of hand protection and the correct type must be used for the task at hand. To make sure you are wearing the most suitable type of glove for the task, you need to look first at what is going to be done and then match the type of glove to that task.

Figure 1.45 Safety gloves

- Wearing lightweight rubber gloves to move glass will not offer much protection, so leather gauntlets must be used.
- Plastic-coated gloves will protect you from certain chemicals.
- Kevlar® gloves offer cut resistance.

Skin and sun protection

Another precaution you can take is ensuring that you wear barrier cream. This is a cream used to protect the skin from damage and infection. Don't forget to ensure that your skin is protected from the sun with a good sunscreen, and make sure your back, arms and legs are covered by suitable clothing.

Whole body protection

The rest of the body also needs protecting when working on site. This will usually involve wearing either overalls or a high-visibility jacket.

High-visibility jackets are essential whenever you are on site or working near traffic. They ensure that the person wearing them is clearly visible at all times. This helps to avoid accidents by making the wearer easier to avoid.

Figure 1.46 High-visibility jacket

Overalls provide protection from dirt and the possibility of minor cuts. In wet or cold conditions you may also need to use waterproof or thermal clothing. Some circumstances will require chemical-resistant clothing.

Knee pads can be worn by workers who will spend a lot of time kneeling, such as carpet fitters. Paper overalls or paper boiler suits can be worn to provide light protection against non-hazardous liquids and dust.

K9. Fire and emergency procedures

Fires can start almost anywhere and at any time, but a fire needs three things to burn:

- fuel
- heat
- oxygen.

Together these elements are known as 'the triangle of fire'. If any one of the three ingredients is missing, fire cannot burn. Remove one side of the triangle, and the fire will be extinguished.

If it can consume all three ingredients from the triangle, a fire will spread. Cutting off the fire's access to fuel, heat or oxygen will stop the spread of the fire.

Fires can be classified according to the type of material involved:

- Class A – wood, paper, textiles etc.
- Class B – flammable liquids, petrol, oil etc.
- Class C – flammable gases, LPG, propane etc.
- Class D – metal, metal powder etc.
- Class E – electrical equipment.

Figure 1.47 The triangle of fire

Fire fighting equipment

There are several types of fire fighting equipment, such as fire extinguishers and fire blankets. Each type is designed to be the most effective at putting out a particular class of fire. Some should never be used in certain types of fire.

Fire extinguishers

A fire extinguisher is a metal canister containing a substance that can put out a fire. There are several different types and it is important that you learn which type should be used on specific classes of fires. This is because if you use the wrong type, you may make the fire worse or risk severely injuring yourself.

Fire extinguishers are now all one colour (red) but they have a band of colour which shows what substance is inside.

Water

The coloured band is red and this type of extinguisher can be used on Class A fires. Water extinguishers can also be used on Class C fires to cool the area down.

Foam

The coloured band is cream and this type of extinguisher can be used on Class A fires. A foam extinguisher can also be used on a Class B fire if the liquid is not flowing, and on a Class C fire if the gas is in liquid form.

> **Find out**
>
> What fire risks are there in the construction industry? Think about some of the materials (fuel) and heat sources that could make up two sides of 'the triangle of fire'

Figure 1.48 Water fire extinguisher

Figure 1.49 Foam fire extinguisher

Figure 1.50 Carbon dioxide (CO_2) extinguisher

Figure 1.51 Dry powder extinguisher

Safety tip

A water fire extinguisher should NEVER be used to put out an electrical or burning fat/oil fire. This is because electrical current can carry along the jet of water back to the person holding the extinguisher, electrocuting them. Putting water on to burning fat or oil will make the fire worse as the fire will 'explode', potentially causing serious injury

Figure 1.52 A fire blanket

Remember

- Remove the fuel – without anything to burn, the fire will go out
- Remove the heat and the fire will go out
- Remove the oxygen and the fire will go out – without oxygen, a fire won't even ignite

Carbon dioxide (CO_2)

The coloured band is black and the extinguisher can be used primarily on electrical fires. However, as well as Class E, it can also be used on Class A, B and C fires.

Dry powder

The coloured band is blue and this type of extinguisher can be used on all classes of fire, but most commonly on electrical and liquid fires. The powder smothers the flames.

Fire blankets

Fire blankets are normally found in kitchens or canteens as they are good at putting out cooking fires. They are made of a fireproof material and work by smothering the fire and stopping any more oxygen from getting to it, thus putting it out. A fire blanket can also be used if a person is on fire.

What to do in the event of a fire

During your induction to any workplace, you will be made aware of the fire procedure as well as where the fire assembly points (also known as 'muster points') are and what the alarm sounds like. Fire drills should be used to practise this procedure.

All muster points should be clearly indicated by signs, and a map of their location clearly displayed in the building. On hearing the alarm you must stop what you are doing and make your way to the nearest muster point. This is so that everyone can be accounted for. If you do not go to the muster point or if you leave before someone has taken your name, someone may risk their life to go back into the fire to get you.

K10. Safety signs and notices

You will see safety signs in many parts of the workplace.

Types of safety sign

There are several different types of safety sign, and they have different purposes.

- **Prohibition signs** – these tell you that something MUST NOT be done. They always have a white background and a red circle with a red line through it.
- **Mandatory signs** – these tell you that something MUST be done. They are also circular, but have a white symbol on a blue background.
- **Warning signs** – these signs are there to alert you to a specific hazard. They are triangular and have a yellow background and a black border.
- **Safe condition signs** (often called information signs) – these give you useful information like the location of things (e.g. a first aid point). They can be square or rectangular and are green with a white symbol.

Figure 1.53 A prohibition sign

Figure 1.54 A mandatory sign

Figure 1.55 A warning sign

Figure 1.56 A safe conditions sign

Figure 1.57 A safety sign with symbol and words

Remember

Make sure you take notice of safety signs in the workplace – they have been put up for a reason!

FAQ

How do I find out what safety legislation is relevant to my job?

Ask your employer or manager, or visit the HSE website (A link to the website has been made available at www.pearsonhotlinks.co.uk).

When do I need to do a risk assessment?

A risk assessment should be carried out if there is any chance of an accident happening as a direct result of the work being done. To be on the safe side, you should make a risk assessment before starting each task.

Do I need to read and understand every regulation?

No. It is part of your employer's duty to ensure that you are aware of what you need to know.

Do I need to attend every toolbox talk?

No, you only need to attend the toolbox talks relevant to you, but if you are unsure or think that you have missed a toolbox talk discuss it with your supervisor.

What do I need to do if my PPE is damaged?

You need to inform your employer immediately so that you can have the PPE replaced. Damaged PPE will not offer sufficient protection.

Check it out

1. Name five pieces of health and safety legislation that affect the construction industry and give a brief explanation of what they do.
2. What is the HSE? Give a brief explanation of its role.
3. Sketch the triangle of fire and explain how these parts of the triangle relate to each other.
4. Describe, with sketches, the major warning signs and explain what they do.
5. Name six different types of PPE and give an example of each.
6. Describe the key items that should be included in a first aid kit.
7. Describe the purpose of a toolbox talk.
8. Describe three key things you should never do with a portable power tool.
9. Using a material that is familiar to you, explain with the aid of sketches if necessary, how that material should be stored.

Getting ready for assessment

The information contained in this unit, as well as continued health and safety good practice throughout your training, will help you with preparing for both your end of unit test and the diploma multiple-choice test. It will also help you to understand the dangers of working in the construction industry. Wherever you work in the construction industry, you will need to understand the dangers of working there. You will also need to know the safe working practices for the work required for your practical assignments.

Your college or training centre should provide you with the opportunity to practise these skills, as part of preparing for the test.

You will need to know about and understand the dangers that could arise and precautions that can be taken:

- the safety rules and regulations
- knowing accident and emergency procedures
- identifying hazards on site
- health and hygiene
- safe handling of materials and equipment
- working at height
- working with electricity
- using personal protective equipment (PPE)
- fire and emergency procedures
- safety signs.

You will need to apply the things that you have learned in this unit to the actual work you will be carrying out in the synoptic test and in your professional life. For example, with learning outcome 6 you have seen why basic working platforms are used and the good practice that you should use when working on these platforms. You have also identified the dangers of working at height.

You will now need to use this knowledge yourself when you are working, by using access equipment to the correct legislation and safeguarding your health, through using the correct PPE. You will also need to use your understanding of how PPE should be stored to maintain it in perfect condition.

Before you start work you should always think of a plan of action. You will need to know the clear sequences of operations for the practical work that is to be constructed, to be sure that you are not making mistakes as you work and that you are working safely at all times.

Your speed in carrying out these tasks in a practice setting will also help to prepare you for the time set for the test. However, you must never rush the test. This is particularly important with health and safety, as you must always make sure that you are working safely. Make sure throughout the test that you are wearing appropriate and correct PPE and using tools correctly.

This unit has explained the dangers that you may face when working. Understanding these dangers and the precautions that can be taken to help protect you from them will not only aid you in your training, but will also help you to remain safe and healthy throughout your working life.

Good luck!

CHECK YOUR KNOWLEDGE

1 Legislation is:
   a a law that must be complied with
   b a guide to tell you what to do
   c a code of practice
   d not your responsibility

2 Accidents are caused by:
   a following all instructions carefully
   b taking care of yourself and others
   c hurrying and not paying attention
   d nothing – accidents just happen

3 Manual handling injuries can be caused by:
   a lifting items that are too heavy
   b lifting an item once
   c lifting an item repetitively
   d all of the above

4 Which regulation deals with lifting components?
   a The Work at Height Regulations
   b The Manual Handling Operations Regulations
   c The PPE Regulations
   d The Electricity at Work Regulations

5 With regards to PPE, the employer must:
   a supply you with it
   b not charge you for it
   c ensure you wear it
   d do all of the above

6 A sign that is circular with a white background and a red circle around the edge with a red line through it is a:
   a warning sign
   b mandatory sign
   c prohibition sign
   d information sign

7 Which of the following regulations deals with chemicals?
   a Control of Substances Hazardous to Health
   b Health and Safety at Work Act
   c Provision and Use of Work Equipment Regulations
   d Control of Noise at Work Regulations

8 Who should carry out risk assessments?
   a no one
   b everyone
   c an untrained supervisor
   d a trained supervisor

9 Welfare facilities must include:
   a washing facilities
   b sleeping area
   c hot food
   d TV room

10 Under current European electrical regulations what colour wire is live?
   a red
   b blue
   c brown
   d black

UNIT 1002

Information, quantities and communicating with others 1

The construction industry contains a great deal of information that you must fully understand to meet the needs of a project. This information can be presented and stored in many ways. Some of the most important information relates to the start of a project, and tells you the type of construction you will be working on, what it will be used for and what you will need to build it. When working with information, you will also be working with other people. You will need to make sure that you use the correct method to communicate different types of information to other people.

This unit contains material that supports the five generic units of the TAPS. It will also support your completion of scaled drawings throughout all TAP units.

This unit will cover the following learning outcomes:

- Interpreting building information
- Determining quantities of materials
- Communicating information in the workplace.

K1. Interpreting building information

Building information is often communicated to others through paper documents. These can be:

- paperwork
- plans
- forms
- diagrams.

To understand all of these documents you need to know what they are used for in a building project.

Diagrams and plans are not drawn to life size, but to scales. So to be able to use diagrams, you need to understand how scales work and what they tell you about the final building.

In this section you will learn about:

- document security
- how to use scales and symbols
- specifications, drawings and schedules.

Document security

A lot of the information we will be looking at in this unit is vital for smooth and safe working on a site. Therefore it is important to store documents safely, securely and correctly. You need to understand this before you begin to work with documents.

Some documents may contain sensitive information such as addresses, National Insurance numbers etc. The Data Protection Act (1998) states that any company that holds personal information must make sure that it is secure and is only used for the purpose that it was provided for. This means that your employer, who will have information such as your bank details, must ensure all of this is kept secure.

Other documents such as drawings should also be kept secure, especially during the duration of the job. This is because these are a permanent record, both of what is happening and what has yet to happen. It is also considered good practice to keep records even after a job has been completed. This is because these can be used for reference at a later date and can be invaluable when estimating the cost of other similar jobs.

One problem with record keeping is obviously storage, and large companies have thousands of documents. However, storage is becoming a lot easier as we can now create and save documents on computers. We can even scan hard copies and save the original documents electronically too.

Scales, symbols and abbreviations

All building plans are drawn to scales and also use various symbols and abbreviations. To draw a building on a drawing sheet, its size must be reduced. This is called a scale drawing.

Using scales

The prefered scales for use in presenting building drawings are shown in Table 2.1.

Type of drawing	Scales
Block plans	1:2500, 1:1250
Site plans	1:500, 1:200
General location drawings	1:200, 1:100, 1:50
Range drawings	1:100, 1:50, 1:20
Detail drawings	1:10, 1:5, 1:1
Assembly drawings	1:20, 1:10, 1:5

Table 2.1 Preferred scales for building drawings

These scales mean that, for example, on a block plan drawn to 1:2500, 1 mm on the plan would represent 2500 mm (or 2.5 m) on the actual building. Some other examples are:

- on a scale of 1:50, 10 mm represents 500 mm
- on a scale of 1:100, 10 mm represents 1000 mm (1.0 m)
- on a scale of 1:200, 30 mm represents 6000 mm (6.0 m).

Accuracy of drawings

Printing or copying of drawings introduces variations that affect the accuracy of drawings. Hence, although measurements can be read from drawings using a rule with common scales marked (Figure 2.1), you should work to written instructions and measurements wherever possible.

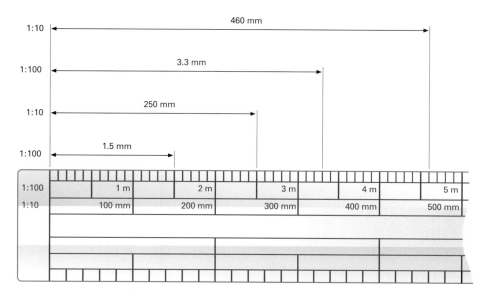

Figure 2.1 Rule with scales for maps and drawings

Scale drawings

Building plans are drawn to scale. Each length on the plan is **in proportion** to the real length.

On a drawing that has been drawn to a scale where 1 mm represents 50 mm:

- a length of 5 mm represents an actual length of $5 \times 50 = 250$ mm
- 12 mm represents an actual length of $12 \times 50 = 600$ mm
- an actual length of 350 mm is represented by a line $350 \div 50 = 7$ mm long.

Scales are often given as **ratios**. For example:

- a scale of 1:100 means that 1 mm on the drawing represents an actual length of 100 mm
- a scale of 1:20 000 means that 1 mm on the drawing represents an actual length of 20 000 mm (or 20 m).

Table 2.2 shows some common scales used in the construction industry.

1:5	1 mm represents 5 mm	5 times smaller than actual size
1:10	1 mm represents 10 mm	10 times smaller than actual size
1:20	1 mm represents 20 mm	20 times smaller than actual size
1:50	1 mm represents 50 mm	50 times smaller than actual size
1:100	1 mm represents 100 mm	100 times smaller than actual size
1:1250	1 mm represents 1250 mm = 1.25 m	1250 times smaller than actual size

Table 2.2 Common scales used in the construction industry

Now look at the following examples.

Did you know?

To make scale drawings, architects use a scale rule (Figure 2.1). The different scales on the ruler give the equivalent actual length measurements for different lengths in cm, for each scale

Key term

In proportion – the correct size in relation to something else

Ratio – one value divided by the other

Find out

With a little practice, you will easily master the use of scales.

Try the following:
- On a scale of 1:50, 40 mm represents: _____
- On a scale of 1:200, 70 mm represents: _____
- On a scale of 1:500, 40 mm represents: _____

Example

A plan is drawn to a scale of 1:20. On the plan, a wall is 4.5 mm long. How long is the actual wall?

1 mm on the plan = actual length 20 mm

So 4.5 mm on the plan = actual length $4.5 \times 20 = 90$ mm.

Example

A window is 3 m tall. How tall is it on the plan?

3 m = 3000 mm

an actual length of 20 mm is 1 mm on the plan

an actual length of 100 mm (5×20) is 5 mm (5×1) on the plan

an actual length of 3000 mm (30×100) is 150 mm (30×5) on the plan.

Therefore, the window is 150 mm tall on the plan.

Symbols and abbreviations

The use of symbols and abbreviations allows the maximum amount of information to be included on a drawing sheet in a clear way. Figure 2.2 shows some recommended drawing symbols for a range of building materials.

Figure 2.3 illustrates the recommended methods for indicating different types of doors and windows and their direction of opening.

Figure 2.4 shows some of the most frequently used graphical symbols and abbreviations, which are recommended in the British Standards Institution standard BS 1192.

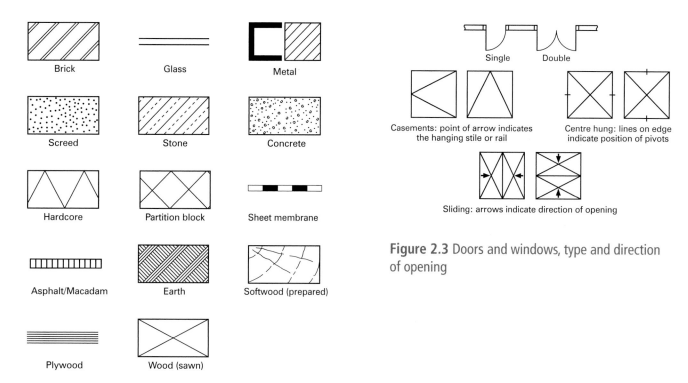

Figure 2.3 Doors and windows, type and direction of opening

Figure 2.2 Building material symbols

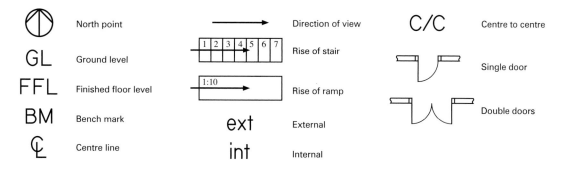

Figure 2.4 Graphical symbols and abbreviations used in the building industry

Remember

It is important to check that the documents you are working with are the most recent. If they have changed in any way, and you haven't been told, what you will be doing will be wrong

Table 2.3 lists some standard abbreviations used on drawings.

Item	Abbreviation	Item	Abbreviation
Airbrick	ab	Hardcore	hc
Asbestos	asb	Hardwood	hwd
Bitumen	bit	Insulation	insul
Boarding	bdg	Joist	jst
Brickwork	bwk	Mild steel	MS
Building	bldg	Plasterboard	pbd
Cast iron	CI	Polyvinyl acetate	PVA
Cement	ct	Polyvinyl chloride	PVC
Column	col	Reinforced condcrete	RC
Concrete	conc	Satin anodised aluminium	SAA
Cupboard	cpd	Satin chrome	SC
Damp proof course	DPC	Softwood	swd
Damp proof membrane	DPM	Stainless steel	SS
Drawing	dwg	Tongue and groove	T&G
Foundation	fnd	Wrought iron	WI
Hardboard	hdbd		

Table 2.3 Standard abbreviations used on drawings

Location drawings, specifications and schedules

Drawings, specifications and schedules are the main reference documents for work on site and are used to plan all the work that takes place during the build. It is important that all these documents are accurate and correct, and that any changes made to them are clearly communicated to everyone working on site.

Location drawings

Location drawings include block plans and site plans, and give a bird's eye view to show what the site will look like when it is completed. They are drawn to a chosen scale.

- **Block plans** – identify the proposed site by giving a bird's eye view of the site in relation to the surrounding area. An example is shown in Figure 2.5.
- **Site plans** – give the position of the proposed building and the general layout of the roads, services, drainage etc. on site. An example is shown in Figure 2.6.

Specifications

The specification or 'spec' is a document produced alongside the plans and drawings and is used to show information that can't be shown on the drawings. Specifications are almost always used, except in the case of very small contracts. A specification should contain:

- **site description** – a brief description of the site, including the address
- **restrictions** – what restrictions apply, such as working hours or limited access
- **services** – what services are available, what services need to be connected and what type of connection should be used
- **materials description** – including type, size, quality, moisture content etc.
- **workmanship** – including methods of fixing, quality of work and finish.

The specification may also name subcontractors or suppliers, or give details such as how the site should be cleared, and so on.

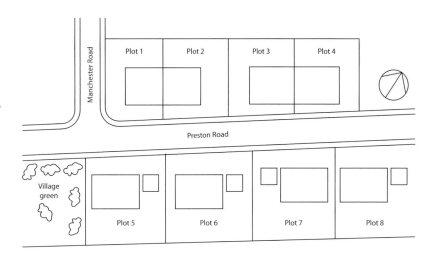

Figure 2.5 Block plan showing location

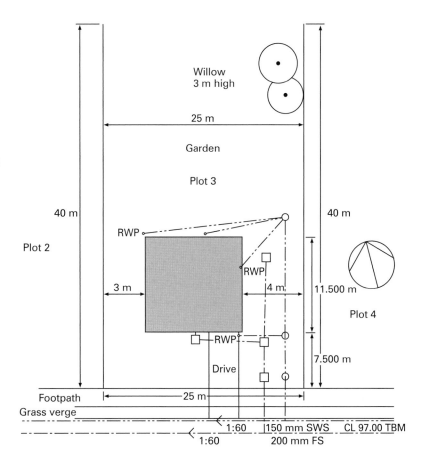

Figure 2.6 Site plan (not to scale)

Figure 2.7 A good 'spec' helps avoid confusion when dealing with subcontractors or suppliers

Schedules

A schedule is used to record repeated design information that applies to a range of components or fittings. Schedules are mainly used on bigger sites where there are multiples of several types of house (four-bedroom, three-bedroom, three-bedroom with dormers etc.), each type having different components and fittings. Schedules avoid the wrong component or fitting being put in the wrong house. Schedules can also be used on smaller jobs such as a block of flats with 200 windows, where there are six different types of window.

The need for a schedule depends on the complexity of the job and the number of repeated designs that there are. Schedules are mainly used to record repeated design information for:

- doors and windows
- sanitary components
- heating components and radiators
- ironmongery
- kitchens
- joinery fitments
- lintels
- windows.

A schedule is usually used with a range drawing and a floor plan.

Figures 2.8–2.10 show basic examples of these documents, using a window as an example.

The schedule in Figure 2.9 shows that there are five types of window, each differing in size and appearance; the range drawing shows what each type of window looks like; and the floor plan shows which window goes where. For example, the bathroom window is a type two window, which is 1200 × 600 × 50 cm with a top-opening sash and obscure glass.

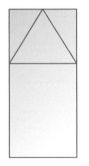

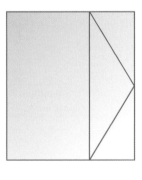
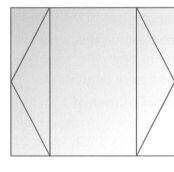

Window 1   Window 2   Window 3   Window 4   Window 5

Figure 2.8 Range drawing

WINDOW SCHEDULE		
WINDOW	LOCATIONS	NOTES
Window 1	Stairwell	
Window 2	Bathroom En-suite	Obscure glass
Window3	Bedroom 1 Bedroom 2	
Window 4	Bedroom 3 Master bedroom	
Window 5	Bedroom 4	

Figure 2.9 Schedule for the windows

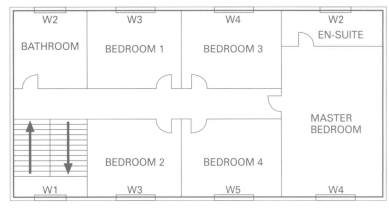

Figure 2.10 Floor plan

Work programme

A work programme is a method of showing very easily what work is being carried out on a building and when. The most common form of work programme is a bar chart. Used by many site agents or supervisors, a bar chart lists the tasks that need to be done down the left side and shows a timeline across the top. A work programme is used to make sure that the relevant trade is on site at the correct time and that materials are delivered when needed. A site agent or supervisor can quickly tell from looking at the chart if work is keeping to schedule or falling behind.

Bar charts

The bar or Gantt chart is the most popular work programme. It is simple to construct and easy to understand. Bar charts have tasks listed in a vertical column on the left and a horizontal timescale running along the top.

Time in days										
Activity	1	2	3	4	5	6	7	8	9	10
Dig for foundation and service routes										
Lay foundations										
Run cabling, piping etc. to meet existing services										
Build up to damp proof course										
Lay concrete floor										

Figure 2.11 Basic bar chart

> **Did you know?**
>
> The Gantt chart is named after Henry Gantt, an American engineer, who, in 1910, was the first to design and use this chart

Did you know?

Bad weather is the main external factor responsible for delays on building sites in the UK. A Met Office survey showed that UK construction companies experience problems caused by the weather on average 26 times a year

Functional skills

FM 1.2.1 relates to using whole numbers. These may be positive or negative numbers. Think of a situation where these numbers would be used – e.g. attendance at a football match or the temperature in both winter and summer.

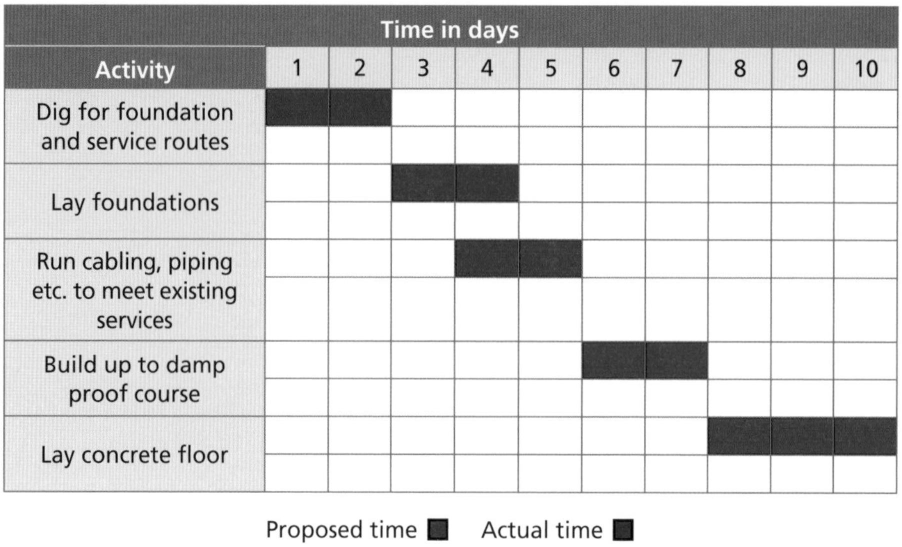
Time in days
Activity
1
2
3
4
5
6
7
8
9
10
Dig for foundation and service routes
Lay foundations
Run cabling, piping etc. to meet existing services
Build up to damp proof course
Lay concrete floor
Proposed time
Actual time

Figure 2.12 Bar chart showing proposed time for a contract

Each task is given a proposed time, which is shaded in along the horizontal timescale. Timescales often overlap as one task often overlaps another.

The bar chart can then be used to check progress. Often the actual time taken for a task is shaded in underneath the proposed time (in a different way or colour to avoid confusion). This shows how what HAS been done matches up to what SHOULD have been done.

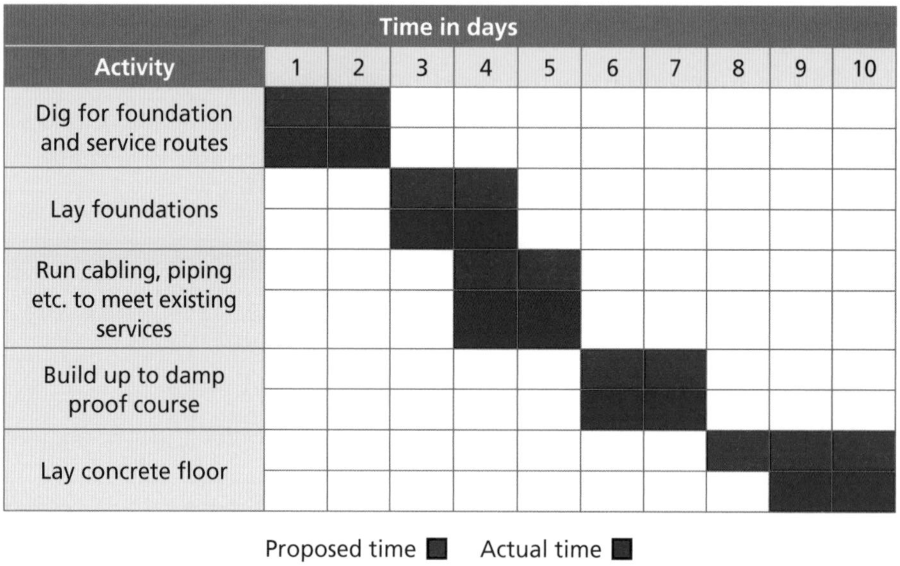
Time in days
Activity
1
2
3
4
5
6
7
8
9
10
Dig for foundation and service routes
Lay foundations
Run cabling, piping etc. to meet existing services
Build up to damp proof course
Lay concrete floor
Proposed time
Actual time

Figure 2.13 Bar chart showing actual time half way through a contract

So a bar chart can help you plan when to order materials or plant, see what trade is due in and when, and so on. A bar chart can also tell you if you are behind on a job; this information is vital if your contract contains a **penalty clause**.

Key term

Penalty clause – a condition written into the contract that states the work must be completed to the required quality by a certain date. If the job over-runs, the contractor will not be paid the full amount for each day the job runs over

When creating a bar chart, you should build in some extra time to allow for things such as bad weather, labour shortages, delivery problems or illness. It is also advisable to have contingency (back-up) plans to help solve or avoid problems, such as:

- capacity to work overtime to catch up time

- bonus scheme to increase productivity

- penalty clause on suppliers to try to avoid late or poor deliveries

- source of extra labour (for example from another site) if needed.

Good planning, with contingency plans in place, should allow a job to run smoothly and finish on time, leading to the contractor making a profit.

K2. Determining quantities of materials

The information contained in the drawings and specification for a project will tell you what materials you will need for the job. You will use this information to determine the quantity of each type of material you will need. To work this out you need to know the methods used to calculate basic **estimates** of material quantity.

When making calculations there are several resources you will find useful. These include:

- diagrams and plans
- calculators
- conversion tables
- scale rules.

Numbers

Place value

0, 1, 2, 3, 4, 5, 6, 7, 8 and 9 are the ten digits we work with. We can write any number you can think of, however huge, using any combination of these ten digits. In a number, the value of each digit depends on its 'place value'. Table 2.4 is a place value table and shows how the value of digit 2 is different, depending on its position.

Key term

Estimate – to assess something, such as a job to be done, and to state a likely price for it

Functional skills

FM 1.2.1a relates to mathematical procedures such as addition and subtraction. You will need to organise numbers in units, tens, hundreds and thousands in order to carry out the task.

Did you know?

Zero is neither positive nor negative

Millions (M)	Hundred thousands (100Th)	Ten thousands (10Th)	Thousands (Th)	Hundreds (H)	Tens (T)	Units (U)	Value
2	9	4	1	3	7	8	2 million
	2	5	3	1	0	7	2 hundred thousand
	7	2	5	6	6	4	2 × ten thousand = 20 thousand
		6	2	4	9	2	2 thousands
		5	6	2	9	1	2 hundreds
			8	4	2	7	2 tens = 20
				1	6	2	2 units

Table 2.4 Place value table for the digit 2

Positive numbers

A positive number is a number that is greater than zero. If we make a number line, positive numbers are all the numbers to the right of zero.

0 1 2 3 4 5 6 7 8 9 10 11 12 13...
Positive numbers

Negative numbers

A negative number is a number that is less than zero. If we make another number line, negative numbers are all the numbers to the left of zero.

...-13 -12 -11 -10 -9 -8 -7 -6 -5 -4 -3 -2 -1 0
Negative numbers

Making calculations

There are several calculation methods that are used to calculate the area of basic shapes. The main ones you will need to use are:

- addition
- subtraction
- multiplication
- division.

These methods are used to calculate the basic areas of a series of shapes that you will encounter on plans and diagrams.

Addition

When adding numbers using a written method, write digits with the same place value in the same column. For example, to work out what is 26 + 896 + 1213, write the calculation:

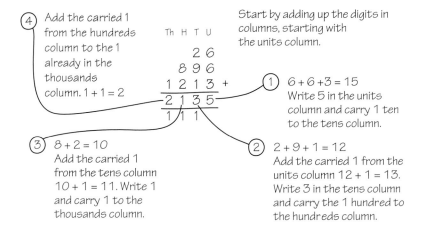

④ Add the carried 1 from the hundreds column to the 1 already in the thousands column. 1 + 1 = 2

Start by adding up the digits in columns, starting with the units column.

① 6 + 6 + 3 = 15
Write 5 in the units column and carry 1 ten to the tens column.

③ 8 + 2 = 10
Add the carried 1 from the tens column 10 + 1 = 11. Write 1 and carry 1 to the thousands column.

② 2 + 9 + 1 = 12
Add the carried 1 from the units column 12 + 1 = 13. Write 3 in the tens column and carry the 1 hundred to the hundreds column.

To add numbers with decimals, write the numbers with the decimal points in line. For example, to work out what is 4.56 + 10.2 + 0.32, write the calculation:

```
  4.56
 10.20      Adding a zero here helps to
  0.32      keep the digits in line.
 ─────
 15.08
```

In a problem, the following words mean you need to add.

- **Total** – What is the total of 43 and 2457? (43 + 2457)
- **Sum** – What is the sum of 56 and 345? (56 + 345)
- **Increase** – Increase 3467 by 521 (3467 + 521)

Subtraction

When subtracting numbers using a written method, write digits with the same place value in the same column For example, to work out what is $314 - 92$, write the calculation;

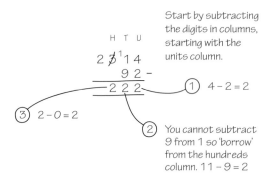

In a problem, the following words and phrases mean you need to subtract.

- **Find the difference** – Find the difference between 200 and 45 $(200 - 45)$

- **Decrease** – Decrease 64 by 9 $(64 - 9)$

- **How much greater than** – How much greater than 98 is 110? $(110 - 98)$

Multiplication

Knowing multiplication tables up to 10×10 helps with multiplying single digit numbers. You can use multiplication facts you already know to work out other multiplication calculations.

To multiply larger numbers you can write the calculation in columns or use the grid method. Both methods work by splitting the calculation into smaller ones.

Example

What is 20×12

You know that $20 = 2 \times 10$

So $20 \times 12 = 2 \times 10 \times 12$

$= 2 \times 12 \times 10$

$= 24 \times 10 = 240$

Multiplying using columns

```
  H T U
    2 5
×   3 6
  ─────
  1 5 0      6 × 25 ⎫ Add these to
  7 5 0     30 × 25 ⎭ find 36 × 25
  ─────
  9 0 0
```

Multiplying using the grid method

$36 \times 25 =$

×	20	5
30	600	150
6	120	30

$30 \times 20 = 600$
$30 \times 5 = 150$
$6 \times 20 = 120$
$6 \times 5 = \underline{30}$
900

Division

Division is the opposite of multiplication. Knowing the multiplication tables up to 10×10 also helps with division. Each multiplication fact gives two related division facts. For example:

$4 \times 6 = 24$ $24 \div 6 = 4$ $24 \div 4 = 6$

Short division

When dividing by a single digit number, use short division. For example, to work out what is $161 \div 7$, write the calculation:

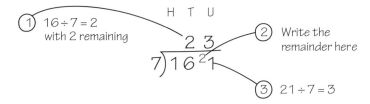

① $16 \div 7 = 2$ with 2 remaining

② Write the remainder here

③ $21 \div 7 = 3$

> **Remember**
>
> Metric units are all based on 10, 100, 1000 – which makes it easy to convert between units

Long division

When dividing by 10 or more, use long division. For example to work out what is $2952 \div 12$, write the calculation:

```
    Th H T U
        2 4 6
12) 2 9 5 2
      2 4
        5 5
        4 8
          7 2
          7 2
            0
```

$2 \times 12 = 24$
$29 - 24 = 5$. Bring down the next 5
$12 \times 4 = 48$
$55 - 48 = 7$. Bring down the 2
$12 \times 6 = 72$

Estimating

Sometimes an accurate answer to a calculation is not required. You can estimate an approximate answer by rounding all the values in the calculation to 1 **significant figure** (s.f.). For example:

Estimate the answer to the calculation 4.9×3.1

4.9 rounds to 5 to 1 s.f.

3.1 rounds to 3 to 1 s.f.

A sensible estimate is $5 \times 3 = 15$

The correct answer is 15.19

> **Key term**
>
> **Significant figure** – a prescribed decimal place that determines the amount of rounding off to be done

> **Did you know?**
>
> You can use values rounded to 1 s.f. to estimate approximate areas and prices

Measures

Quantities of material are presented in measurements, which are used when ordering and in plans and specifications. The mathematic skills described above will enable you to use these units of measurement.

Units of measurement

The metric units of measurement are shown in Table 2.5. The most common units you will work with are millimetres and metres.

Length	millimetres (mm) centimetres (cm) metres (m) kilometres (km)
Mass (weight)	grams (g) kilograms (kg) tonnes (t)
Capacity (the amount a container holds)	millilitres (ml) centilitres (cl) litres (l)

Table 2.5 Metric units of measurement

milli means one thousandth	$1mm = \frac{1}{1000}$ m	$1ml = \frac{1}{1000}$ litre
centi means one hundredth	$1cm = \frac{1}{100}$ m	$1cl = \frac{1}{1000}$ litre
kilo means one thousand	$1kg = 1000$ g	$1km = 1000$ m

For calculations involving measurements, you need to convert all the measurements into the same unit.

Table 2.6 shows some useful metric conversions.

Length	Mass	Capacity
1 cm = 10 mm	1 kg = 1000 g	1 l = 100 cl = 1000 ml
1 m = 100 cm = 1000 mm	1 tonne = 1000 kg	
1 km = 1000 m		

Table 2.6 Useful metric conversions

Example

A plasterer measures the lengths of cornice required for a room. He writes down the measurements as 175 cm, 2 m, 2250 mm, 1.5 m. To work out the total length of cornice needed, we first need to write all the lengths in the same units:

175 cm = 175 ÷ 100 = 1.75 m

2 m

1.5 m

2250 mm = 2250 ÷ 1000 = 2.25 m

So the total length is:

1.75 + 2 + 1.5 + 2.25 = 7.5 m

Did you know?

A useful rhyme to help you remember the pints to litre conversion is: 'a litre of water is a pint and three quarters'

To convert 2657 mm to metres:	2657 ÷ 1000 = 2.657 m
To convert 0.75 tonnes to kg:	0.75 × 1000 = 750 kg

Imperial units

In the UK we still use some imperial units of measurement (see Table 2.7).

Length	Inches Feet Yards Miles
Mass (weight)	Ounces Pounds Stones
Capacity (the amount a container holds)	Pints Gallons

Table 2.7 Some imperial units of measurement

To convert from imperial to metric units, use the approximate conversions shown in Table 2.8.

Length	Mass	Capacity
1 inch = 250 mm	2.2 pounds = 1 kg	1.75 pints = 1 litre
1 foot = 300 mm	1 ounce = 25 g	1 gallon = 4.5 litres
5 miles = 8 km		

Table 2.8 Converting imperial measurements to metric

Calculating perimeters and areas

Perimeter of shapes with straight sides

The perimeter of a shape is the distance all around the outside of the shape. To find the perimeter of a shape, measure all the sides and then add the lengths together.

Units of area

The area of a two-dimensional (2-D; flat) shape is the amount of space it covers. Area is measured in square units, such as square millimetres (mm²) and square metres (m²).

The area of this square is 10 × 10 = 100 mm².

> **Remember**
> - To convert from a smaller unit to a larger one – divide
> - To convert from a larger unit to a smaller one – multiply

> **Example**
> If a wall is 32 feet long, what is its approximate length in metres?
>
> 1 foot = 300 mm
>
> So 32 feet = 32 × 300 mm
> = 9600 mm = 9.6 m.

> **Remember**
> 1 cm² = 100 mm²
>
> 1 m² = 10 000 cm²

> **Example**
>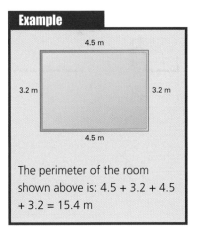
>
> The perimeter of the room shown above is: 4.5 + 3.2 + 4.5 + 3.2 = 15.4 m

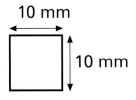

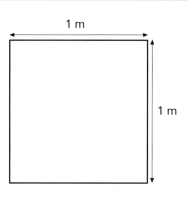

The area of this square is $1 \times 1 = 1 \text{ m}^2$.

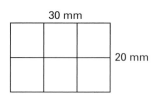

Area of shapes with straight sides

This rectangle is drawn on squared paper. Each square has an area of 10 mm².

You can find the area by counting the squares:

Area = 6 squares = 60 mm²

You can also calculate the area by multiplying the number of squares in a row by the number of rows:

$3 \times 2 = 6$

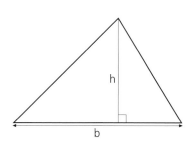

The area of a rectangle with length l and width w is:

$A = l \times w$

Example

If the length of a rectangular room is 3.6 m and the width is 2.7 m, the area is:

$A = 3.6 \times 2.7 = 9.72 \text{ m}^2$

Area of a triangle

The area of a triangle is given by the formula:

$$A = \frac{1}{2} \times h \times b$$

where h is the **perpendicular** height and b is the length of the base. The perpendicular height is drawn to meet the base at right angles (90°).

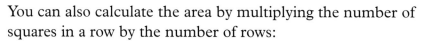

Key term

Perpendicular – at right angles to

Example

What is (a) the area and (b) the perimeter of the triangle below?

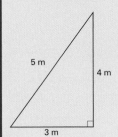

Perpendicular height = 4 m, base = 3 m

$$A = \frac{1}{2} \times h \times b$$

$$= \frac{1}{2} \times 4 \times 3$$

$$= 6 \text{ m}^2$$

Perimeter = 5 + 4 + 3 = 12 m

Pythagoras' theorem

You can use Pythagoras' theorem to find unknown lengths in right-angled triangles. In a right-angled triangle:

- one angle is 90° (a right angle)
- the longest side is opposite the right angle and is called the **hypotenuse**.

Pythagoras' theorem says that for any right-angled triangle with sides a and b and hypotenuse c, $c^2 = a^2 + b^2$.

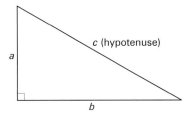

Key term

Hypotenuse – the longest side of a right-angled triangle

a^2 is 'a squared' and is equal to $a \times a$.

In the example a is '3 squared' and is equal to 3×3. The opposite or inverse of squaring is finding the square root. $\sqrt{25}$ means 'the square root of 25': $5 \times 5 = 25$, so $\sqrt{25} = 5$.

Example

What is the length of the hypotenuse of this triangle?

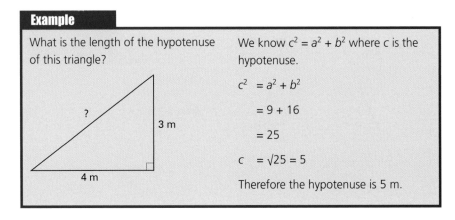

We know $c^2 = a^2 + b^2$ where c is the hypotenuse.

$$c^2 = a^2 + b^2$$

$$= 9 + 16$$

$$= 25$$

$$c = \sqrt{25} = 5$$

Therefore the hypotenuse is 5 m.

Example

What is the length of side a in the right-angled triangle below?

12 m · a · 6 m

$a^2 = c^2 - b^2$

$\quad = 12^2 - 6^2$

$\quad = 144 - 36 = 108$

$a \quad = \sqrt{108} = 10.3923\ldots$ (using the $\sqrt{}$ key on a calculator)

$\quad = 10.4$ m (to 1 decimal place [d.p.])

Learning these squares and square roots will help with Pythagoras' theorem calculations. Table 2.9 shows some squares and square roots you will often find useful to know.

$1^2 = 1 \times 1 = 1$	$\sqrt{1} = 1$
$2^2 = 2 \times 2 = 4$	$\sqrt{4} = 2$
$3^2 = 3 \times 3 = 9$	$\sqrt{9} = 3$
$4^2 = 4 \times 4 = 16$	$\sqrt{16} = 4$
$5^2 = 5 \times 5 = 25$	$\sqrt{25} = 5$
$6^2 = 6 \times 6 = 36$	$\sqrt{36} = 6$
$7^2 = 7 \times 7 = 49$	$\sqrt{49} = 7$
$8^2 = 8 \times 8 = 64$	$\sqrt{64} = 8$
$9^2 = 9 \times 9 = 81$	$\sqrt{81} = 9$
$10^2 = 10 \times 10 = 100$	$\sqrt{100} = 10$

Table 2.9 Useful squares and square roots

Using Pythagoras' theorem to find the shorter side of a triangle

You can rearrange Pythagoras' theorem like this:

$$c^2 = a^2 + b^2$$

$$a^2 = c^2 - b^2$$

Example

You can also use Pythagoras' theorem to find the perpendicular height of a triangle. For example, if we wanted to find the area of the triangle below, we would need to find the perpendicular height:

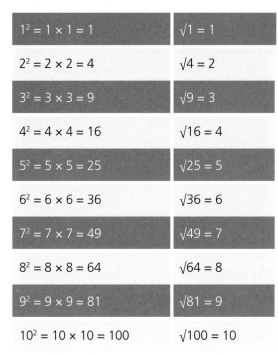

6 m · h · 3 m · 2 m

Using Pythagoras theorem:

$h^2 = 6^2 - 3^2$

$\quad = 36 - 9 = 27$

$h = \sqrt{27} \quad = 5.196\ldots = 5.2$ m (to 1 d.p. using the $\sqrt{}$ key on a calculator)

Area $= \frac{1}{2} \times b \times h$

$\quad = \frac{1}{2} \times 5 \,(3 + 2) \times 5.2$

$\quad = 13$ m^2

Areas of composite shapes

Composite shapes are made up of simple shapes such as rectangles and squares. To find the area, divide up the shape and find the area of each part separately. For example, to work out the area of the L-shaped room below:

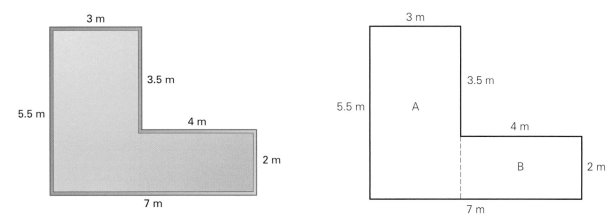

First divide it into two rectangles, A and B:

Area of rectangle A = $3 \times 5.5 = 16.5$ m^2

Area of rectangle B = $4 \times 2 = 8$ m^2

Total area of room = $16.5 + 8 = 24.5$ m^2

You could also divide the rectangle in the example above into two different rectangles, C and D, like this:

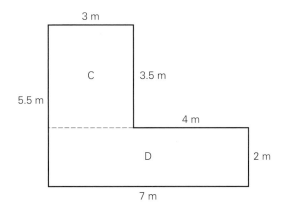

Check that you get the same total area.

Some shapes can be divided into rectangles and triangles. For example, to find the area of the wooden floor below:

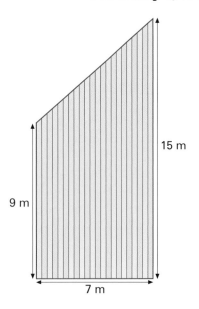

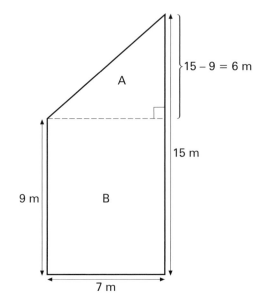

15 – 9 = 6 m

15 m

9 m

B

7 m

Divide the floor into a right-angled triangle A and a rectangle B.

Triangle A has vertical height 6 m and base 7 m.

Area of the triangle A $= \dfrac{1}{2} \times b \times h$

$$= \dfrac{1}{2} \times 7 \times 6 = 21 \text{ m}^2$$

Area of the rectangle B = 9 × 7 = 63 m²

Total area = 21 + 63 = 84 m².

Circumference of a circle

The formula for the **circumference** of a circle of **radius** r is:

$C = 2\pi r$

The diameter is the distance across the circle through the centre (diameter = 2 × radius).

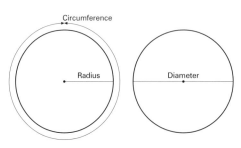

Circumference

Radius

Diameter

$\pi = 3.141\ 592\ 654\ldots$

To estimate the circumference of a circle, use $\pi = 3$. For more accurate calculations use $\pi = 3.14$, or the π key on a calculator.

Key terms

Radius – the distance from the centre of a circle to its outside edge

Circumference – the perimeter of a circle, the distance all the way around the outside

Did you know?

If you are given the diameter of the circle, you need to halve the diameter to find the radius

Area of a circle

The formula for the area of a circle of radius r is:

$$\text{Area} = \pi r^2$$

We can calculate the area of a circle with radius 3.25 m as:

$$\text{Area} = \pi r^2$$

$$= \pi \times r^2$$

$$= 3.14 \times 3.25 \times 3.25 = 33.166\ 25$$

$$= 33\ \text{m}^2 \text{ (to the nearest metre).}$$

Area and circumference of part circles and composite shapes

You can use the formulae for circumference and area of a circle to calculate perimeters and areas of parts of circles, and shapes made from parts of circles. For example, we can work out the perimeter and area of the semicircular window (right).

The diameter of the semicircle is 1.3 m, so the radius is $1.3 \div 2 = 0.65$ m.

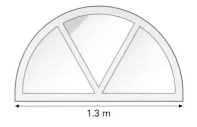

1.3 m

The length of the curved side is half the circumference of the circle with radius 0.65 m.

$$\text{Length of curved side} = \frac{1}{2} \times 2\pi r$$

$$= \frac{1}{2} \times 2 \times \pi \times r$$

$$= \frac{1}{2} \times 2 \times 3.14 \times 0.65 = 2.041\ \text{m}$$

Circumference of the semicircle = curved side + straight side

$$= 2.041 + 1.3 = 3.341\text{m}$$

$$= 3.34\ \text{m}$$

Area of semicircle = half the area of the circle with radius 0.65m

$$= \frac{1}{2} \times \pi\, r^2$$

$$= \frac{1}{2} \times \pi \times r^2$$

$$= \frac{1}{2} \times 3.14 \times 0.65 \times 0.65 = 0.663\ 325\ \text{m}^2$$

$$= 0.66\ \text{m}^2 \text{ (to 2 d.p.)}$$

Example

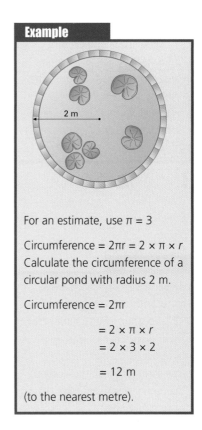

2 m

For an estimate, use π = 3

Circumference = 2πr = 2 × π × r

Calculate the circumference of a circular pond with radius 2 m.

Circumference = 2πr

$$= 2 \times \pi \times r$$
$$= 2 \times 3 \times 2$$
$$= 12\ \text{m}$$

(to the nearest metre).

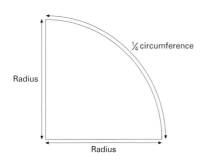

To find the area of a quarter circle, use $\frac{1}{4}\pi r^2$.

To find the perimeter of a quarter circle, work out $\frac{1}{4}$ circumference + 2 × radius.

To find the area of a composite shape including parts of circles, divide it into circles and simple shapes and find the areas separately.

K3. Communicating information in the workplace

Functional skills

Communicating effectively is an essential skill in everyday work. **FE** 1.1.1 and **FE** 1.1.3 – 4 relate to speaking and listening. You might be expected to take part in discussions about your work and be asked for your opinions. You will also be required to write information, such as messages to supervisors, and present information such as material orders or accident reports. The writing skills **FE** 1.3.1 –1.3.5 will enable you to communicate information, ideas and opinions effectively.

Communication, in the simplest of terms, is a way or means of passing on information from one person to another. Communication is very important in all areas of life and we often do it without even thinking about it. You will need to communicate well when you are at work, no matter what job you do. What would happen if someone couldn't understand something you had written or said? If we don't communicate well, how will other people know what we want or need and how will we know what other people want?

Companies that do not establish good methods of communicating with their workforce, or with other companies, will not function properly. They will also end up with bad working relationships. Co-operation and good communication are vital to achieve good working relationships.

Message taking

One of the most common reasons for communicating is to give a message to someone. You could often be the 'channel' passing a message from one person to another (the 'third party').

To ensure good and efficient communication there are certain things you can do when taking messages. When a phone call is made, many things may be discussed. Some of these things may need to be passed on to a third party.

The main things you should record when taking a phone call are:

- date
- time
- contact name and details.

Remember

Making sure messages are as clear and complete as possible is an important rule to remember when you communicate with anyone – either through speaking (oral communication), writing or any other form of communication

The topic of conversation can also be recorded but, if it's complex or lengthy, this may not be possible. The most important thing to take is the person's contact details. This will allow the person the message is for to get in direct contact with the person sending the message, so that further conversations can take place.

Taking accurate information from a conversation is important as other people may use this as a source of information for making decisions. For example, a person receiving a message may decide when to call back, based on a message. If the message didn't indicate the matter was urgent, the person may delay returning the call, which could have serious consequences.

Did you know?

Some companies have their own forms to cover such things as scaffolding checks

Information relevant to communication

There are a number of different sources of information on site that are important to effective communication. By using these sources of information, you can improve the effectiveness of your communication.

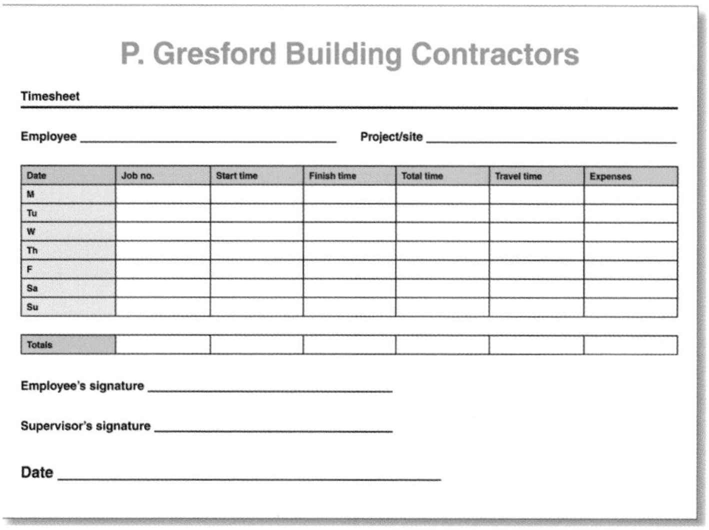

P. Gresford Building Contractors

Timesheet

Employee ______ Project/site ______

Date	Job no.	Start time	Finish time	Total time	Travel time	Expenses
M						
Tu						
W						
Th						
F						
Sa						
Su						
Totals						

Employee's signature ______

Supervisor's signature ______

Date ______

Figure 2.14 Timesheet

General site paperwork

No building site could function properly without a certain amount of paperwork. Here is a brief description of some of the documents you may encounter, besides the ones already mentioned in the first part of this unit.

Timesheets

Timesheets record hours worked, and are completed by every employee individually. Some timesheets are basic, asking just for a brief description of the work done each hour, but some can be more detailed. In some cases timesheets may be used to work out how many hours the client will be charged for.

Day worksheets

Day worksheets are often confused with timesheets. However, they are different as day worksheets are used when there is no price or estimate for the work and so enable the contractor to charge for the work. Day worksheets record work done, hours worked and, sometimes, the materials used.

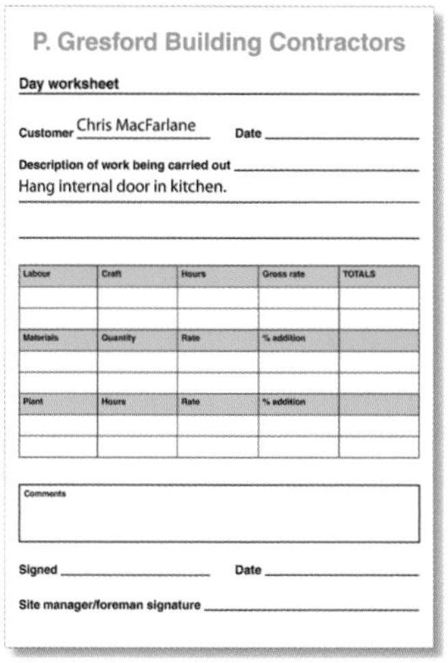

P. Gresford Building Contractors

Day worksheet

Customer Chris MacFarlane Date ______

Description of work being carried out ______
Hang internal door in kitchen.

Labour	Craft	Hours	Gross rate	TOTALS
Materials	Quantity	Rate	% addition	
Plant	Hours	Rate	% addition	

Comments

Signed ______ Date ______

Site manager/foreman signature ______

Figure 2.15 Day worksheet

P. Gresford Building Contractors

Job sheet

Customer Chris MacFarlane

Address 1 High Street
         Any Town
         Any County

Work to be carried out
Hang internal door in kitchen

Special conditions/instructions
Fit with door closer
3 × 75mm butt hinges

Figure 2.16 Job sheet

Job sheet

A job sheet is similar to a day worksheet but is used when the work has already been priced. Job sheets show what needs to be done and what has been completed.

Variation order

A variation order is used by the architect to make any changes to the original plans, including omissions, alterations and extra work.

Confirmation notice

This is given to the contractor to confirm any changes that have been made in the variation order, so that the contractor can carry out the work.

Orders/requisitions

These are used to order materials from a supplier.

Delivery notes

These are given to the contractor by the supplier, and list all the materials being delivered. Each delivery note should be checked for accuracy against the order (to ensure what is being delivered is what was asked for) and against the delivery itself (to make sure that the delivery matches the delivery note).

Invoices

Invoices come from a variety of sources such as suppliers or subcontractors, and state what has been provided and how much the contractor will be charged for it.

Remember

If there are any discrepancies or problems with a delivery, such as poor quality or damaged goods, you should write on the delivery note what is wrong BEFORE you sign it. You should also make sure that the site agent is informed so that they can rectify the problem

Remember

Invoices may need paying by a certain date – fines for late payment can sometimes be incurred. So it is important that they are passed on to the finance office or financial controller promptly

Delivery Note

Bailey & Sons Ltd
Building materials supplier
Tel: 01234 567890

Your ref: AB00671

Our ref: CT020   Date: 17 Jul 2006

Order no: 67440387

Invoice address: Delivery address:
Carillion Training Centre,   Same as invoice
Deptford Terrace, Sunderland

Description of goods	Quantity	Catalogue no.
OPC 25kg	10	OPC1.1

Comments:

Date and time of receiving goods:
Name of recipient (caps):
Signature:

Figure 2.17 Delivery note

INVOICE		JARVIS BUILDING SUPPLIES		
L Weeks Builders				3RD AVENUE
4th Grove				THOMASTOWN
Thomastown				

Quantity	Description	Unit price	Vat rate	Total
30	Galvanised joist hangers	£1.32	20%	£47.52
			TOTAL	£47.52

To be paid within 30 days from receipt of this invoice

Please direct any queries to 01234 56789

Figure 2.18 Invoice

Delivery records

These list all deliveries over a certain period (usually a month), and are sent to the contractor's head office so that payments can be made.

Daily report/site diary

This is used to pass general information (deliveries, attendance etc.) to a company's head office.

JARVIS BUILDING SUPPLIES
3rd AVENUE
THOMASTOWN

Customer ref__________

Customer order date__________

Delivery date__________

Item no	Qty Supplied	Qty to follow	Description	Unit price
1	30	0	Galvanised joist hangers	£1.32

Delivered to: L Weeks Builders
4th Grove
Thomastown

Customer signature..........................

Figure 2.19 Delivery record

DAILY REPORT/SITE DIARY

PROJECT__________
DATE__________

Identify any of the following factors, which are affecting or may affect the daily work activities and give a brief description in the box provided

WEATHER ( ) ACCESS ( ) ACCIDENTS ( ) SERVICES ( )
DELIVERIES ( ) SUPPLIES ( ) LABOUR ( ) OTHER ( )

SIGNED ....
POSITION ....

Figure 2.20 Daily report or site diary

Policies and procedures

Most companies will have their own policies and procedures in the workplace. All employees will be expected to follow these.

A policy states what the company expects to be done in a certain situation. Companies usually have policies for most things ranging from health and safety to materials orders. For example, in a health and safety policy the company will expect all employees to abide by rules and regulations and be safe.

To ensure that the policies are followed, the company will use certain procedures for working. For example, using a certain form to record data or using a certain method of working.

These policies and procedures are vital in a large organisation that may be doing work in several different sites in different locations. A senior manager should be able to walk into any site at any location and see exactly the same set-up with the same forms and procedures being used everywhere.

Site rules

Site rules will cover most things ranging from safety to security. The company will have general policies covering rules that everyone on site must follow. These include important but basic things such as hours of work, behaviour etc.

However, a local site may have additional rules that apply only to that site. This is because each site will have some different situations. Site rules deal with those situations that could occur ONLY on that site.

Remember

Your company's rules should be explained to you when you first start work. Any additional site rules should be made clear at your site induction (see Unit 1001, page 12)

Positive and negative communication

You can communicate in a variety of ways, and the main methods of communication are explained below, with the advantages and disadvantages of each method.

The key point to remember is to make all your communication positive. Positive communication will basically have a positive

Messages

To Andy Rogers

Date Tues 10 Nov   Time 11.10am

Message Mark from Stokes called with a query about recent order. Please phone asap (tel 01234 567 890)

Message taken by: Lee Barber

Figure 2.21 A message is a form of written communication

Key terms

Fax – short for facsimile, which is a kind of photocopy that can be sent by dialling a phone number on a fax machine

outcome with the message being communicated successfully. This will lead to things getting done right first time. Negative communication will have the opposite effect and may lead to costly delays.

For positive communication, you need to ensure that no matter what method you use, the communication is clear, simple and – importantly – communicated to the right people.

Methods of communication

There are many different ways of communicating with others and they all generally fit into one of these four categories:

- verbal communication (speaking), for example talking face to face or over the telephone or radio
- written communication, for example sending a letter or a memo
- body language, for example the way we stand or our facial expressions
- electronic communication, for example email, **fax** and text messages.

Each method of communicating has some good points (advantages) and some bad points (disadvantages).

Verbal communication	
Verbal communication is the most common method we use to communicate with each other. If two people don't speak the same language or if someone speaks very quietly or not very clearly, verbal communication cannot be effective. Working in the construction industry you may communicate verbally with other people face to face, over the telephone or by radio/walkie-talkie.	
Advantages	**Disadvantages**
Verbal communication is instant, easy and can be repeated or rephrased until the message is understood.	Verbal communication can be easily forgotten as there is no physical evidence of the message. Because of this it can be easily changed if passed to other people. A different accent or use of slang can sometimes make it difficult to understand what a person is saying.

Written communication	
Written communication can take the form of letters, messages, notes, instruction leaflets and drawings among others.	
Advantages	**Disadvantages**
There is physical evidence of the communication and the message can be passed on to another person without it being changed. It can also be read again if it is not understood.	Written communication takes longer to arrive and understand than verbal communication and body language. It can also be misunderstood or lost. If it is handwritten, the reader may not be able to read the writing if it is messy.

Body language

It is said that, when we are talking to someone face to face, only 10% of our communication is verbal. The rest of the communication is body language and facial expression. This form of communication can be as simple as the shaking of a head from left to right to mean 'no' or as complex as the way someone's face changes when they are happy or sad or the signs given in body language when someone is lying.

We often use hand gestures as well as words to get across what we are saying, to emphasise a point or give a direction. Some people communicate entirely through a form of body language called sign language.

Advantages	Disadvantages
If you are aware of your own body language and know how to use it effectively, you can add extra meaning to what you say. For example, when you are talking to a client or a work colleague, even if the words you are using are friendly and polite, if your body language is negative or unfriendly, the message that you are giving out could be misunderstood. By simply maintaining eye contact, smiling and not folding your arms, you have made sure that the person you are communicating with has not got a mixed or confusing message. Body language is quick and effective. A wave from a distance can pass on a greeting without being close, and using hand signals to direct a lorry or a load from a crane is instant and doesn't require any equipment such as radios.	Some gestures can be misunderstood, especially if they are given from very far away. Also, some gestures that have one meaning in one country or culture can have a completely different meaning in another.  **Figure 2.22** Try to be aware of your body language

Electronic communication

Electronic communication is becoming more and more common and easy with advances in technology. Electronic communication can take many forms, such as text messages, email and fax. It is now possible to send and receive emails via mobile phones, which allows important information to be sent or received from almost anywhere in the world.

Advantages	Disadvantages
Electronic communication takes the best parts from verbal and written communication in as much as it is instant, easy and there is a record of the communication being sent. Electronic communication goes even further as it can tell the sender if the message has been received and even read. Emails in particular can be used to send a vast amount of information and can even give links to websites or other information. Attachments to emails allow anything from instructions to drawings to be sent with the message.	There are a few disadvantages to electronic communication, the obvious ones being no signal or a flat battery on a mobile phone and servers being down which prevent emails being sent etc. Not everyone is up to speed on the latest technology and some people are not comfortable using electronic communication. You need to make sure that the person receiving your message is able to understand how to access the information. Computer viruses can also be a problem, as can security, where hackers can tap into your computer and read your emails and other private information. A good security set-up and anti-virus software are essential.

Did you know?

Meetings can be an informal 30 minute gathering over a cup of tea or last a full day

FAQ

Why not just write the full words on a drawing?

This would take up too much space and clutter the drawing, making it difficult to read.

When working out the prices or materials for quotes is it important to be exact?

No. When estimating things it is easier to round up to the nearest whole number.

Which form of communication is the best?

No one way can be classed as best as it will depend on the circumstances, e.g. you wouldn't send a text regarding a job interview and you wouldn't send a formal letter to a friend asking them to meet. Always choose the method of communication that works best with the situation you are in.

Check it out

1. Describe four different methods of communication.
2. Describe the information that a schedule might give you.
3. Briefly explain why drawings are used in the construction industry.
4. What do the following abbreviations stand for: DPC; hwd; fnd; DPM?
5. Sketch the graphical symbols which represent the following: brick; metal; sawn wood; hardcore.
6. Explain the difference between day worksheets and timesheets.
7. What does a block plan show? Sketch an example of a block plan to show this.
8. Explain the importance of a Gantt chart.
9. What kind of information would you expect to find in a delivery note?
10. Describe and explain the type of information that can be found in specifications.
11. Describe the purpose of the Data Protection Act (1998).

Getting ready for assessment

The information contained in this unit, as well as continued practical assignments that you will carry out in your college or training centre, will help you with preparing for both your end of unit test and the diploma multiple-choice test. It will also aid you in preparing for the work that is required for the synoptic practical assignments.

Working with contract documents such as drawings, specifications and schedules is something that you will be required to do within your apprenticeship and even more so after you have qualified.

You will need to know about and be familiar with:

- interpreting building information
- determining quantities of material
- relaying information in the workplace.

To get all the information you need out of these documents you will need to build on the maths and arithmetic skills that you learned at school. These skills will give you the understanding and knowledge you will need to complete many of the practical assignments, which will require you to carry out calculations and measurements.

You will also need to use your English and reading skills. These skills will be particularly important, as you will need to make sure that you are following all the details of any instructions you receive. This will be the same for the instructions that you receive for the synoptic test, as it will for any specifications you might use in your professional life.

Communication skills have been a particular focus of this unit and of learning outcome 3. This unit has explained the reasons behind recording a message and using relevant information to keep communication clear. You have also seen the benefits of positive communication over negative communication and the benefits of effective communication.

When working either professionally or for your practical assignments, you will need to communicate effectively with the people you are working with and alongside. While studying for your qualification, you will use a range of communication methods. These will include face to face, email, phone and writing. You will also need to know about the message you give to people with your body language.

The communication skills that are explained within the unit are also vital in all tasks that you will undertake throughout your training and in life.

Good luck!

CHECK YOUR KNOWLEDGE

1 A drawing that shows you a bird's eye view of a site and its surrounding area is known as a:
   a location drawing
   b component range drawing
   c assembly drawing
   d detail drawing.

2 What does the abbreviation 'ct' stand for?
   a concrete
   b cupboard
   c column
   d cement

3 A scale of 1 to 50 means that 1 mm represents:
   a 5 mm
   b 50 mm
   c 500 mm
   d 5000 mm

4 Add together the following dimensions:
   3 m + 60 cm + 9 mm.
   a 36 090 mm
   b 3690 mm
   c 3609 mm
   d 30 609 mm

5 Calculate the following: 6 m – 60 cm.
   a 540 mm
   b 5400 mm
   c 5.54 m
   d 5440 mm

6 What is 250 x 8?
   a 1750
   b 2000
   c 2250
   d 2500

7 What is 12^2?
   a 144
   b 156
   c 160
   d 172

8 What is the area of a room that is 4 m long and 3.4 m wide?
   a 13 m²
   b 1.36 m²
   c 13.6 m²
   d 136 m²

9 Which of these is an advantage of spoken communication?
   a It is quick.
   b It can be forgotten.
   c There is no record of it.
   d All of the above.

10 The written form of communication that tells us the layout of a building is known as a:
   a specification
   b timesheet
   c drawing
   d schedule

UNIT 1003

Building methods and construction technology 1

Whatever type of building is being constructed there are certain principles that must be followed and certain elements that must be included. For example, both a block of flats and a warehouse have a roof, walls and a floor. These basic principles are applied across all the work carried out in construction and will apply to nearly all the possible projects you could work on.

This unit contains material that supports TAP Unit: Set Out for Masonry Structures. It also contains material that supports the delivery of the five generic units.

This unit will cover the following learning outcomes:

- Foundations, walls and floor construction
- Construction of internal and external masonry
- Roof construction.

Did you know?

The whole of the UK is mapped in detail and the Ordnance Survey places datum points (bench marks) at suitable locations from which all other levels can be taken

Functional skills

While working through this unit, you will be practising the functional skills **FE** 1.2.1–1.2.3. These relate to reading and understanding information.

Key term

Datum point – any fixed reference point at a known height, from which calculations or measurements can be taken.

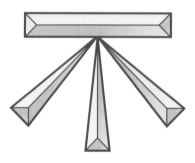

Figure 3.1 Ordnance bench mark

K1. Foundations, walls and floor construction

The majority of buildings need to be constructed so that they have a level internal surface and walls. To do this, we need to have a standard level across the whole site, to ensure that all construction is being carried out to this same height. This information is given by datum points on the construction site.

Datum points

The need to apply levels is required at the beginning of the construction process and continues right up to the completion of the building. **Datum points** are used to transfer levels for a range of construction jobs, including the following:

- roads
- brick courses
- paths
- excavations
- finished floor levels.

The same basic principles are applied throughout all these jobs.

Ordnance bench mark (OBM)

OBMs are found cut into locations such as walls of churches or public buildings. The height of the OBM can be found on the relevant Ordnance Survey map or by contacting the local authority planning office. Figure 3.1 shows the normal symbol used, though it can appear as shown in Figure 3.2.

Site datum

It is necessary to have a reference point on site to which all levels can be related. This is known as the site datum and is usually positioned at a convenient height, such as the finished floor level (FFL). The site datum must be set in relation to some known point, preferably an OBM, and must be positioned where it cannot be moved. Figure 3.2 shows a site datum and OBM, illustrating the height relationship between them.

If no suitable position can be found a datum peg may be used. Its accurate height is transferred by surveyors from an OBM, as with the site datum. The datum peg is usually a piece of timber or steel rod positioned accurately to the required level and then set in concrete. However, it must be adequately protected and is generally surrounded by a small fence for protection (Figure 3.3).

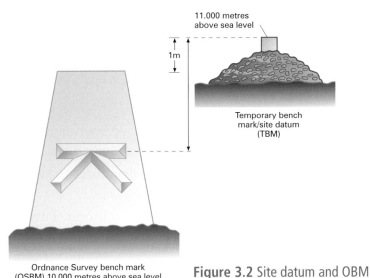

Figure 3.2 Site datum and OBM

11.000 metres above sea level

1m

Temporary bench mark/site datum (TBM)

Ordnance Survey bench mark (OSBM) 10.000 metres above sea level

10.000 metres above sea level

Steel or wooden peg concreted in and protected by fence

Figure 3.3 Datum peg suitably protected

Key terms

Substructure – all of the structure below ground and up to and including the damp proof course (DPC)

Superstructure – the main building above the ground

Load-bearing – something that carries a load, such as a wall that supports the structure above

Temporary bench mark (TBM)

When an OBM cannot be conveniently found near a site, a temporary bench mark (TBM) is usually set up at a height suitable for the site. Its accurate height is transferred by surveyors from the nearest convenient OBM.

All other site datum points can now be set up from this TBM using datum points, which are shown on the site drawings. Figure 3.4 shows datum points on drawings.

Substructure

All buildings will start with the **substructure**. The purpose of the substructure is to receive the loads from the **superstructure** and transfer them safely down to a suitable **load-bearing** layer of ground.

The main material used in foundations and floors is concrete. Concrete is made up of sand, cement, stones and water.

The main part of the substructure is the foundations. When a building is at the planning stage, the entire area – including the soil – will be surveyed to check what depth, width and size of foundation will be required.

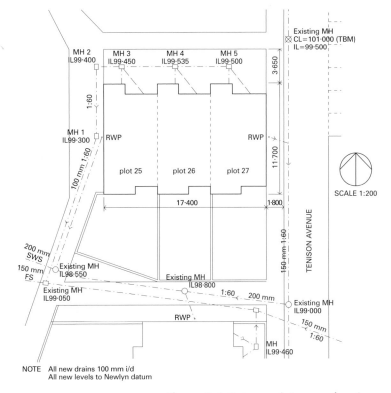

NOTE   All new drains 100 mm i/d
All new levels to Newlyn datum

Figure 3.4 Datum points on a drawing

Figure 3.5 All buildings have a substructure

This is vital: the wrong foundation could lead to the building subsiding or even collapsing.

The main type of foundation is a strip foundation. Depending on the survey reports and the type of building, one of three types of foundation will usually be used.

- **Narrow strip foundation** – the most common foundation used for most domestic dwellings and low-rise structures.
- **Wide strip foundation** – used for heavier structures or where weak soil is found.
- **Raft foundation** – used where very poor soil is found. This is basically a slab of concrete that is thicker around the edges.

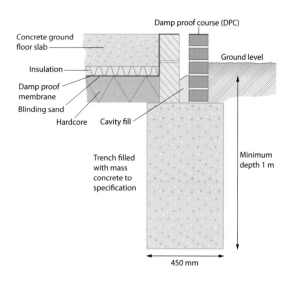

Figure 3.6 Narrow strip foundation

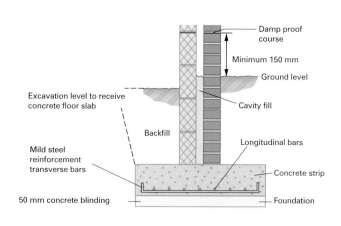

Figure 3.7 Wide strip foundation

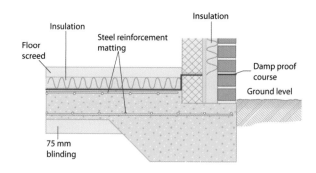

Figure 3.8 Raft foundation

Damp proof course

A damp proof course (DPC) and damp proof membranes are used to prevent damp from penetrating into a building. Flexible DPC may be made from polythene, **bitumen** or lead and is supplied in rolls of various widths for different uses.

Slate can also be used as a DPC. Older houses often have slate, but modern houses normally have polythene.

Damp proof membrane is used as a waterproof barrier over larger areas, such as under the concrete on floors etc.

Floors

There are two main types of floor: ground and upper.

Ground floors

There are several types of ground floor. The ones you will most often come across are:

- **Suspended timber floor** – this is a type of floor where timber joists are used to span the floor. The size of floor span determines the depth and thickness of the timbers used. The joists are either built into the inner skin of brickwork, seated upon small walls (dwarf/sleeper wall), or some form of joist hanger is used. The joists should span the shortest distance; sometimes dwarf/sleeper walls are built in the middle of the span to give extra support or to go underneath load-bearing walls. The top of the floor is decked with a suitable material (usually chipboard or solid pine tongue and groove boards). As the floor is suspended, usually with crawl spaces underneath, it is vital to have air bricks fitted, allowing air to flow under the floor, preventing high moisture content and timber rot.

Key terms

Bitumen – also known as pitch or tar, bitumen is a black sticky substance that turns into a liquid when it is heated. It is used on flat roofs to provide a waterproof seal

Slate – is a natural stone composed of clay or volcanic ash that can be machined into sheets and used to cover a roof

Figure 3.9 Damp proof course (DPC)

Did you know?

DPC is usually made of 1000-gauge polythene, and comes in large rolls, usually black or blue in colour

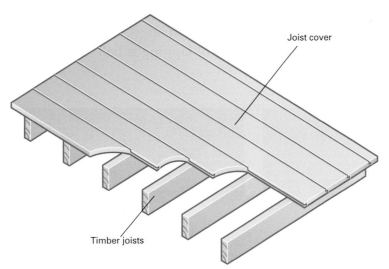

Joist cover

Timber joists

Figure 3.10 Suspended timber floor

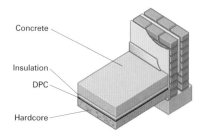

Figure 3.11 Section through a concrete floor

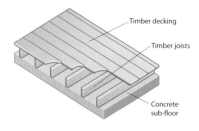

Figure 3.12 Floating floor

Key term

Regularised joists – joists that are all the same depth

- **Solid concrete floor** – concrete floors are more durable and are constructed on a sub-base incorporating hardcore, damp proof membranes and insulation (Figure 3.11). The depth of the hardcore and concrete will depend on the building and will be set by the Building Regulations and local authority. Underfloor heating can be incorporated. You must take great care when finishing the floor to ensure it is even and level.

- **Floating floor** – basic timber floor constructions that are laid on a solid concrete floor. The timbers are laid in a similar way to joists, though they are usually 50 mm thick maximum as there is no need for support. The timbers are laid at predetermined centres, and are not fixed to the concrete base (hence floating floor); the decking is then fixed on the timbers. Insulation or underfloor heating can be placed between the timbers to enhance the thermal and sound properties.

Upper floors

Solid concrete slabs can be used in larger buildings, but the most common type of upper floor is the suspended timber floor. The joists are either built into the inner skin of brickwork or supported on some form of joist hanger. Spanning the shortest distance, with load-bearing walls as supports, it is vital that **regularised joists** are used because a level floor and ceiling are required. The tops of the joists are decked out, with the underside being clad in plasterboard and insulation placed between the joists.

K2. Construction of internal and external masonry

Bonding

Bonding is the term given to the different patterns produced when lapping bricks to gain the most strength from the finished item. The most common type of lapping is half brick lap – better known as half bond.

Figure 3.13 Unbonded wall

Figure 3.14 Stretcher bond wall

If bricks were just put one on top of the other in a column, there would be no strength to the wall, and with sideways and downward pressure this type of wall would collapse. The main reasons for bonding brickwork are:

- strength
- distribution of heavy loads
- help resist sideways and downward pressure to the wall.

Other types of brick bonding are:

- stretcher bond walling
- English bond walling
- Flemish bond walling.

Walls

External walls come in a variety of styles but the most common is cavity walling. Cavity walling is simply two brick walls built parallel to each other, with a gap between acting as the cavity. The cavity wall acts as a barrier to weather, with the outer leaf preventing rain and wind penetrating the inner leaf. The cavity is usually filled with insulation to prevent heat loss.

External walling is often load-bearing. Loadings from the floors and the roofs are transferred to the inner leaf in common cavity-wall construction.

Internal walls

There are several different designs of internal walls. Each has advantages and disadvantages. These methods include:

- **Block work** – simple block work, covered with plasterboard or plastered over for a smooth finish. Its disadvantage is low thermal and sound insulation.
- **Timber stud partition** – this is preferred when dividing an existing room, as it is quicker to erect. It is clad in plasterboard and plastered to a smooth finish. Insulation can make the partition more fire and sound resistant. It can be load-bearing.
- **Metal stud partition** – this is similar to timber, but metal studs are used.

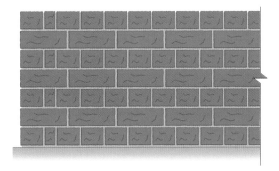

Figure 3.15 English bond wall

Figure 3.16 Flemish bond wall

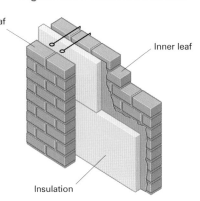

Outer leaf

Inner leaf

Insulation

Figure 3.17 A cavity wall

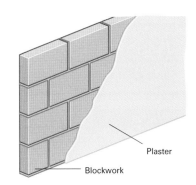

Plaster

Blockwork

Figure 3.18 Cross section of block work

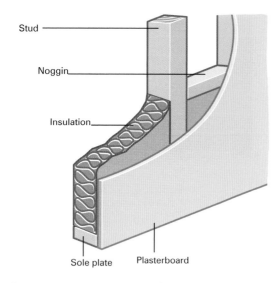

Figure 3.19 Cross section of timber stud partition

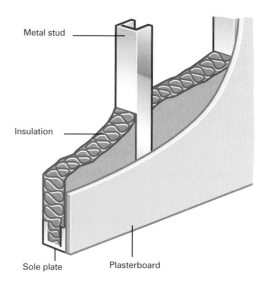

Figure 3.20 Cross section of metal stud partition

Figure 3.21 General purpose tie wire

Figure 3.22 Stacked lintels

Key term

Gauging – measuring the amount of each of the components required to complete the mortar using a specific ratio, such as 1:4

Tie wires

Tie wires are a very important part of a cavity wall. They tie the internal and external walls together, resulting in a stronger job. If we built cavity walls to any great height without connecting them together, the walls would be very unstable and could possibly collapse.

Pre-cast concrete lintels

Lintels are components placed above openings in brick and block walls to bridge the opening and support the brick or block work above. Concrete lintels have a steel reinforcement placed near the bottom for strength, which is why pre-cast concrete lintels have a 'T' or 'Top' etched into the top surface. They come in a variety of sizes to suit the opening size.

Mixing mortar

Mortar is used in bricklaying for bedding and jointing the bricks when building a wall. Mortar is made of sand, cement, water and plasticiser. Mortar must be 'workable' so that it can roll and spread easily. The mortar should hold on to the trowel without sticking. Mortar can be mixed to the appropriate strength through two methods.

Gauging materials

Accurate measuring of materials to the required proportion before mixing is important to ensure consistent colour, strength and durability of the mortar. The most accurate method of **gauging** the mortar materials is by weight.

However, this method is usually only used on very large sites. The next best way to gauge the materials is by volume using a gauge box.

A gauge box is a bottomless box made to the volume of sand required (to a proportion of a bag of cement). The box is placed on a clean, level, flat surface and filled with the sand. The sand is levelled off and any spillages cleaned away. The box is then removed, leaving the amount of sand to be mixed with the bag of cement. If a gauge box is not available, a bucket could be used. A bucket is filled with sand and emptied on a clean, flat surface for the number of times specified in the proportion. A separate bucket should be used to measure the cement.

Mixing by hand

The materials should be gauged first into a pile with the cement added. The cement and sand should then be 'turned' to mix the materials together. The pile should be turned a minimum of three times to ensure the materials are mixed properly. The centre of the pile should be 'opened out' to create a centre hole.

Gradually add the water, mixing it into the sand and cement, making sure not to 'flood' the mix. Turn the mix another three times, adding water gradually to gain the required consistency.

Mixing by machine

This can be carried out by using an electric mixer or a petrol or diesel mixer. Always set the mixer up on level ground.

- **Electric mixer** – the voltage should be 110 V and all cables and connections should be checked before use for splits or a loose connection (see Unit 1001, page 33). Cables should not be in contact with water and the operation should not be carried out if it is raining.
- **Petrol or diesel mixer** – make sure the fuel and oil levels are checked and topped up before starting. If using the mixer for long periods, the levels should be checked regularly.

Gauge the materials to be used, fill the mixer with approximately half of the water required (add plasticiser if being used). Add half the amount of cement to the water and add half of the sand. Allow to mix, and then add the remaining cement, then sand. Add more water if required, allowing at least two minutes for the mix to become workable and to ensure all the materials are thoroughly mixed together.

Once the mix has been taken out of the mixer, part fill the mixer with water and allow the water to run for a couple of minutes to

Did you know?

A 'shovel full' of material is not a very accurate method of gauging materials and should be avoided

Remember

It is easier to add more water than to try to remove excess water.

All aggregates should be 'well graded' – they should range from small to large grains so they fill in all the voids in the concrete

Remember

Never hit the mixer drum with a hammer etc. to clean it out – this could result in costly repairs to the drum remove any mortar sticking to the sides. If the mixer will not be used again that day, it should be cleaned thoroughly, either using water (and adding some broken bricks to help remove any mortar stuck to the sides) or ballast and gravel (which should then be cleaned out and the mixer washed with clean water). This will keep the mixer drum clean, and any future materials used will not stick to the drum sides so easily. On most large sites, mortar is brought in already mixed.

K3. Roof construction

Although there are several different types of roofing, all roofs will either technically be a flat roof or a pitched roof.

Flat roofs

A flat roof is a roof with a **pitch** of 10° or less. The pitch is usually achieved through laying the joists at a pitch, or by using **firring pieces**.

The main construction method for a flat roof is similar to that for a suspended timber floor, with the edges of the joists being supported either via a hanger or built into the brickwork, or even a combination of both. Once the joists are laid and firring pieces are fitted (if required), insulation and a vapour barrier are put in place. The roof is then decked on top and usually plasterboarded on the underside. The decking on a flat roof must be waterproof, and can be made from a wide variety of materials, including fibreglass or bitumen-covered boarding with **felt** layered on it.

Drainage of flat roofs is vital. The edge where the fall leads to must have suitable guttering to allow rainwater to run away without draining down the face of the wall.

Pitched roofs

There are several types of pitched roof, from the basic gable roof to more complex roofs such as mansard roofs. Whichever type of roof is being fitted to a building, it will most likely be constructed in one of the following ways.

Did you know?

As hot air rises, the majority of heat loss that occurs is through a building's roof. Insulation such as mineral wool or polystyrene must be fitted to roof spaces and ideally any intermediate floors

Key terms

Pitch – the angle or slope of the roof

Firring pieces – tapered strips of timber

Felt – a bitumen-based waterproof membrane

Did you know?

A flat roof without drainage will have a lot of strain on it when rain water collects there. This could lead the roof to collapse

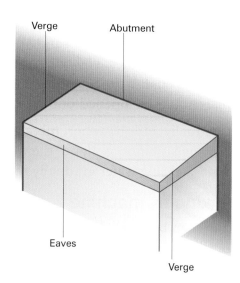

Figure 3.23 Flat roof terminology

Figure 3.24 Duo pitch roof with gable ends

Prefabricated truss roof

As the name implies, this is a roof that has prefabricated members called trusses. Trusses are used to spread the load of the roof and to give it the required shape. Trusses are factory-made, delivered to site and lifted into place, usually by a crane. They are also easy and quick to fit: they are either nailed to a wall plate or held in place by truss clips. Once fitted, bracing is attached to keep the trusses level and secure from wind. Felt is then fixed to the trusses and tiles or slate are used to keep the roof and dwelling waterproof. Metal trusses can also be used for industrial or more complex buildings.

Traditional/cut roof

This is an alternative to trusses and uses loose timbers that are cut in situ to give the roof its shape and spread the relevant load. More time-consuming and difficult to fit than trusses, the cut roof uses rafters that are individually cut and fixed in place, with two rafters forming a sort of truss. Once the rafters are all fixed, the roof is finished with felt and tiles or slate.

Finishing roofs

To finish a roof where it meets the exterior wall (eaves), you must fix a vertical timber board (fascia) and a horizontal board (soffit) to the foot of the rafters or trusses. The fascia and soffit close off the roof space from insects and birds.

Ventilators are attached to the soffits to allow air into the roof space. This prevents rot. Guttering is attached to the fascia board to channel the rainwater into a drain.

Roof components

Ridge

A ridge is a timber board that runs the length of the roof and acts as a type of spine. It is placed at the apex of the roof structure. The uppermost ends of the rafters are then fixed to this. This gives the roof central support and holds the rafters in place.

Purlin

Purlins are horizontal beams that support the roof at the mid point. They are placed midway between the ridge and the wall plate. They are used when the rafters are longer than 2.5 m. The purlin is supported at each end by gables.

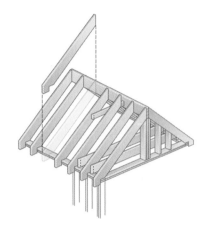

Figure 3.25 Prefabricated wooden roof truss

Figure 3.26 Individually cut rafters

Figure 3.27 Fascia and soffit in roof construction

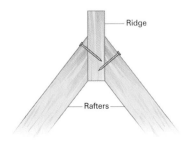

Figure 3.28 A ridge

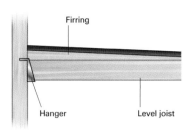

Figure 3.29 Firrings

Figure 3.30 Felt and battens on a roof

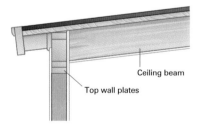

Figure 3.31 Simple diagram of a wall plate and roof

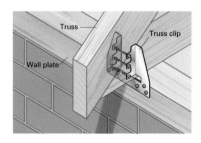

Figure 3.32 Truss clips

Firrings

A firring is an angled piece of wood, laid on top of the joints on a flat roof. They provide a fall. This supplies a pitch of around 10° or less to a roof. This pitch will allow the draining of flat roofs of water. This drainage is vital. The edge where the fall leads to must have suitable guttering to allow rainwater to run away and not down the face of the wall.

Batten

Battens are wood strips that are used to provide a fixing point for roof sheet or roof tiles. The spacing between the battens depends on the type of roof and they can be placed at right angles to the trusses or rafters. This makes them similar to purlins.

Some roofs use a grid pattern in both directions. This is known as a counter-batten system.

Wall plate

Wall plates are timber plates laid flat and bedded on mortar. These plates run along the wall to carry the feet of all trusses, rafters and ceiling joists. They can serve a similar role as lintels, but their main purpose is to bear and distribute the load of the roof across the wall. Wall plates are held in place by restraint straps along the wall. These anchor the wall plates in place to prevent movement.

Hangers and clips

Hangers, or clips, are galvanised metal clips that are used to fix trusses or joists in place on wall plates. This anchors the trusses and joists to the wall plate, which is in turn firmly anchored to the wall. This gives the roof a stable and firm construction and helps it withstand the pressures of wind and weather.

Bracing

Bracing are lengths of timber attached along the trusses. This holds them in place and helps to prevent any movement in high winds. Combined with the wall plates and truss clips, bracing is a major part of ensuring the stability of the roof in all conditions.

Felt

Felt is rolled over the top of the joists to provide a waterproof barrier. It is then fastened down to provide a permanent barrier. Overlapping the felt strips when placing them will help make this barrier even more effective, as will avoiding air bubbles in the felt.

Slate and tile

Slate is flat and easy to stack. The supplier will recommend the spacing between the battens on the roof. The slate is laid onto the battens, with the bottom of each tile overlapping the top of the one below. The top and bottom rows are made up of shorter slates to provide this lapping for the slate below/above. This provides waterproofing to the roof. Slate is often nailed into place.

Roofing tiles are made from concrete or clay. They are moulded or formed into a shape that allows them to overlap each other. This provides weatherproofing to the roofs, similar to the technique used for slate.

Flashings

Flashings are made from aluminium or lead. They are used to provide water resistance around openings in a roof, such as chimneys or dormer windows or when a roof butts up to an existing wall.

Metal flashing can be purchased in rolls or in sections specifically designed for certain roles – such as around a chimney.

Figure 3.33 Bracing

Figure 3.34 Dormer window flashing and tiles

FAQ

How do I know what type of foundation is needed?

A site survey, including taking soil samples and checking the area for tree roots etc., will help determine which type of foundation is used. A site survey will need to be carried out before you begin any construction work. Without it you may overlook a potential problem with the area you are planning to build on.

How do I know what height things should be on site?

The site datum will give you a baseline to which all measurements can be taken and the drawing will give you a measurement such as 1000 mm above site datum. You can use this information to set the height that things will need to be on site in relation to each other.

Check it out

1 Explain the main purpose of substructure.
2 List the three different types of foundation. Sketch each type and explain the differences between them.
3 Give a brief description of external walling.
4 Explain the difference between a truss roof and a cut roof.
5 Sketch English and Flemish brick bonds.

6 Describe the purpose of a gauge box.
7 Describe the purpose of a site datum.
8 List four materials which can be used as DPC.
9 Sketch diagrams showing the cross section of two types of internal wall.
10 Describe what mortar is used for and explain what it is made from.

Getting ready for assessment

The information contained in this unit, as well as continued practical assignments that you will carry out in your college or training centre, will help you with preparing for both your end of unit test and the diploma multiple-choice test. It will also aid you in preparing for the work that is required for the synoptic practical assignments.

The information in this unit will help you to understand the basics of your own trade as well as the basic information on several other trade areas.

You will need to be familiar with:

- foundations, walls and floor construction
- construction in internal and external masonry
- roof construction.

It is important to understand what other trades do in relation to you and how the work they do affects you and your work. It is also good to know how the different components of a building are constructed and how these tie in with the tasks that you carry out. You must always remember that there are a number of tasks being carried out on a building site at all times and many of these will not be connected to the work you are carrying out. It is useful to remember the communication skills you learnt in Unit 1002, as these will be important for working with other trades on site. You will also need to be familiar with specifications and contract documents and to know the type of construction work that other trade workers will be doing around you on site.

For learning outcome 1 you saw how datum points work on site and the purpose that they serve in construction. You have seen that these are vital when building a range of constructions, such as roads, brick courses, paths and excavations for floor levels. You have also seen the materials used in concrete foundations and floors and the reasons for DPM and DPC.

You will need to use this knowledge to demonstrate your understanding of construction on site. Part of this is being able to sketch basic cross sections of strip foundations and concrete floors. You will also need to be able to sketch the different types of foundation found in domestic buildings, including strip and raft concrete floor slab.

Remember that a sound knowledge of construction methods and materials will be very useful during your training as well as in later life in your professional career.

Good luck!

CHECK YOUR KNOWLEDGE

Unit 1003 Building methods and construction technology 1

1   What is a datum point?
   a   A point from which you take all your levels.
   b   A point from which you take the time and date.
   c   A point that tells you which way is north.
   d   A point from which you draw.

2   The most common type of foundation is:
   a   raft foundation
   b   wide strip foundation
   c   narrow strip foundation
   d   none of the above.

3   The type of foundation used when the soil is very poor is called:
   a   raft foundation
   b   wide strip foundation
   c   narrow strip foundation
   d   none of the above.

4   What can damp proof course (DPC) be made from?
   a   Slate
   b   Lead
   c   Polypropylene
   d   Any of the above

5   What are tie wires used in?
   a   Brick walls
   b   Timber stud walls
   c   Block walls
   d   Cavity walls

6   What is the component placed above openings in brick and block walls called?
   a   Lintel
   b   Cavity tray
   c   DPC
   d   Wall tie

7   What is a roof with a pitch of 10° or less called?
   a   Lean to roof
   b   Pitched roof
   c   Flat roof
   d   Domed roof

8   What is the horizontal timber board called that is fixed to the foot of a rafter and finishes the roof?
   a   Soffit
   b   Fascia
   c   Eaves
   d   Gable

9   Which of these statements about fixing slates to a roof is *not* correct?
   a   The bottom of each tile should overlap the top of the one below.
   b   The architect will specify the spacing between the battens on the roof.
   c   The top and bottom rows are made up of shorter slates.
   d   Slate is often nailed into place.

10 A roof made with loose timbers and cut in situ is a:
   a   cut roof
   b   truss roof
   c   gable roof
   d   flat roof.

Know how to erect and dismantle access equipment and working platforms 1

Most construction trades require frequent use of some type of working platform or access equipment, and painting and decorating is no different. Working off the ground can be very dangerous and the greater the height, the more serious the risk of injury.

The unit also contains material that supports NVQ Unit QCF 250A Erect and Dismantle Access/Working Platforms. This unit also supports TAP Unit Erect and Dismantle Working Platforms

This unit will cover the following learning outcomes:

- Interpreting guidance information for using access equipment and working platforms
- Inspecting components and identifying defects
- Erecting and working from access equipment and working platforms
- Dismantling and storing components.

Safety tip

If any faults are revealed when checking a stepladder, take it out of use, report it to the person in charge and attach a warning notice to it to stop anyone else using it

Did you know?

Stepladders should be stored under cover to protect them from damage such as rust or rotting

Figure 7.1 British Standards Institution Kitemark

K1. Interpreting guidance information for using access equipment and working platforms

Suitable access equipment and working platforms

When working at height, there are a number of different types of access equipment and working platforms that can be used for both internal and external work. This section will look at the most common of these in detail.

Stepladders and ladders

Stepladders

A stepladder has a prop, which when folded out allows the ladder to be used without having to lean it against something. Stepladders are one of the most frequently used pieces of access equipment in the construction industry and are often used every day. This means that they are not always treated with the respect they demand. Stepladders are often misused – they should only be used for work that will take a few minutes to complete. When work is likely to take longer than this, a sturdier alternative should be found.

When stepladders are used, the following safety points should be observed:

- Ensure that the ground on which the stepladder is to be placed is firm and level. If the ladder rocks or sinks into the ground, it should not be used for the work.
- Always open the steps fully.
- Never work off the top tread of the stepladder.
- Always keep your knees below the top tread.
- Never use stepladders to gain additional height on another working platform.
- Always look for the Kitemark, which shows that the ladder has been tested independently and audited to ensure it meets the appropriate standards.

A number of other safety points need to be observed, depending on the type of stepladder being used.

Wooden stepladder

Before using a wooden stepladder:

- check for loose screws, nuts, bolts and hinges
- check that the tie ropes between the two sets of **stiles** are in good condition and not frayed
- check for splits or cracks in the stiles
- check that the treads are not loose or split
- never paint any part of a wooden stepladder as this can hide defects, which may cause the ladder to fail during use, causing injury.

Aluminium stepladder

Before using an aluminium stepladder:

- check for damage to stiles and treads to see whether they are twisted, badly dented or loose
- avoid working close to live electricity supplies because aluminium will conduct electricity.

Fibreglass stepladder

Before using a fibreglass stepladder, check for damage to stiles and treads. Once damaged, fibreglass stepladders cannot be repaired and must be disposed of.

Ladders

A ladder, unlike a stepladder, does not have a prop and so has to be leant against something in order for it to be used. Along with stepladders, ladders are one of the most common pieces of equipment used to carry out work at heights and gain access to the work area.

As with stepladders, ladders are also available in timber, aluminium and fibreglass and require similar checks before use.

Pole ladder

These are single ladders and are available in a range of lengths. They are most commonly used for access to scaffolding platforms. Pole ladders are made from timber and must be stored under cover and flat, supported evenly along their length to prevent them sagging and twisting. They should be checked for damage or defects every time before being used.

Key term

Stiles – the side pieces of a stepladder into which the steps are set

Figure 7.2 Wooden stepladder

Figure 7.3 Aluminium stepladder

Figure 7.4 Pole ladder

Unit 1007

Know how to erect and dismantle access equipment and working platforms 1

Figure 7.5 Aluminium extension ladder

Extension ladder

Extension ladders have two or more interlocking lengths, which can be slid together for convenient storage or slid apart to the desired length when in use.

Extension ladders are available in timber, aluminium and fibreglass. Aluminium types are the most popular because they are lightweight yet strong and available in double and triple extension types. Fibreglass versions are very strong but they are heavy, making them difficult to manoeuvre.

Erecting and using a ladder

The following points should be noted when considering the use of a ladder:

- As with stepladders, ladders are not designed for long spells of work. Consider alternative working platforms if the work will take longer than a few minutes.
- Don't use a ladder to do work that requires the use of both hands. You need one free hand to hold the ladder.
- You should be able to do the work without stretching.
- Make sure that the ladder can be properly secured to prevent it slipping on the surface it is leaning against.

Pre-use checks

Before using a ladder, check its general condition. Make sure that:

- no rungs are damaged or missing
- the stiles are not damaged
- no **tie-rods** are missing
- no repairs have been made to the ladder.

In addition, for wooden ladders, ensure that:

- they have not been painted, which may hide defects or damage
- there is no decay or rot
- the ladder is not twisted or warped.

Erecting a ladder

Observe the following guidelines when erecting a ladder:

- Ensure that you have a solid, level base.
- Do not pack anything under either (or both) of the stiles to level a stepladder.
- If the ladder is too heavy to put it in position on your own, get someone to help.
- Ensure that there is at least a four-rung overlap on each extension section.

Safety tip

Ladders must *never* be repaired once damaged and must be disposed of

Key term

Tie-rods – metal rods underneath the rungs of a ladder that give extra support to the rungs

Did you know?

On average in the UK, 14 people a year die at work falling from ladders; nearly 1200 suffer major injuries (source: Health and Safety Executive)

- Never rest the ladder on plastic guttering as this may break, causing the ladder to slip and you to fall.
- Where the base of the ladder is in an exposed position, ensure that it is adequately guarded so that no one knocks it or walks into it.
- Secure the ladder at both the top and bottom. The bottom of the ladder can be secured by a second person. However, this person must not leave the base of the ladder while it is in use.
- The angle of the ladder should be a ratio of 1:4 (or 75°). This means that the bottom of the ladder is 1 m away from the wall for every 4 m in height (see Figure 7.6).
- The top of the ladder must extend at least 1 m above its landing point.

Roof work

When carrying out any work on a roof, a roof ladder or **crawling board** must be used. Roof work also requires the use of edge protection or, where this is not possible, a safety harness.

The roof ladder is rolled up the surface of the roof and over the ridge tiles, just enough to allow it to be turned over and the ladder hook allowed to bear on the tiles on the other side of the roof. This hook prevents the roof ladder sliding down the roof once the roof is accessed.

Trestle platforms

A trestle is a frame upon which a platform or other type of surface, for example, a table top, can be placed. A trestle should be used rather than a ladder for work that will take longer than a few minutes to complete. Trestle platforms are composed of the frame and the platform (sometimes called a stage).

Frames

A-frames

These are most commonly used by carpenters and painters. As the name suggests, the frame is in the shape of a capital A and can be made from timber, aluminium or fibreglass. Two are used together to support a platform (a scaffold or staging board). See Figure 7.8.

> **Remember**
> You must carry out a thorough risk assessment before working from a ladder. Ask yourself, 'Would I be safer using an alternative method?'

4 m

1 m

Figure 7.6 Correct angle for a ladder

> **Key term**
> **Crawling board** – a board or platform (placed on roof joists), which spreads the weight of the worker, allowing the work to be carried out safely

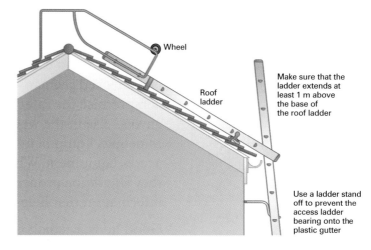

Wheel

Roof ladder

Make sure that the ladder extends at least 1 m above the base of the roof ladder

Use a ladder stand off to prevent the access ladder bearing onto the plastic gutter

Figure 7.7 Roof work equipment

Safety tip

An A-frame trestle should never be used as a stepladder as it is not designed for this purpose

Figure 7.8 A-frame trestles with scaffold board

Figure 7.9 Steel trestle with staging board

When using A-frames:

- they should always be opened fully and, in the same way as stepladders, must be placed on firm, level ground
- the platform width should be no less than 450 mm
- the overhang of the board at each end of the platform should be not more than four times its thickness.

Steel trestles

These are sturdier than A-frame trestles and are adjustable in height. They are also capable of providing a wider platform than timber trestles – see Figure 7.9. As with the A-frame type, they must be used only on firm and level ground, but the trestle itself should be placed on a flat scaffold board on top of the ground. Trestles should not be placed more than 1.2 m apart.

Platforms

Scaffold boards

Check that scaffold boards provide a safe working platform before you use them. Ensure that they:

- are not split
- are not twisted or warped
- have no large knots, which cause weakness.

Staging boards

These are designed to span a greater distance than scaffold boards and can offer a 600 mm-wide working platform. They are ideal for use with trestles.

Hazards associated with access equipment and working platforms

You will need to be able to identify potential hazards associated with working at height, as well as hazards associated with equipment. It is essential that access equipment is well maintained and checked regularly for any deterioration or faults, which could compromise the safety of someone using the equipment and anyone else in the work area. Although obviously not as important as people, equipment can also be damaged by the use of faulty access equipment. When maintenance checks are carried out, they should be properly recorded. This provides very important information that helps to prevent accidents.

Good housekeeping is *vitally* important when working at height, in order to prevent slips and trips. Not only are you at added risk, but materials and tools that are left on a working platform can be knocked off the platform onto people working below. There is a risk of causing serious head injuries to people below – and not just the workforce as, in some cases, the working platform may be in an area that is used by the general public.

When working in a public area, you must protect the public from hazards by putting barriers around the work area. You must also ensure that the sides of any working platforms are sealed off to prevent any materials or objects from falling.

Risk assessment

Before any work is carried out at height, a thorough risk assessment needs to be completed. Your supervisor or someone else more experienced than you will do this while you are still training, but it is important that you understand what is involved so that you are able to carry out an assessment in the future.

For a risk assessment of working at height to be valid and effective, a number of questions must be answered:

- How is entering and exiting the work area to be achieved?
- What type of work is to be carried out?
- How long is the work likely to last?
- How many people will be carrying out the task?
- How often will this work be carried out?
- What is the condition of the existing structure (if any) and the surroundings?
- Is adverse weather likely to affect the work and workers?
- How competent are the workforce and their supervisors?
- Is there a risk to the public and work colleagues?

Duties

Your employer has a duty to provide and maintain safe plant and equipment, which includes scaffold access equipment and systems of work.

You have a duty:

- to comply with safety rules and procedures relating to access equipment
- to take positive steps to understand the hazards in the workplace and report things you consider likely to lead to danger, for example a missing handrail on a working platform
- not to tamper with or modify equipment.

Did you know?

Only a fully trained and competent person is allowed to erect any kind of working platform or access equipment. You should therefore not attempt to erect this type of equipment unless this describes you!

Hazard identification records

A hazard identification record is literally a record of all the possible hazards that have been identified on site. It is used to keep check of any risks or hazards associated with the work being carried out (for example, working at height). If an accident or near miss occurs while tasks are carried out, the record shows what problems had been identified and what measures had been put in place to prevent it occurring.

Manufacturer's specifications and Work at Height Regulations

The Work at Height Regulations were covered in Unit 1001, page 10. Under the Work at Height Regulations, the employer has a duty to carry out an assessment before anyone starts any work at height. If there is no alternative to working at height, then a suitable scaffold system should be selected that takes into account the nature of the work. However, you should always look to avoid working at height whenever possible.

As an employee, you must follow any training given to you, report any hazards to your supervisor and use any safety equipment made available to you. You will need to remember that:

- mobile access towers should be used if possible because they can provide an effective and safe means of gaining access to work at height
- inappropriate erection and misuse of towers is the cause of most accidents at work every year
- the manufacturers of scaffold systems have to abide by the working at height law and therefore will provide the correct information needed to erect and dismantle safely all scaffold equipment.

Scaffold manufacturers by law should be certified by the BSI (British Standards Institution) and comply with the requirements of (European Standard) BS EN 1004 2004 or BS 1139-6 2005. The new Work at Height Regulations were introduced into the industry in April 2005. The equipment you are using should have a BSI Kitemark to identify that it meets the appropriate standards.

Every manufacturer should provide an instruction manual with their equipment that shows how to erect and dismantle the equipment correctly. Some manufacturers actually attach a step-by-step guide to the frame of a tower scaffold to aid in the correct, safe method of erecting and dismantling the tower.

K2. Inspecting components and identifying defects

When working at height, there are several parts of ladders and working platforms that you will need to be familiar with. It will also be important that you are able to recognise any defects in components and materials. This will help to avoid possible accidents while you are working, and ensure that you stay safe.

Components for internal and external work

All of the material you will use to work at height is made up from several different components. This section will look at types of scaffolding and the components that make up both scaffolding and ladders.

Scaffolding

Tubular scaffold is the most commonly used type of scaffolding within the construction industry. There are two types of tubular scaffold:

- **Independent scaffold** – free-standing scaffold that does not rely on any part of the building to support it (although it must be tied to the building to provide additional stability).
- **Dependent scaffold** – scaffolding that is attached to the building with poles (putlogs) inserted into the brickwork and given a bearing of 75 mm. The poles stay in position until the building is complete and give the scaffold extra support.

No one other than a qualified **carded scaffolder** is allowed to erect or alter scaffolding. Although you are not allowed to erect or alter this type of scaffold, you must be sure that it is safe before you work on it. You should ask yourself a number of questions to assess the condition and suitability of the scaffold before you use it:

- Are there any signs attached to the scaffold that state it is incomplete or unsafe?
- Is the scaffold overloaded with materials such as bricks?
- Are the platforms cluttered with waste materials?
- Are there adequate guardrails and scaffold boards in place?
- Does the scaffold actually *look* safe?
- Is there the correct access to and from the scaffold?
- Are the various scaffold components in the correct place (see Figure 7.10)?
- Have the correct types of fittings been used (see Figure 7.11)?

Key term

Carded scaffolder – someone who holds a recognised certificate showing competence in scaffold erection

Did you know?

It took 14 years of experimentation to settle finally on 48 mm as the diameter of most tubular scaffolding poles

Mobile tower scaffolds

These are so called because they can be moved around without being dismantled (see Figure 7.12). Lockable wheels make this possible. Mobile towers are used extensively throughout the construction industry. A tower can be made from either traditional steel tubes and fittings or aluminium, which is lightweight and easy to move. The aluminium tower is normally specially designed and is referred to as a 'proprietary tower'.

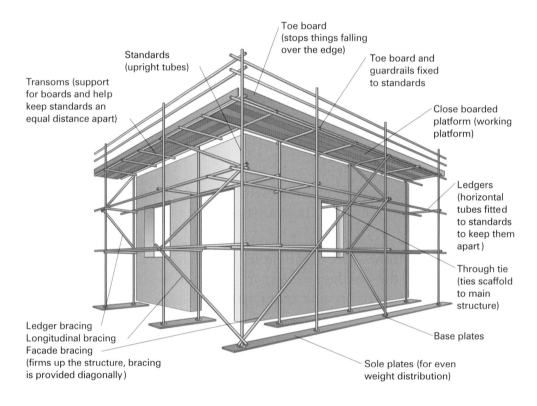

Figure 7.10 Components of a tubular scaffolding structure

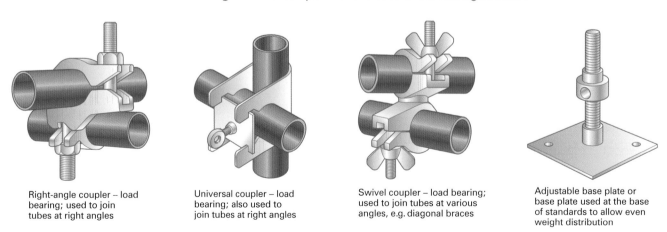

Right-angle coupler – load bearing; used to join tubes at right angles

Universal coupler – load bearing; also used to join tubes at right angles

Swivel coupler – load bearing; used to join tubes at various angles, e.g. diagonal braces

Adjustable base plate or base plate used at the base of standards to allow even weight distribution

Figure 7.11 Types of scaffold fittings

Low towers (podiums)

These are smaller versions of the standard mobile tower scaffold and are designed specifically for use by one person. They have a recommended working height of no more than 2.5 m and a safe working load of 150 kg. They are lightweight and easily transported and stored (see Figure 7.13).

These towers require no assembly other than the locking into place of the platform and handrails. However, you still require training before you use one and you must ensure that the manufacturer's instructions are followed when setting up and working from this type of platform.

There are several important points you should observe when working from a scaffold tower:

- Any working platform must be fitted with guardrails and toe boards. Guardrails must be fitted at a minimum height of 950 mm.
- Guardrails and toe boards must be positioned on all four sides of the platform.
- Any tower higher than 9 m must be secured to the structure.
- Towers must not exceed 12 m in height unless they have been specifically designed for that purpose.
- The working platform of any tower must be fully boarded and be at least 600 mm wide.
- If the working platform is to be used for materials, then the minimum width must be 800 mm.
- All towers must have their own access and this should be by an internal ladder.

Figure 7.12 Mobile tower scaffold

Figure 7.13 Podium scaffold

Remember

Aluminium can be damaged – you must be careful that you inspect it fully before use

Safety tip

Never climb a scaffold tower on the outside as this can cause it to tip over

Working life

Sanjit has been asked by a client to take a look at all the fascia boards on a two-storey building. Depending on the condition of the fascia boards, they will need either repairing or replacing. The job will probably take Sanjit between two and six hours, depending on what he has to do.

- What types of scaffolding do you think might be suitable for Sanjit's job?
- Can you think of anything that Sanjit will need to consider while he prepares for and carries out this task?

He will need to think about things such as access and egress points, whether the area will be closed off to the public, how long he will need to work at height, and so on.

- Take a look through the information here on types of scaffold. What type of scaffold do you think Sanjit should use for this task?

Safety tip

Remember, you should never paint a ladder, as this can disguise or cover possible faults in the ladder, making it more unsafe to use

Components of ladders and platforms

You must always check these components are not damaged before you use a ladder, to avoid accidents or the collapse of the ladder.

Component	Purpose
Stile	Found on both sides of a ladder and stepladder and combine to form the main body of the ladder. Joined by either rungs or treads. Always check they are free from damage and not bent or twisted.
Rung	Round or rectangular sections you climb up on any type of ladder. As these will take your weight, you must always check that rungs are not split or missing.
Tie rod	Steel rods fitted beneath, and supporting, the rungs. Check they are fitted below the second rung of a ladder at regular intervals and are free from damage.
Rope	Usually made from hemp sash cord or a material of equivalent strength. Used to prevent stepladders from collapsing when in use. Make sure they are not frayed or loose and are fitted correctly. Use a firm knot at each end and make sure ropes are the same length and thickness.
Tread	Steps on a stepladder, made from both timber and aluminium. These will take your full weight, so check there are no splits and they are not painted out to hide defects. They need to be at least 90 mm deep and spaced at 250 mm intervals.
Hinge	Fixed to both parts of a stepladder and prevent it from collapsing. Make sure they are free moving and fixed correctly to both components of the ladder.
Swingback	Type of timber or aluminium stepladder without a platform, made in two parts. One part is the climbing part and the other the back frame. Aluminium swingbacks are lighter but very strong and will not twist, warp, burn or rust. Damage is usually caused by misuse, e.g. dropping, which can dent the material.
Non-slip inserts	Fitted to the ends of the stiles on most ladders. Make sure the fixed ones are free from damage and the hinged ones can move freely.
Pulley	Wheels that guide the smooth running of the ropes used on certain types of scaffold and hoisting equipment. Also attached to some rope-operated ladders. Make sure the pulleys are turning freely and are not loose or corroded.
Locking boards	Boards which interlock staging boards when used for platforms on static scaffold. Check that the locking mechanism is free from damage.
Scaffold boards	Usually used on static scaffold and made from timber and aluminium. When using timber boards, check for twists, warps and split ends. Timber should be straight grained and free from large knots.
Platform	Normally used for mobile towers. Made from aluminium and gives a non-slip advantage over other types of board, making it hard to damage.

Table 7.1 Ladder and scaffold components

Inspections

Before using any scaffolding equipment, you should check it thoroughly to make sure it is safe. Carry out this check before you begin the assembly of any scaffolding. You should also regularly check any scaffolding in use, to make sure that it is still safe and secure.

Inspection report	
1. Name and address of person for whom the inspection was carried out	Name: Address:
2. Site address of inspection	Address:
3. Date and time of inspection	Date: Time:
4. Location and description of place of work	Location: Description:
5. Type of scaffold inspected	Type:
6. Health and safety risks associated with equipment	Risks:
7. Can work be carried out safely?	YES .... NO ....
8. If not, who has been informed?	Name:
9. Details of any actions taken as a result of risks identified in question 6 above	Details:
10. Details of any further action considered necessary	Details:
11. Name of person making the report	Name:
12. Position of person making the report	Position:
13. Date and time report completed and handed in	Date: Time:
14. Name of person receiving report	Name:
15. Position of person receiving report	Position:

Figure 7.14 Inspection report

Remember

You will need to remember that timber swingbacks can get twisted, warped and burned.

With aluminium structures, you will need to be aware of the same issues that could arise

Working life

Georgia has just been promoted to site manager and as part of her duties she has to make safety checks on all access equipment and materials used on site. Her manager has asked her to carry out a scaffold inspection report because of bad weather over the weekend. The site has a number of static scaffold systems in place and has also got a tower scaffold for internal work. There are a number of stepladders and pole ladders in storage awaiting the start of internal work activities.

The job has been in progress for four months now and the weather is starting to turn bad due to the time of year.

- Is Georgia qualified to make these checks? You will need to think about the responsibilities that come with Georgia's new job. What types of check should Georgia make?
- Does she need to check all the access equipment on site?
- What documentation will Georgia need to carry out her checks?
- What should she do if she finds faulty or damaged scaffold?

The inspection carried out on scaffolding before use is called a pre-erection inspection. Any static scaffold is checked to make sure that all the components are fit for use. A pre-erection inspection is carried out by a qualified and carded scaffolder.

At this stage, providing there are no issues, the scaffold can be erected. However, if there are issues with any components of the scaffold, they need to be removed and classed as condemned. A notice is then placed on the actual part and the issue reported to the site manager. The scaffold cannot be erected until a replacement part is acquired.

To carry out a pre-erection inspection, check that all components are in place to build or erect the scaffold. You will also need to check that there are no missing parts or damage to the components. This also applies to stepladders, ladders, podiums and towers. Inspection requirements for small towers under 2 m are different from those for towers of 2 m and above.

Platforms less than 2 m high should be inspected:

- prior to use
- after assembly in any position
- after any event liable to have affected their stability
- at suitable intervals depending on frequency and conditions of use.

Platforms of 2 m and above should be checked:

- prior to use
- after assembly in any position
- after any event liable to have affected their stability
- at intervals not exceeding seven days.

It is important to carry out pre-erection inspections on any scaffolding equipment to avoid any injury to workers when the scaffold is in use for the first time. This will also identify any faults in the scaffolding components, allowing these to be rectified before use. By inspecting the scaffolding before use, you will also be saving time and labour, both of which could be wasted if you put up scaffolding then discover it to be unsafe.

In-use inspections

Inspections carried out while the scaffolding is being used will help ensure it has not been damaged after assembly and that it is safe to use. Damage can be caused by movement or loosening of components when people are working on the scaffold, adding extra weight and pressure to the structure. Scaffold left outside can also be damaged because it is open to the elements.

Inspection time periods

Each type of scaffolding inspection is carried out over slightly different time periods. You will need to follow these to make sure that you are working safely at all times.

- The correct time for a scaffolding pre-erection inspection is always before any component is fixed together or built up so a thorough check can be carried out.
- When a scaffold system is erected, it should be inspected at intervals not exceeding seven days.

These two inspection periods should be repeated when handing over the responsibility of the scaffold to others. They should also be repeated after any accident or incident when a thorough check of the scaffold should be made as soon as possible.

If a scaffold has collapsed, you should treat the area like a crime scene. Do not touch anything until either the HSE or the local authority inspectors have seen it. You should also carry out a new check after bad weather, such as strong winds, to make sure that the scaffolding is still safe to use.

K3. Erecting and working from access equipment and working platforms

When using access equipment and working platforms, you must be particularly careful that you are wearing the correct PPE; steel toe-capped safety boots, manual handling gloves and a safety helmet. PPE was covered in detail in Unit 1001, pages 48–50. Refer back to this section for more details.

Secure bases

It is essential that tower scaffolds are situated on a firm and level base. The stability of any tower depends on the height in relation to the size of the base:

- For use inside a building, the height should be no more than three-and-a-half times the smallest base length.
- For outside use, the height should be no more than three times the smallest base length.

The height of a tower can be increased provided the area of the base is increased proportionately. The base area can be increased by fitting outriggers to each corner of the tower.

The wheels of a mobile tower must be in the locked position while the tower is in use and unlocked only when the tower is moved.

Remember

Scaffolding can also be damaged by unsupervised members of the public using or climbing on it and through vandalism. You should carry out a check after leaving the scaffolding unsupervised to ensure that it has not been damaged in any way during your absence

Safety tips

Before carrying out any check after an accident, you must ensure that the workplace has been deemed safe

Mobile towers can be moved *only* when they are free of people, tools and materials

Suitable bases

Bases and sole plates are used for the bottom of standards and diagonal bracing. These form the key part of a static scaffold system, and support the entire structure as it stands.

Loading and storing of platforms

The correct way to load or stack any scaffold equipment is in methodical order. This allows the operative to store the components in the correct sequence. It also helps with the identification of the parts of the scaffolding. This system of loading keeps all the components stored in a safe manner and allows for them to be visually checked again for faults.

Manual handling access equipment and working platforms

Manual handling was covered in Unit 1001, pages 29–32. Refer back to this section for some general information on carrying out manual handling tasks. The correct manual handling technique used for erecting and moving ladders is as follows:

Step 1 – Grip the ladder firmly by holding the stiles at an angle, with one hand higher up the ladder than the other.

Step 2 – Gently ease the ladder into your shoulder and raise it from the ground, taking care not to lift it quickly, as this could knock you off balance. Once you have the ladder off the ground, position it so you can safely move away.

Step 3 – When you have reached the area where you want to place the ladder, gently set it down. Take care to position it and then place it against the surface you are working on. You will need to position it correctly at 75 degrees.

Working with extension ladders

When raising an extension ladder, you should make sure that the sections are closed and then ask for assistance. To lift a ladder, first lay it flat on the ground. One person should stand on the bottom rung of the ladder, holding the stiles to steady the ladder when it is being lifted. A second person stands at the top of the ladder and lifts the end of it over their head. They then walk towards the foot of the ladder, moving their hands one at a time down the ladder, raising it at the same time. This continues until the ladder is upright.

> **Remember**
>
> Storage of materials was covered in Unit 1001, pages 34–43. Refer back to this section for more information

> **Safety tip**
>
> Before moving any access equipment, you must make sure that it is safe to do so. Check your surroundings for any hazards, such as overhead cables or blocked walkways. Once you are sure everything is safe, you can carry out the task of erecting or moving scaffold

> **Safety tip**
>
> When erected, an extension ladder should be placed at the correct angle of 75 degrees

Stepladders

To erect a stepladder, you lean the equipment forward slightly, hold onto the stiles of the front frame and pull the back frame away from the front. Once the ladder is in position, make sure that all components are in place.

When erecting an A-frame trestle for a scaffold, first lift it into position. Hold it so it is balanced then pull apart both sides. Make sure that the parts are fully opened and secure in the area of work.

K4. Dismantling and storing components

Dismantling ladders and platforms

Ladders

To dismantle a ladder make sure it is footed on the bottom rung and then lift it from the surface it is resting on. Hold onto a stile, then walk slowly backwards from the position while feeding the stiles through your hands until the ladder is in a position to lay it safely on the ground. Then move it into storage.

Platforms and platform steps

To dismantle platform steps, lean them forwards then release the locking mechanism, if fitted, or make sure that the rope is free to move. Place the back frame onto the front frame then lift the steps into position to move off to storage or to a new area of work.

A trestle can be dismantled in a similar way to the method used for ladders above. Lean one side of the trestle forwards then close the two frames together. You can then move it or store it.

Storing access equipment and working platforms

Ladders should be stored under cover. They can be laid flat and supported in three places along their length. They can also be hung by the stiles, again in three equal places along their length.

Stepladders, platform steps and trestles should be stored in their standing position in a covered store, off the ground if possible to avoid the effects of dampness and other weather conditions.

Remember

To lower a ladder, reverse the raising process. If the ladder is to be moved, the two operatives should position the ladder between them equally for the load, then move off

Safety tip

When erecting a stepladder, take care not to move too quickly in case you lose your balance. Then, when the stepladder is fully apart, stand it down and carry out a visual check to see if there are any faults

Safety tip

Take care when moving backwards not to move too fast and lose balance

Unit 1007

Know how to erect and dismantle access equipment and working platforms 1

FAQ

Am I protected from electrocution if I am working on a wooden stepladder?

No. If you are working near a live current on a wooden stepladder, if any metal parts of the ladder, such as tie rods, come into contact with the current, they will conduct electricity and you may be electrocuted. Take every precaution possible in order to avoid the risk of electrocution – the simplest precaution is turning off the electricity supply.

What determines the type of scaffolding used on a job?

As you will have read in this unit, only a carded scaffolder is allowed to erect or alter scaffolding. The carded scaffolder will select the scaffolding to be used according to the ground condition at the site, whether or not people will be working on the scaffolding, the types of materials and equipment that will be used on the scaffolding and the height to which access will be needed. However, if you are working for yourself, you will have to determine what type of scaffold is needed for the job at hand; for example, stepladders to reach ceilings in rooms, a staircase ladder system to decorate a staircase, a tower scaffold to reach higher areas if working in a warehouse.

Check it out

1. Write a method statement explaining the process you need to follow before working at height. You should make sure that your statement includes full reference to the health and safety issues you must follow when working.

2. Explain why you should not use a ladder for long spells of work at height.

3. Explain, with the use of a diagram, why a ratio of 1:4 is used when erecting a ladder.

4. State when a trestle platform should be used.

5. In order to increase the height of a tower scaffold, what else has to be increased and by how much?

6. Explain how some of the safeguards used when working at height operate, and what benefits they bring for safe working.

7. Explain how risk assessments are used when working at height.

8. Write a method statement explaining the process used by inspectors when checking scaffolding and access equipment.

9. Explain the correct manual handling processes that should be used with access equipment.

10. With the use of diagrams, demonstrate the correct methods that should be used when storing ladders, explaining why these procedures are necessary.

Getting ready for assessment

The information contained in this unit, as well as continued practical assignments that you will carry out in your college or training centre, will help you to prepare for both your end of unit test and the diploma multiple-choice test. It will also aid you in preparing for the work required for the synoptic practical assignments.

Working at different height levels is something you will be required to do in many of the painting and decorating tasks you will encounter while working in the construction industry. You will need to be familiar, not only with the safe working practices for these jobs, but also with the correct methods of working in these conditions.

You will need to know about and be familiar with:

- interpreting guidance information for using access equipment and working platforms
- inspecting components and identifying defects
- erecting and working from access equipment and working platforms
- dismantling and storing components.

This unit has introduced the concepts you will need to think about when working with access equipment and working platforms. In your work, you will need to use the knowledge you have gained from this unit.

For learning outcome 1, you have learned why it is important to inspect components and identify defects. When carrying out practical work, you will need to be able to recognise all the component parts of scaffolding and access equipment, and be familiar with their function, in order to use them correctly. You will also need to use this knowledge when carrying out inspections of these materials, both before and after use. You will need to be able to report any problems of potential hazards verbally to your supervisor.

Before you carry out any work at height, think of a plan of action, which will tell you the order you need to do things in. It will also record a rough timescale for the work you need to carry out, in order to make sure that you complete everything you need to do safely. You will need to refer back to this plan at each stage to make sure that you are not making any mistakes as you work, or missing out any part of the process that you need to work through. Without checking this, you could make some serious mistakes that could have an impact on the final build.

Your speed in carrying out any tasks in a practice setting will also help to prepare you for the time set for the test. However, you must never rush the test! Always make sure that you are working safely. Make sure throughout the test that you are wearing the appropriate PPE and using tools correctly.

Good luck!

CHECK YOUR KNOWLEDGE

1 When working from a stepladder, you must not:
- **a** open the steps fully
- **b** work from the top step
- **c** ensure the steps are on a level surface
- **d** check the steps before use

2 Which of the following are part of a stepladder?
- **a** stiles
- **a** rungs
- **b** toe boards
- **c** guardrails

3 Why should you not paint a wooden ladder?
- **a** It will hide the manufacturer's stamp.
- **b** It will make the ladder slippery.
- **c** It will make the ladder weaker.
- **d** It will hide any defects.

4 A ladder should be:
- **a** secured at the top
- **b** secured at the bottom
- **c** not rested against guttering
- **d** all of the above

5 Scaffold boards must be checked for:
- **a** splits
- **b** twists or warps
- **c** large knots
- **d** all of the above

6 Who is authorised to alter a scaffold?
- **a** anyone
- **b** the site agent
- **c** a health and safety inspector
- **d** a qualified, carded scaffolder

7 When working from a mobile tower scaffold, you must not:
- **a** climb up the outside
- **b** move it when there are people on it
- **c** throw things from the platform to the ground
- **d** do any of the above

8 When working at height for a long time, the best type of access equipment to use is a:
- **a** wooden stepladder
- **b** fibreglass stepladder
- **c** pole ladder
- **d** tower scaffold

9 What does BSI stand for when associated with scaffolding:
- **a** Best Scaffold Intended
- **b** Big Sturdy Instruments
- **c** British Scaffold Information
- **d** British Standards Institution

10 When erected, an extension ladder should be placed at an angle of:
- **a** 90°
- **b** 45°
- **c** 75°
- **d** 60°

UNIT 1008

Know how to prepare surfaces for decoration 1

The correct preparation of a surface is essential if you are going to produce work that looks good and lasts well. It is important that all surface contaminants such as dirt, oil, rust and loose or flaking existing coatings are removed. If contaminants are not removed, the ability of paint or paper to adhere (stick) to the surface will be affected.

This unit supports NVQ Unit QCF330 Prepare New Surfaces for Paint Systems in the Workplace.

This unit also supports TAP Unit Prepare Surfaces for Painting and Decorating

This unit will cover the following learning outcomes:

- Preparing a range of bare and previously painted and decorated surfaces to receive coatings/covering systems
- Correcting defects in surfaces and surface coatings
- Repairing and making good surfaces.

K1. Preparing a range of bare and previously painted and decorated surfaces to receive coatings/covering systems

Surface preparation is a very important task; if you prepare a surface thoroughly, you will end up with a high-quality finish and a good reputation. In this section we will look at some typical surfaces you may find yourself working on during your career, along with appropriate preparation tasks for each.

Identifying different substrates

In the building industry the following substrates are used widely. All of these play vital roles in the actual construction of most buildings and structures.

Timbers (softwoods and sheet materials) – used in **first fixing** and **second fixing** operations. This includes the building and installing of roofs, rafters, joists, bargeboards, fascias, soffits, flooring, stud walls, carcassing structures for boxing in pipes and so on. It also includes the fitting of window frames, window sills, door linings, door frames and doors, skirting boards and dado/picture rails. It can also include the fitting of kitchens and bathrooms.

Metal (ferrous and non-ferrous) – used in the industry for various items of structural work. A good example of this is formwork, which holds in place freshly placed and compacted concrete in the foundation stage of the building work. Metal is also used in the building of timber and metal roofs, as well as being the main material for some purpose-built structures, such as warehouses.

Plaster and plasterboard – used in the construction of internal and external walls on most buildings, as well as ceilings. Plasterboards are used during the construction of dividing walls within buildings and also fixed to ceiling joists to construct the ceilings in all rooms. These structures are then either taped and dry-lined or completely plastered to finish the job. Plaster is also placed directly on brick and block substrates to create a surface that can then be decorated.

Brick and blockwork – this forms the major part of the structure of a variety of buildings, with their main purpose being the construction of internal and external walls. This is also used to divide rooms within buildings. Blockwork usually refers to breeze

---

Key terms

First fixing – refers to work that is carried out before the plastering of a new structure

Second fixing – the joinery work carried out after the plastering of a new structure

---

Did you know?

Ferrous metals include iron. Non-ferrous metals do not

blocks and thermalite blocks, which are used internally. They are then either plastered over or have plasterboards fixed to them prior to decoration. In many cases, they are then simply painted over.

Appropriate materials needed to prepare surfaces

Before you start work on any painting or decorating task, you need to prepare the area and surfaces you are going to work on. If you don't do this, the results will be poor and you may have to start again, which will cost time and money.

Materials

Stoppers

Stoppers is a term used to describe a variety of materials used to repair or fix items during decorating. A stopper is usually a stiff material used to 'make good' and 'fill gaps' or 'large holes' on surfaces. It dries with the minimum amount of shrinkage. Areas on timber such as **open joints** and splits need to be filled and made flush prior to decoration. Splits can occur in timber for various reasons but it is the decorator who has to repair them during decoration.

Solvents

Solvents, such as white spirit, are used to remove grease and oil from metal surfaces prior to decoration. Solvents are used instead of water-based solutions to clean and wash down the surface of metals to avoid rust. These materials are very toxic so make sure that the area you are working in is well ventilated and that you are wearing gloves and a fume mask.

Single-pack filler

Single-pack filler usually refers to fillers used on internal timber floors. They are usually mixed with sanding dust to fill any gaps, cracks or knots in the timber. This is an extremely fast-drying, solvent-based filler.

Shellac, patent and white knotting

Normally referred to as knotting solution, these are used to seal any resinous knots or streaks in timber. They can also be used to seal any staining or discolouration on surfaces prior to decoration. This solution is used in the first stage of painting new softwood structures such as skirting boards. As well as using suitable PPE, make sure that the area is well ventilated when using these products.

> **Key term**
>
> **Open joints** – gaps in timber structures

> **Remember**
>
> Stoppers are used for stopping, which is a preparation process you will need to use on a range of building substrates

> **Safety tip**
>
> Whenever you use solvents, you must always make sure that you wear the correct PPE, that is, gloves, knee pads and so on. Look back at Unit 1001, pages 48–50 to remind yourself about PPE

Figure 8.1 Stripping knife/scraper

Figure 8.2 Putty knife

Figure 8.3 Chisel knife

Figure 8.4 Nail punch

Etching primer-mordant solution

This material is sometimes known as etch primer or T-wash and is used to give new galvanised metal a **key** prior to applying any paint systems. The mordant solution chemically etches and prepares the surface, providing adhesion for the subsequent paints. Make sure that you are wearing a face mask and the area you are working in is well ventilated, as this solution is very toxic and should not be inhaled.

Stabilising solutions

These are highly penetrating, clear, solvent-based solutions. They are normally used on external masonry structures to prevent defects such as chalking, and can be used to prime surfaces that are flaking. By using this material for both internal and external surfaces, you can save time and money during the preparation stage. Make sure the area you are working in is ventilated and you are wearing a suitable mask and gloves.

Tools and equipment

Stripping knife/scraper

A stripping knife (or scraper) is used to remove old or flaking paint, wallpaper and other loose debris from surfaces to be decorated. When not in use, clean off the knife and protect the tip with a suitable cover.

Putty knife

A putty knife is a tool used for applying putty to window rebates. It is also used to scrape away unwanted putty from glass surfaces after fixing glass to frames. It can also be used to force stoppers and putty into small holes and cracks.

On one side, it has a straight blade and on the other a curved blade. This aids in the application of both bedding putty and facing putty when glazing. It can also be used to apply stoppers/putty into small holes and cracks and help force the material in.

Chisel knife

A chisel knife is a good all-round preparation tool and can be used for a variety of tasks, such as scraping off paint or wallpaper in areas where a standard stripping knife could not fit and removing drawing pins, staples and so on from surfaces prior to decoration.

Nail punch

A nail punch enables you to countersink any nail heads that are protruding on timber surfaces while preparing for painting.

Shave hooks

Shave hooks are used to scrape off loose deposits and old coatings from beadings and mouldings during burning off or basic paint removal processes. They can also be used to prepare areas that are to receive fillers. Shave hooks are available in three different shapes: triangular, pear-shaped and combination. The blade edges should be kept sharp to ensure maximum performance and avoid unnecessary damage to surfaces.

Figure 8.5 Shave hooks

Hot air gun/stripper

Hot air guns or strippers produce hot air via an electrical element rather than a naked flame. This reduces the risk of fire and scorching of surfaces such as timber. In addition, hot air guns/strippers are more suited to use on surfaces where there is a risk of **combustion** or where there is glass present, which could crack due to the high temperature.

Figure 8.6 Hot air gun/stripper

Chipping hammer

Chipping hammers are used to remove heavy rust, mill scale and loose rust while preparing surfaces before painting. These tools come in both hand-held and powered versions.

Figure 8.7 Chipping hammer

Dusting brush

Dusting brushes are used to remove loose dust, grit and other fine debris from surfaces before applying paint. They are an important part of a decorator's tool kit.

Figure 8.8 Dusting brush

Roller trays

Roller trays are used to hold and transport coatings while decorating with rollers. By using this equipment, it is easier to apply coatings to surfaces via a roller. These trays come in various sizes to accommodate the different-sized roller heads.

Figure 8.9 Roller tray

Dustpan and brush

A dustpan and brush can be used for general cleaning before and after decorating. If you fail to remove dust and debris from your work area, it may result in the contamination of surfaces and paint systems, leading to poor workmanship and a damaged reputation.

Figure 8.10 Dustpan and brush

Figure 8.11 Knotting brush

Figure 8.12 Wire brush

Figure 8.13 Rotary wire brush

Figure 8.14 Filling knife

Figure 8.15 Using a filling board

Brushes

All brushes need to be cleaned thoroughly after use. Leaving traces of material on the bristles could damage them, making the brush useless. Care of brushes depends upon the material from which they are made. It is therefore best to read any manufacturer's instructions on cleaning and storage.

Knotting brush

This is usually a 1-inch brush or small round brush. It is used when applying knotting solution to knots, stains and so on.

Wire brush

A wire brush is used to remove loose rust and corrosion from various types of metalwork. Wire brushes are available with either steel wire or bronze wire bristles. Bronze wire versions are well suited where there is a fire hazard as they will not cause sparks.

Rotary wire brush

Rotary wire brushes are used in the same way as ordinary wire brushes, although they are more powerful and less manually demanding to use (that is, they do some of the work for you).

Filling knife

A filling knife looks very similar to a stripping knife but is used to apply fillers as part of the preparation process. The blade is made of a thinner gauge metal, which makes it more flexible, allowing manipulation of the filler. A filling knife requires the same cleaning and protection as a scraping knife.

Filling board

This tool can be used to apply a variety of fillers/stoppers to areas such as open-grain timbers, cracks, small holes, shallow indentations and uneven surfaces prior to decoration.

The filling board is used to hold large amounts of filler while you are filling any holes or cracks in surfaces. These boards are usually used for mixing and holding large amounts of fillers and stoppers when applying to surfaces. Having a filling board allows the painter to cover large areas at a time.

Woven fabric

Woven fabric refers to the material used to make the dust sheets and fire blankets that are used in preparing a work area. They are available in cotton and flame-retardant fabric.

Buckets

Buckets are used in preparation of surfaces for holding water and other mixtures used when stripping old wall coverings and washing down surfaces prior to decoration.

Rubbing blocks

Rubbing blocks are used to support both wet and dry abrasive papers and make handling and working with abrasive papers easier. They are available in wood, plastic, cork or rubber versions.

Figure 8.16 Rubbing block

Preparation processes for building substrates

To prepare substrates for work, you will need to be familiar with some of the common preparation processes and defects you may encounter as part of your work.

Wet and dry abrading

Abrading a surface means wearing away the top layer by rubbing (that is, creating friction). This is a very important part of surface preparation and provides a key for the coating and covering to be applied and smooths the surface in order to give a good-quality finish.

It is important that the correct type of abrading material is used:

- An abrasive that is too rough can leave scratches on surfaces that show through to the finish.
- An abrasive that is too fine can result in preparation time taking longer than necessary and may be ineffective at removing or levelling rough surface imperfections.

Cheap, inadequate abrasives such as glasspaper can greatly extend the preparation time of any job because they tend to get blunt and clog very quickly.

Wet and dry abrasives can be used in both wet and dry conditions. A waterproof adhesive fixes the abrasive particles to the backing, which means that the paper doesn't lose the particles when it gets wet. In fact if wet and dry paper is used dry, it tends to clog up and so is more suited to wet use.

Types of abrasive

The aggregates (abrasive particles) used in wet and dry abrasive paper have traditionally been silicon carbide, but aluminum oxide is becoming increasingly popular. Aluminium oxide abrasive, sometimes called production paper, is usually available 'open

Remember

When washing a surface, you should always start at the bottom and work upwards. This avoids streaking of painted surfaces, which can damage the finish coated'. This is where the particles of aggregate are spaced apart on the backing paper. This reduces the risk that a lubricant, such as water or oil, might become clogged as the paper is used.

Abrasive paper

Sometimes known as sandpaper, abrasive paper is grit on flexible backing sheets used to wear down a surface. Abrasive paper is available with different sizes of grit, each suited to a different type of task (e.g. for coarse or fine abrasion). Wet abrasive paper can be used with water to give a very fine abrasion or, when used with mineral oil, for smoothing and polishing metals.

Always use the correct type of abrasive paper for the job and never use hand abrasive paper in a power tool such as an orbital or belt sander. Abrasive papers should be stored in a cool dry place and replaced regularly.

Silicon carbide and glasspaper are classed as sandpapers and are a form of paper where an abrasive has been fixed to them. The abrasive or grit comes in various sizes and is referred to by a number. The size of grit is used to classify the sandpaper by 'grade'.

These papers come in individual sheets, rolls, discs, belts, blocks and special shaped pads (which can be attached to power tools).

Glasspaper is an inexpensive soft abrasive, normally used for sanding painted or natural timber or metal surfaces. It wears out quickly and is normally used to provide a rough finish before using a finer grade paper to finish the job.

Silicone carbide paper, also known as 'wet and dry' paper, is suitable for both dry and wet abrading. It can be used for sanding substrates such as hardwoods, plywood, brass, aluminum, plastic and glass edges. It is very hard wearing and, when used with water, gives a very fine finish between coats of varnish and paint. It can also be used with mineral oil for smoothing and polishing metals. When the paper is used with a lubricant it helps with keeping dust down as well as giving a smoother finish.

Pole sander

A pole sander is used when preparing surfaces with sandpaper or abrasive paper, to help you reach high areas such as ceilings and the tops of walls.

Grit size	Grade
80–100	Medium course
120–150	Medium
180–200	Fine
240 upwards	Very fine

Table 8.1 Types of sandpaper

Figure 8.17 Pole sander

Sanders

There are two main types of sander used for abrading:

- Orbital sander
- Belt sander

The orbital sander is the slower of the two, but is lighter and easier to use. It can be used to prepare surfaces ready for painting, including timber, plastic, most metals and previously painted surfaces. This type of sander is more suited to small areas. The belt sander is much faster than the orbital sander and is more suited to larger surface areas.

Figure 8.18 Orbital sander

Figure 8.19 Belt sander

Working life

As part of her training, Helen has been placed on a new building site to gain evidence for her qualification. While on site, she has been asked to prepare all the new plaster work and new second-fix joinery work in one of the properties. She will then assist in coating the surfaces with a suitable paint system. Helen wants to impress her new supervisor so she can gain more evidence on site so starts preparing the surfaces straight away instead of waiting for her colleague, who will be working with her. Helen decides to abrade the new plaster walls with a coarse sandpaper, because she remembers that surfaces need a key prior to applying coatings. After a few minutes, she realises that she has made a mistake so then starts rubbing down the woodwork instead. At this point, her supervisor walks in and tells her to stop what she is doing!

- What has Helen done wrong? Should she have waited for her colleague? Why has her supervisor told her to stop? What mistake has Helen realised she has done?
- What would you have done? What defects have been created? How should the preparation have been done?

Safety tip

When using electrical equipment, always follow the manufacturer's instructions and check the equipment before you use it to ensure that there are no faults, either with the equipment or its power supply lead

Knotting

During the preparation of timber surfaces, you may notice knots in the wood. A knot is a place in the timber where a branch was joined to the tree. If you paint bare timber without preparing the knots first, the sap will bleed from the knot, staining the paint finish. Knotting solution must be applied to knots in order to seal them.

A knotting solution can also be applied to a surface which has suffered **resin** exudation (discharge). This is caused by heat, which makes the resin rise out of timber and discolour the surface.

Safety tip

Knotting solution is highly flammable and so should not be exposed to naked flames. You must also make sure that you wear the appropriate PPE when handling this material

Key term

Resin (also known as sap) – a very sticky substance that comes from trees/timber and becomes very hard when exposed to the air

Remember

If you're not sure what preparation is required for a particular sort of timber, always seek advice before starting the task

Key term

Spot primed – the application of primer (base coat) to small areas of metal, timber or plaster to seal them. On metals this prevents rust or corrosion from returning

Key term

Flush – when one surface is level and even with another surface

Priming

Priming is the first coat of paint applied to a surface. If the surface preparation for the priming coat or the application and choice of the primer is incorrect in any way, the durability of the paint system will be reduced.

Some manufacturers market their primers as 'universal', meaning they can be used for a wide range of surfaces. These should not be expected to out-perform primers specifically designed for a particular surface. For example, when painting on an aluminum surface, a two-pack etch primer designed specifically for use on aluminum would be far better than a universal primer.

Filling

You may find the surface you are working on is in good condition (also known as sound), and will not need any repair, but even sound surfaces can have patchy areas where the existing coating has peeled off or is flaking.

In these situations the flaking paint has to be removed to form a solid edge. The bare areas then need to be **spot primed**. When the primer has dried, the edges of the repaired area can be surface-filled with a suitable filling agent. The filling agent will remove any indentations in the surface by 'filling' the gap.

If a hole or crack on a surface is not filled 'proud' (see below), it can shrink with the drying process, and will need filling all over again.

Proud filling

Whenever you fill any holes or cracks you should overfill and leave proud. This means that you leave a raised amount of material filler. The reason you do this is that after the drying process has occurred, the filler will reduce or shrink back. Some filler will still be proud and you will need to rub it down to leave it **flush** or level with the surface.

Back filling

This refers to filling a large hole or gap with a filler, rendering, mortar or stopper by pressing the material deep into the area then leaving it to dry. You will then need to repeat the process until you either make the surface proud or level.

Flush filling

This refers to filling any small indentations on surfaces where you would use a filling knife or caulk board to apply the filler and make the surface flush prior to applying coatings.

Knife filling

This is also used when applying stoppers/fillers to defective areas such as splits in timber, open joints in timber, holes, cracks, gaps and indentations.

Tools used for filling

Hand-held hawk and trowel

Painters use hawks and trowels to repair small holes in plastered walls or plasterboards before painting.

Figure 8.20 Hand hawk

Pointing trowel

Pointing trowels are used by painters to repair lightly damaged brickwork while preparing before painting or protecting. They are usually used by both bricklayers and plasterers, but painters can use pointing trowels to make good large cracks and holes in trowelled surfaces when decorating. They are made from forged steel and come with a wooden or rubber handle.

Figure 8.21 Pointing trowel

Caulking tool

Made up of a flexible flat metal or plastic blade set in a wooden or plastic handle, a caulking tool is used for applying filler and jointing materials. It is also sometimes used to smooth out decorative coverings applied to plasterboard surfaces. A caulking tool should be maintained in the same way as a filling knife.

Figure 8.22 Caulking tool

Removal of rust

During your inspection of the work surface, you may notice areas where the surface has **corroded**, usually due to **rust**. This will have to be cleaned and removed before work can be carried out.

Rust can be removed with either hand or power tools.

> **Key term**
>
> **Corroded** – destroyed or damaged by chemical reaction
>
> **Rust** – a red or yellowish-brown coating of iron oxide

Needle gun

Needle guns are used to remove rust from around corroded nuts, bolts, rivets and welds. They can also be used in the preparation of stonework. There are various types of needles available for use with the gun depending on the surface to be prepared. Needle guns are powered by compressed air and great care must be taken to ensure safe operation.

Figure 8.23 Needle gun

Raking out

When there is any defective rendering, such as cracked rendering, loose rendering and perished rendering, you should rake out the brick joints. This will give a consistent depth to all the joints and remove any inconsistencies or debris.

After work, flush the area with clean water, particularly where the rendering is now missing or removed. This will also give the area a key prior to re-rendering with a suitable mortar. Make sure that the new render is flush with the existing render.

Wetting in

When removing wall coverings, you need to wet in first. This means you apply water to the wallpapered area after first **scoring** the paper. This water then penetrates the paper, making it softer and easier to remove. You can also wet in holes and cracks in rendering prior to applying filler, to help prevent the filler drying out before it sets.

Removal of paint and wall coverings

If the surface you are going to work on already has a coating of paint that is in poor condition (that is, it has a brittle paint film or paint actually flaking off), it will be necessary to remove the entire paint coating in order to produce a good finished effect. This can be done using heat or chemical means.

Paint can be burned off with heat, using a LPG (liquefied petroleum gas) burning off torch or a hot air stripper.

LPG torch/gun

LPG torches or guns are used to remove old paint and varnish. They do this by producing a naked flame that heats the area being treated, allowing the paint or varnish to be scraped off with a stripping knife or shave hook.

Some LPG torches run from a large gas canister (see Figure 8.24). Smaller, disposable, cartridge-type gas torches are also available. These are light and easy to use, although they do produce less heat and have a shorter burning time.

Steam stripper

Using a steam stripper is a very efficient way of removing surface coverings from both walls and ceilings. Take care when using a steam stripper because over-application of the steam process can result in damage to the covered surface, leading to blistering and/ or removal of small areas of plaster finishes. You must also take care when using these strippers on ceilings because you can be at risk from burns or scalding due to the hot water/steam produced by the stripper.

Figure 8.24 LPG torch/gun

Preparing surfaces

New softwoods/hardwoods

Abrading a new softwood or hardwood may result in damage due to scratching or furring (the lifting of wood fibres). For this reason, it is better simply to dust off the surface prior to painting. If you notice any raised nail heads, they will need to be punched down below the surface and filled with a suitable filling agent prior to painting.

Rough sawn timber

Rough sawn timber should be dry brushed thoroughly to remove soil, vegetation and dust.

New plaster and plasterboard

New plaster and plasterboard should be dry scraped with a scraper to remove any bits and nibs and then dusted down. Never abrade the surface as this will scratch it.

Brickwork, block work, stonework, rendering, pebbledash and concrete finishes

These types of surface can be thoroughly cleaned with scrapers and dry brushing in order to remove dirt and powdery residue. The surface may need to be scrubbed if efflorescence is present (see page 141) or washed if mould is present, but it should be allowed to dry thoroughly before being worked on. Dusting off should be carried out prior to painting.

Ferrous metalwork

Ferrous metals contain iron. They include cast iron, wrought iron, mild steel and stainless steel. These surfaces are prone to rusting and will need to be cleared of all rust prior to painting. Depending upon the extent of the rust, it can be removed with a wire brush, mechanical wire brush, abrasive papers and/or scrapers.

New metalwork needs to be cleaned down with white spirit or an emulsifying agent to remove grease and oily residues.

Non-ferrous metalwork

Non-ferrous metals do not contain iron. They include aluminium, zinc, copper and brass. These should be dry and free from grease prior to painting. Previously painted non-ferrous metals need to be abraded and any corrosion deposits found should be scraped back to a firm edge where any flaking paint is evident.

Figure 8.25 Steam stripper

> **Safety tip**
>
> Always follow the manufacturer's instructions regarding the correct use and maintenance of LPG torches

> **Remember**
>
> Take care when scrubbing with a wire brush so as not to damage surfaces with scratches

> **Remember**
>
> The over-burnishing of rust when preparing steelwork results in reduced adhesion of metal primer

Painted wood

Painted wood should be washed down using sugar soap and warm water and then rinsed with clean water. The surface should then be abraded to provide a key and then dusted down to remove surface dust.

Painted plaster

Painted plaster should be washed down with sugar soap and warm water, then rinsed off with clean water. The surface should then be abraded. Any indentations, cracks, holes etc. should be filled with a filling agent. Once dry, areas filled should be sanded down and dusted off ready for painting.

Plastic

Plastic surfaces might include guttering and down pipes. Although, normally, plastic guttering and down pipes are used because they are virtually maintenance-free, there may be occasions when a client wants a colour change. Special primers are required for preparing plastic surfaces to receive paint finishes, because good adhesion is hard to achieve. Plastic surfaces should be degreased and abraded using wire wool and a suitable degreaser to provide a key before application of the primer.

Glazed tiles

These should be washed down using a detergent, for example sugar soap.

Polystyrene tiles

Polystyrene tiles should be dusted off and filled with a plaster-based filler where any damage is evident. Oil-based fillers should not be used because they will dissolve the polystyrene.

New wallpaper

Wallpapered surfaces, including those covered with embossed and blown vinyl paper, should be dusted off and any paste marks washed off before painting.

Old wallpaper

Old wallpaper is best stripped off using either water and a scraper or a steam stripper and a scraper. Some papers, such as vinyl, can be peeled off, leaving the backing paper on the surface.

Primer and coating systems for a range of surfaces

There is a range of primers that can be used for the substrate surfaces you will encounter as a painter. Some of the most common are covered below.

Solvent-based primers

Primer	Description
Aluminium	Spirit-based primers used to seal oily hardwoods. Also suitable for chipboard, creosoted timber, hardboard, plywood and softwood fixings. Used to seal areas with previously applied coatings, such as **bituminous paints**, which can soften or bleed through subsequent new coatings or coverings
White and pink	General-purpose wood primers for both interior and exterior timber fixtures and provide good adhesion for further coats in the paint system
Zinc phosphate	Metal (steel, iron and non-ferrous) primer that has a rust-inhibitive pigment added to it to aid in the prevention of corrosion and rust

Table 8.2 Solvent-based primers

Alkali and alkali-resisting (ARP) primer

The chemical nature of surfaces like concrete, cement rendering, asbestos sheeting and some plasters is **alkaline**. This can cause problems if a solvent-based paint system is to be applied because the alkalinity in the surface can attack the paint rather like a paint stripper, causing a paint defect known as **saponification**.

To prevent saponification, it is necessary to apply an alkali-resistant primer, which forms a barrier between the surface and the paint. Acrylic surface coatings are resistant to alkalis, so you would think an alkali-resistant primer wouldn't be needed, but the **permeable** nature of the coatings allows any alkalinity through if the surface becomes damp.

Key terms

Bituminous paints – coatings used to protect both steelwork and timber from moisture and corrosive atmospheres, usually used on roof work. They are also known as 'coal tar' and are highly water resistant, and therefore applied on rainwater pipes and guttering, railings, storage tanks, concrete posts, fencing, roofs and also used on car and caravan vehicle chassis work

Alkaline – having a pH greater than 7 (an acid has a pH of less than 7)

Saponification – a chemical reaction that makes soap and so foams up as a result

Permeable – allowing things to pass through it

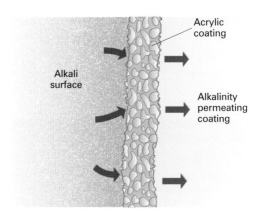

Figure 8.26 Alkalinity permeating an acrylic coating

Water-based primers

Primer	Description
Metal primer	Specially formulated coatings, low in volatile organic compounds (VOCs), non-toxic and virtually odourless. Expensive to purchase and can only be applied on properly prepared metal surfaces. When you spot-prime metal surfaces, the following primers can be used: • Calcium plumbate primer for galvanised iron • Etch primer/mordant solution for all non-ferrous metals • Zinc phosphate metal primer for all ferrous/non-ferrous metals • Zinc rich epoxy primer for new blast-cleaned metals.
Size primer	Used to seal porous surfaces prior to decoration. Used when using starch paste prior to paper hanging. Thinned-down adhesives (PVA or cellulose) to act as sealer on new plaster and plasterboard
Acrylic primer	Water-based alkali-resisting primer made from high-quality pigments and a tough acrylic resin. Low odour, fast air drying and easily applied; available in white and pink
Emulsion primer	Used as a primer when diluted with water and for finishes to internal domestic surfaces. Available in matt or silk varieties, easy to apply, air drying and water-based. Best suited for surfaces that do not need shine, particularly uneven or imperfect areas. Silk emulsion leaves an attractive sheen when dry and is more durable and washable than matt emulsion

Table 8.3 Water-based primers

> **Remember**
>
> Some materials that have been applied previously may have had toxics added to them and, therefore, you need to take great care when using any new material

Coating systems

Coating systems are paint systems that refer to the type of coating, method of application and number of layers of various paints/coatings required for a particular job. Examples include:

- new timber – knotting solution to seal any exposed knots followed by a primer then an undercoat and finally finished with a gloss or eggshell finish
- new plastered wall area – a plaster primer followed by two or three coats of coloured emulsion.

Coating system	Description
Solvent-based	Oil-based paints and coatings. Solvent helps with application and curing of coating. Thinners used to help speed up drying and get the correct viscosity (thickness). Used widely in various industries and have a long life span when used correctly. Very high in VOCs and a hazard if used incorrectly
Water-based	Water-based paints and coatings. Use water to help disperse the resin in the coating. Thinned by adding water and low in VOCs. Any spillages can be cleaned away with water. Help to reduce the risk of fire
Coating system	**Description**
Preservative	Used on timber to protect it from insects and fungus. Can extend the life of timber. Can be both solvent- and water-based (more common). Can swell the timber when applied or injected and cause it to twist and split. Many methods used to preserve timber such as steeping, soaking, dipping, brushing, spraying and using pressure
Paper	Usually, different grades of lining paper are used as a cheap preparation method of covering damaged and uneven surfaces prior to paper hanging or painting. Can save both time and money

Table 8.4 Coating systems

K2. Correcting defects in surfaces and surface coatings

There are a large number of defects that you will encounter when working with surfaces. This section will introduce some of the most common defects and the methods used to correct them.

Types and causes of common defects

During your career as a painter and decorator, there may be occasions when the surface coating you have applied fails in some way. This may be because you did not adequately prepare the surface prior to applying the coating, because the environmental conditions (for example the weather) were not favourable or because your tools or materials were of poor quality. Figure 8.27 shows some common surface coating defects and their causes.

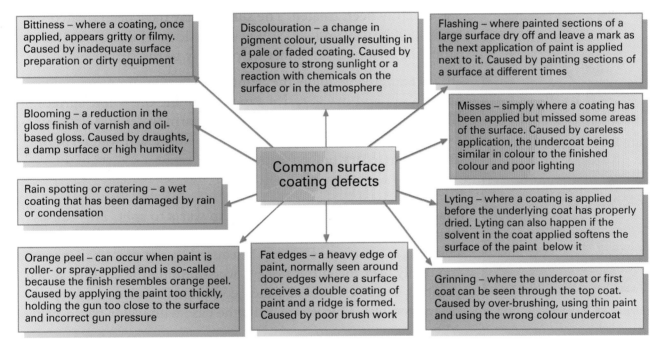

Bittiness – where a coating, once applied, appears gritty or filmy. Caused by inadequate surface preparation or dirty equipment

Blooming – a reduction in the gloss finish of varnish and oil-based gloss. Caused by draughts, a damp surface or high humidity

Rain spotting or cratering – a wet coating that has been damaged by rain or condensation

Orange peel – can occur when paint is roller- or spray-applied and is so-called because the finish resembles orange peel. Caused by applying the paint too thickly, holding the gun too close to the surface and incorrect gun pressure

Discolouration – a change in pigment colour, usually resulting in a pale or faded coating. Caused by exposure to strong sunlight or a reaction with chemicals on the surface or in the atmosphere

Common surface coating defects

Fat edges – a heavy edge of paint, normally seen around door edges where a surface receives a double coating of paint and a ridge is formed. Caused by poor brush work

Flashing – where painted sections of a large surface dry off and leave a mark as the next application of paint is applied next to it. Caused by painting sections of a surface at different times

Misses – simply where a coating has been applied but missed some areas of the surface. Caused by careless application, the undercoat being similar in colour to the finished colour and poor lighting

Lyting – where a coating is applied before the underlying coat has properly dried. Lyting can also happen if the solvent in the coat applied softens the surface of the paint below it

Grinning – where the undercoat or first coat can be seen through the top coat. Caused by over-brushing, using thin paint and using the wrong colour undercoat

Figure 8.27 Common surface coating defects

Efflorescence

Efflorescence is the appearance of white patches on cement-based surfaces and can occur on brickwork, rendering and internal plaster. Cement is porous; moisture such as rain can penetrate the cement, dissolving some of the lime and creating calcium hydroxide. The calcium hydroxide rises to the surface when the cement dries out and, once all the moisture has disappeared, calcium carbonate is left on the surface as the white patch you can see.

Figure 8.29 Cissing

Figure 8.30 Flaking

Figure 8.31 Bittiness

> **Did you know?**
>
> Flaking can also be caused by poor preparation when mixing the paint

> **Key term**
>
> **Tack rag** – a small muslin cloth coated with an oil and sticky to the touch, used to remove dust and small debris from surfaces prior to painting

Although efflorescence will eventually disappear on its own, if a surface is to be decorated, any efflorescence will need to be removed during preparation. The treatment for surfaces affected by efflorescence is removal by scrubbing with a stiff fibre brush or a wire brush. Never try to remove efflorescence by washing the surface as the calcium carbonate will simply dissolve in the water and sink back into the cement.

Figure 8.28 Efflorescence

Cissing

This is caused by applying paint over a contaminated surface that has recently been treated. The surface may have been treated with polish, oil or wax and will still have a residue of this on it. This stops the coating from adhering properly to the surface.

To correct cissing, allow the painted surface to dry again before using a wet and dry abrasive paper to abrade the whole surface. Then wash it down with a solution of warm water and detergent before applying a final rinse of the area with clean water. Allow the surface to dry before reapplying the paint.

Flaking

Flaking is caused when the paint film starts to split. This causes hairline cracks to appear in the paint, which leads to flaking paint chips on the surface. This can be caused by the paint being spread too thinly over the surface or by over-thinning the coating. When painting exteriors, cool or windy conditions can lead to the paint drying too fast. This is especially the case with water-based paints.

To rectify remove the loose or flaking coating with a scraper or wire brush, then abrade the areas affected. You will need to prime any bare spots then repaint.

Bittiness

Bittiness is caused by small particles of dirt and debris, which have either landed on the wet surface of the coating or not been fully removed from a surface prior to applying coatings. To remove this defect, lightly abrade the surface and then fully dust down and use a **tack rag** to remove all traces of dirt from the surface and then repaint.

Runs, sags and curtains

These are all names for a similar defect. They are caused by poor application of a coating to a surface. They occur when too much coating has been applied and gravity makes the coating move down the surface in a 'curtain' effect. To prevent this make sure you have not overloaded your brush or roller and you fully spread out the coating.

Figure 8.32 Curtain defect

Mould

Mould is a furry growth of micro-organisms (fungus), which often grows in moist or warm conditions, as Figure 8.33 shows. If mould is found during surface preparation, all traces of it must be removed. If it is not totally removed, the mould can quickly re-establish itself underneath an applied coating, which can then lead to the premature failure of that coating.

This procedure should be followed to remove mould growth:

Figure 8.33 Mould growth

- Wet the mould to avoid the spread of spores to other areas.
- Remove heavy patches of mould with a scraper or wire brush.
- Apply a fungicidal wash to the affected area and allow it to dry.

If possible, the affected area should be left for a week or so and re-treated if the mould reappears. In most cases, only one application will be necessary. This is because fungicidal wash has a residue effect on the surface, which means that traces of it remain, continually removing mould growth from the surface.

> **Safety tip**
>
> Make sure that you are wearing the correct PPE throughout to avoid irritants coming into contact with your skin or you inhaling any dust while using the abrasive paper

Materials and cleaning agents needed for rectification processes

As well as these materials, you will also need to use many of the same tools as you used for preparing surfaces (see pages 128–131). Primers (pages 139–140) are also important materials for rectification.

> **Remember**
>
> Sometimes it may be necessary to remove all of the coating using, for example, a heat gun and start the whole application system again

Sterilising fluids and fungicidal washes

These are used to kill and remove mould, algae, fungus, moss and so on from surfaces prior to applying coatings. After the surfaces have been wiped down with the solutions, you then need to apply a good-quality fungicidal paint to help prevent further outbreaks of mould and other problems.

> **Safety tip**
>
> Fungicidal washes are poisonous and should be treated with extreme care. Wear suitable PPE and always wash your hands after using these products

Solvents

Solvents (white spirit and methylated spirits) are used to clean down metal surfaces prior to applying coatings. These help to prevent corrosion and rust occurring and dry very quickly, meaning the application of coatings can be performed straight after cleaning the surfaces. Methylated spirits are also used to clean brushes after applying knotting solution to surfaces. White spirit cannot remove knotting from brushes, due to the ingredients used to create knotting.

Acetone

Acetone is a type of solvent used as a heavy-duty degreaser during the preparation of some metal structures and can also be used to remove residues from glass. Grease must be removed from all surfaces before painting because, if it is left in place, it can lead to cissing and other defects once the paint is applied.

Stain blocks

Stain blocks (**proprietary** and **non-proprietary**) are used to prevent and cure stains (for example, nicotine stains, other colours bleeding through, felt-tip pen marks, adhesive marks, fire damage marks and damp patches). (See Aluminium primer on page 139). Usually, stain blocks are available in a spray can for easier application.

Detergents

When washing a surface down, it is important to use the correct washing agent. Dirt can be removed with a mild detergent. After using a detergent, make sure that the area is thoroughly rinsed and allowed to dry completely.

Abrading surfaces

Wet and dry abrasive paper is used during the application of coatings to surfaces where a perfect finish is desirable. It is also used when a **feathered edge** is required after filling surfaces and spot priming. This type of abrasive paper has a longer life span than other abrasive papers.

K3. Repairing and making good surfaces

Making good processes for defective areas

There are several processes that you will often need to use when carrying out repairs and making good surfaces. Some processes have been covered earlier in this unit (pages 131–38).

Sinking nail heads

When nail heads have been left protruding above the surface use a nail punch and a hammer to sink the head of the nail back into the wood. Place the nail punch squarely on the nail head, making sure that you have covered the whole head. Then carefully hammer the nail until the nail head is below the surface of the timber. Then apply a stopper or filler to the hole.

Scraping

There are various sizes and types of scraper, such as a 6-inch linblade scraper, used to remove heavy wall coverings, to a 1-inch scraper used to remove staples from walls. Scrapers are used for many different tasks, such as removal of wallpaper, rust, nibs from plaster surfaces and scraping away flaking paint and pastes from surfaces prior to redecoration. You will need to scrape off defects before you can begin painting.

Undercutting

When there is damaged rendering on any surface, you must first brush down the area to remove any loose rendering and dust. If possible, rake out the mortar joints to form a key. Then remove the plaster to form an undercut under the existing plaster. To do this, cut back the plaster at an angle on either edge of the defective rendering to form a wedge-like area to refill with rendering.

Applying caulk and sealants

Caulk is a waterproof filler and sealant used in cracks and gaps. Mastic is an acrylic type of caulk and is applied using a mastic gun – a frame that holds and helps dispense mastic from its tube. Dry mastic feels a bit like rubber.

Mastic is available in various colours and is used to seal gaps around external windows and doors. It is not normally primed and is very flexible and waterproof.

Remember

Make sure you fully bed in, or fill the hole with, the stopper or filler with a putty knife

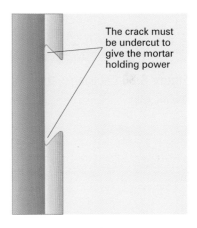

The crack must be undercut to give the mortar holding power

Figure 8.34 Undercutting

Did you know?

Flexible caulk is used to fill gaps around skirting boards, door and window frames, architrave, dados and picture rails. A suitable primer for this filler would be acrylic primer/undercoat

You must make sure that you apply a finished edge as this material cannot be rubbed down.

A mastic gun is easy to use. Surplus caulk can be removed with a filling knife and a damp cloth should be used to soften the edges. Any remaining material can then be sponged off.

Figures 8.35 and 8.36 show two examples of how caulking can be applied to skirting boards.

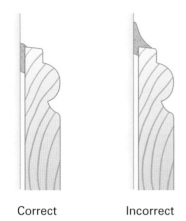

Correct   Incorrect

Figure 8.35 Correct and incorrect caulking

Defective areas

Common defective areas are outlined below.

Defective area	Description
Open joints	Gaps that have developed in timber
Splits	Defects found in timber. Caused by bad workmanship
Indentations	Small holes and gaps in the surface, rectified by flush filling
Open grained timber	Refers to timber such as oak and mahogany with wider grains. Needs to be filled flush with a wood filler prior to staining or coating, so there will be no faults visible when the structure is decorated
Putties	Around windows and glass, can become defective with age and must be removed. Hack off the defective putty using a hacking knife and hammer and clean the area before replacing
Stale paste	Careless paper hanging has been carried out and the decorator leaves paste residue on the surface without cleaning with damp cloth. May need to be removed using wet and dry abrasive paper and a scraper

Figure 8.36 Caulking with a mastic gun

Table 8.5 Common defective areas

Commonly used stoppers

A decorator will use a wide range of stoppers and fillers. Some of these have been covered earlier in this unit (see pages 127–28).

This section will look at other types of stopper and will explain the primers that can be used with these stoppers.

Plaster and plaster-based stoppers

Plaster and plaster-based stoppers are used on internal surfaces only. They are very smooth fillers and come ready-mixed. Primers used for this filler are the same as caulk. Plaster, used for gypsum and lime plaster repairs, is quick setting and drying. A suitable primer for this repair could be one of the following:

- acrylic primer/undercoat
- alkali-resisting primer

Unit 1008 Know how to prepare surfaces for decoration 1

Repairing a crack in plaster

If you come across any cracks in trowelled (plaster-finished surfaces), you need to repair ('make good') the area.

Step 1: Rake out the crack, running the edge of your scraper along the crack to remove any loose plaster and so on.

Step 2: Dust down the area to remove any flaking and fine dust, so the filler is not contaminated and therefore defective.

Step 3: 'Wet in' the area to aid the adhesion stage for the filler when you fill the crack.

- all-purpose primer
- primer sealer
- plaster sealer.

Plaster-based stoppers are used on plaster and for filling grains on timber. They must be mixed with clean water. The primers that can be used for this repair are:

- acrylic primer/undercoat
- aluminium wood primer
- all-purpose primer
- wood primer.

Cement/vinyl-based stopper

This is used for external surfaces only. It is waterproof, making it perfect for dealing with a wide range of weather conditions, but it is hard to rub down when dry. Primers used for this repair are:

- acrylic primer/undercoat
- all-purpose primer.

Cement mortar can be used to repair deep holes in plaster and to repair external rendering and brickwork. Primers used for this type of filler could be:

- stabilising solution
- plaster sealer
- primer sealer
- all-purpose primer.

> **Remember**
> If you don't 'wet in', the filler could dry out too quickly due to the porous surface and then shrink drastically and fall out. You only need to brush the crack with water and not soak the area

> **Remember**
> The tools you will use when working with stoppers are:
>
> Filling knife (page 130)
>
> Filling board (page 130)
>
> Putty knife (page 128)
>
> Pointing trowel (page 135)
>
> Caulking tool (page 135).

Functional skills

When deciding on the best plan to use for practical work you may need to explain in writing why you are doing what you are doing. This will allow you to practise **FE** 1.3.1–1.3.5 – Write clearly with a level of detail to suit the purpose.

By looking at problems and coming up with solutions, you will also practise **FM** 1.3.1 – Judge whether findings answer the original problem and **FM** 1.3.2 – Communicate solutions to answer practical problems

Tinted stopper

This is used for repairing defects in stained timbers that will be varnished with clear wood finishes.

Oil- and solvent-based filler

This is used for internal and external painted surfaces and comes ready-mixed. Primers used for this material could be:

- all-purpose primer
- primer sealer
- plaster sealer
- wood primer.

Ready-mixed lightweight

Ready-mixed lightweight is used for internal and external surfaces. It is a smooth paste that can be worked to a fine feathered edge. Primers for this material are the same as for plaster.

Lightweight filler

Lightweight filler used on plaster, wallboards and timber comes ready-mixed. This filler does not shrink or sag and needs little sanding. The primers used are the same as for plaster.

Linseed oil putty

This is used for stopping and filling holes, filling indentations on timber surfaces and also for fixing or bedding in glass. It comes ready-mixed and should always be covered up when not in use as it dries out very quickly.

Primers used for this material could be:

- wood primer
- acrylic primer/undercoat
- all-purpose primer
- aluminium wood primer
- primer sealer.

Replacing glass in a window

If and when you have to replace glass in a window make sure that the rebate where the glass is going to be fixed is clean and dust-free before you prime the area. Allow the primer to dry before you apply putty.

Replacing glass in a window

Step 1 Apply bedding putty directly to the rebate usually by hand-pressing the putty into place.

Step 2 Place the glass into the frame carefully, pressing the glass around the edges into the bedding putty until the glass is firmly fixed.

Step 3 Using your putty knife, remove any excess putty from the glass where it has spread out from the pressure. This putty will then be used again as part of the facing putty.

Step 4 Apply sprigs to each side of the glass. Sprigs are metal wires that help hold the glass in place.

Step 5 Apply the facing putty around the outer edge of the frame and glass. Once this has been completed, use your putty knife to bevel the facing putty pressing the putty into an angled position to finish off and leave a clean smooth finish.

Step 6 Once dry, apply a suitable paint system to protect and decorate the putty and frame.

Unit 1008

Know how to prepare surfaces for decoration 1

Working life

Amy, Leon and Lydia have been given the job of preparing the walls and ceilings of a property and Lynne is preparing all new and existing woodwork. Lydia notices there are a number of fine cracks running through some of the walls. Amy and Leon notice some of the ceilings are looking yellowish in colour. Lynne has identified four new doors being replaced in the property and the skirting boards need attention due to damage and scuff marks.

Amy and Leon work in one room and Lydia and Lynne agree to work together in a separate room. After all the ceilings have been painted twice with a white emulsion, the yellowish stain starts to reappear. Amy suggests applying a third coat to cover this up. In the other room, Lynne is applying caulk to the tops of the skirting board. Lydia asks Lynne whether she can fill the deep cracks with caulk while she is filling the tops of the skirting board. Lydia has not feathered the filler out in places and not left the filler proud in others.

- Why did the group split up to do the tasks?

- What has caused the yellowish stain on the ceilings? Will applying a third coat cure this problem? What should Amy and Leon have done before applying the emulsion to the ceilings?

- Should Lynne fill the deep cracks above the skirting board as Lydia has suggested? Give reasons for your answer. What will happen to the filler that has not been left proud?

FAQ

Can I use caulk to fill holes in surfaces?

No! It is not advisable to use caulk to fill holes and cracks because you cannot abrade caulk when it dries. This is because its flexible properties do not let it harden off. Caulk is only recommended for filling the tops of skirting board and around architrave to seal any gaps.

How long do you leave a steam stripper on a surface when removing wall coverings?

It depends on how many layers of wallpaper are on the surface. However, you should not allow the steam stripper to stay in any one place too long as you can cause the plaster on the surface to 'blow'. This is when the plaster lifts off the surface, therefore creating a much bigger defect that will need repairing.

Why do you have to 'wet in' prior to applying fillers to holes and cracks?

You 'wet in' to help with the adhesion of the filler and to remove any excess dust and debris that has not been fully removed during the preparation stage.

When removing rust from metal, why don't you remove all traces of it and make the surface clean and shiny?

Although the rust has to be removed from the metal, it is not advisable to make sure that the surface is clean and shiny. This is because when you try to apply the paint system, the primer will not be able to adhere to the surface as there will be no key for the paint to stick to.

Check it out

1   Write a method statement describing the steps that need to be followed when preparing new timber fixtures and fittings and new plasterboards and plastered surfaces.

2   Explain the different types of substrates a decorator may need to prepare for decoration. Use diagrams to help with your answers.

3   Describe the sequence of actions to be followed when filling holes and cracks in rendered surfaces. What tools and equipment might you need?

4   Describe some of the different types of filler that are available and state some of the different uses they have.

5   Explain when and where a colour stopper would be used and explain the functions of a stopper.

6   Prepare a method statement on removing rust and millscale, describing what could go wrong when preparing these defects. Explain the dangers that could be present when removing these defects and state what PPE would be needed.

7   Describe how to remove runs and sags from paint work.

8   When spot priming metal surfaces, name two different primers used and which metals they would be applied to.

9   How would you prevent staining from happening to your newly painted surfaces? Name four different reasons for the defect staining.

10 Write a method statement for removing old wallpaper. Name two different methods of removing wallpaper, stating what precautions should be followed and listing the tools and equipment needed.

Getting ready for assessment

The information contained in this unit, as well as continued practical assignments that you will carry out in your college or training centre, will help you in preparing for both your end of unit test and the diploma multiple-choice test. It will also aid you in preparing for the work required for the synoptic practical assignments.

When painting and decorating, you will need to be able to prepare a range of surfaces to receive coatings. This will include not only new surfaces made from a range of materials, but also surfaces that have previously been painted or decorated. To carry this out, you will need to know the techniques and methods used to prepare these surfaces, as well as repairing and making good any defects or damage to the surface before work.

You will need to be familiar with:

- preparing a range of bare and previously painted surfaces to receive coatings
- correcting defects in surfaces and surface coatings
- repairing and making good surfaces.

For learning outcome 2, you have learned how to identify the type and cause of a range of defects as well as the rectification process used to repair the damage. You will need to have the ability to use this knowledge practically, to recognise defects when you encounter them and select the correct tools, equipment and materials to repair the damage. When working practically, you will need to be able to protect the work

area, ensuring that nothing else around you is damaged. You will also need to make sure that you are working within all the relevant health and safety legislation.

The knowledge you have gained about the different types of surfaces, and the preparation techniques needed for each, will prepare you for any aspect of the practical test where you will need to prepare or repair a surface. These same skills will be vital throughout your career as a painter and decorator.

Before you carry out any work, think of a plan of action that will tell you the order you need to do things in. It will also record a rough timescale for the work you need to carry out, in order to make sure that you complete everything you need to do safely. You will need to refer back to this plan at each stage to make sure that you are not making any mistakes as you work, or missing out any part of the process that you need to work through. Without checking this, you could make some serious mistakes that could have an impact on the final build.

Your speed in carrying out any tasks in a practice setting will also help to prepare you for the time set for the test. However, you must never rush the test! Always make sure that you are working safely. Make sure throughout the test that you are wearing the appropriate PPE and using tools correctly.

Good luck!

CHECK YOUR KNOWLEDGE

1 Which tool is used to scrape off loose deposits and old coatings from beadings and mouldings during the paint removal process?

a stripping knife

b caulking blade

c trimming knife

d shave hook

2 Why must you take care when using a steam stripper on ceilings?

a The surface can quickly become too hot, because steam rises.

b The user is at risk from burns or scalding.

c Ceilings are more likely to blister than walls.

d all of the above

3 What is the purpose of a needle gun?

a removing rust

b applying fillers

c removing old putty

d joining materials

4 Which of these tools would not be used in the preparation of rusty steel?

a scraper

b chipping hammer

c filling knife

d wire brush

5 The main ingredient in knotting solution is:

a filler

b dye

c shellac

d emulsion

6 Mould growth and wet rot are fungal growths caused by:

a moisture

b cold

c wind

d pollution

7 Which defects can be found in cement rendering?

a saponification

b efflorescence

c cracks

d all of the above

8 Decorator's caulk is:

a a flexible filler

b a powder filler

c a wood stopper

d a metal sealant

9 The abrasive particles on abrasive paper are made of:

a silicon carbide

b aluminium oxide

c glass

d any of the above

10 What advantage has a hot air gun got over a LPG gun when removing coatings from a window frame?

a does not scorch the surface

b does not crack the glass

c less risk of a fire

d all of the above

UNIT 1009

Know how to apply paint systems by brush and roller 1

Paint can be applied to a surface in a variety of different ways. Each method of application has its own advantages and disadvantages and should be chosen according to the type of surface, paint and finished effect. Applying the surface coating can be one of the cheapest, quickest, easiest and most effective tasks a decorator can perform.

This unit contains material that supports NVQ Unit QCF 331 Apply Paint Systems to New Surfaces by Brush and Roller in the Workplace.

This Unit also supports TAP Unit Apply Paint systems by Brush and Roller.

This unit will cover the following learning outcomes:

- Preparing a work area and protecting surrounding areas, furniture and fittings
- Preparing materials for application, and applying water-based and solvent-based coatings by brush and roller
- Cleaning, maintaining and storing brushes and rollers
- Storing paint materials.

Functional skills

When protecting areas you will need to make sure you have enough material to cover all the areas that could be damaged. You may need to take measurements and check special precautions for some materials. This will allow you to practise **FM** 1.2.1b relating to interpreting information.

Safety tip

Make sure that you use the correct manual handling techniques when lifting and moving items and use stepladders correctly when taking down pictures or covering light fittings. See Unit 1001 (pages 29–32) and Unit 1007 (pages 106–107)

Remember

Preparing the work area can help prevent defects, such as bittiness, which you would otherwise need to rectify later

Find out

Using the Internet and other resources, find out what impact certain weather conditions, such as high temperatures and rain, can have on painting

K1. Preparing a work area and protecting surrounding areas, furniture and fittings

Before any decoration is done, the most important task for the decorator is the protection of any areas, items, fixtures and fittings that are not being worked on and could be damaged.

Common items that need protecting include:

- carpets, rugs and other types of flooring
- sofas, curtains, chairs, tables, electrical equipment
- pictures, shelving, wall lights and sockets
- ceiling light fittings, shades and fire alarms/smoke detectors
- door furniture (handles, hinges, locks etc.)
- plant pots, garden seats and patio areas.

It is very important that, before you start any work, you look around and make sure that all items are protected by removing them or covering them with the appropriate material. Damage caused during decorating could be very costly, both to the decorator's pocket and reputation.

Preparing the working area

When preparing internal or external work areas prior to carrying out the application of paint systems, you need to make sure that all dust and debris (flakes of paint, bristles, pieces of abrasive paper etc.) have been removed so that no contamination can occur to the surfaces while coatings are still wet.

If you are working externally, you will also need to make sure that you protect the area from the impact of weather. One of the possible ways of doing this is through tenting. This involves putting up a full cover that protects the job from rain, wind, snow and also the effects of the sun (see Figure 9.1). It will also help to protect the general public from hazards.

For external painting jobs, the weather is a particular concern as it can have a direct impact on the final quality of the job. When applying coatings to surfaces, it is not only damp and cold weather that can cause defects; sunlight and high humidity conditions can lead to defects such as blistering, cracking, flashing and flaking.

On some contracts, you will find that other trades are working alongside you, for example joiners, electricians and plasterers. When working on this type of set-up, you will need to have an access and exit point from the premises. This will allow all trades to access and exit the area safely and avoid any accidents.

You may also need to be able to seal off your working area if you are working with paints or coatings that are toxic. This is to protect the general public. Decorators may also need to wear appropriate PPE when working in these areas. The working area will need to have sufficient ventilation and extraction systems installed to disperse the build-up of any fumes.

Any extraction system used will need to be masked to prevent damage from coatings prior to starting any decoration work.

When you have finished decorating, always place items back in their original position. This will leave the client with a good impression of your work and can help to develop good relationships. You may then benefit from customer recommendation.

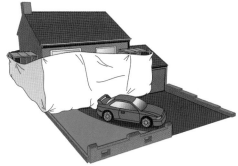

Figure 9.1 Tent used to protect paintwork

> **Did you know?**
>
> An example of an area that will need ventilation and extraction systems set up could be a room or corridor that needs to be decorated with a specialist coating

Common items requiring protection and methods used

As previously stated, you should always assess a work area for items that need to be protected before starting your work. Figure 9.2 shows some examples.

> **Safety tip**
>
> You need to be especially careful for the safety of the general public if the contract is in a hospital or shopping centre or other area where there is a great deal of contact with the general public

> **Safety tip**
>
> Site preparation can result in injury. Always be aware of the risks involved with the work you do, such as slips, trips, falls and manual handling injuries

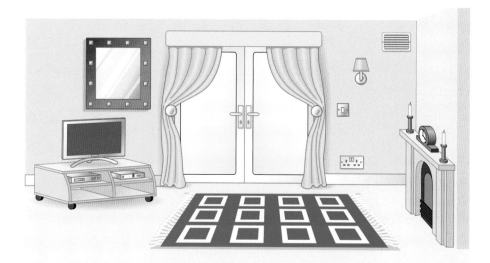

Figure 9.2 What do you think may need protecting in this room?

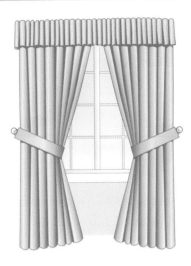

Figure 9.3 Curtains and a pelmet should ideally be removed

Figure 9.4 A wooden curtain pole

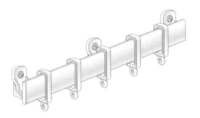

Figure 9.5 A curtain track

Figure 9.6 Roller blind

Door furniture

Any items on an internal or external door – such as handles, finger plates, letter boxes, numbers, knockers, hinges, kick plates, push plates, door bell buttons and spy holes – are known as door furniture.

The easiest way to protect door furniture from paint, varnish or scratches is to remove it. To avoid the loss of or accidental damage to any door furniture and screws, pack them straight into a box or crate, covering individual items with newspaper, bubble wrap or something similar. Store the container in a safe and dry place.

If the removal of door furniture is impossible or inappropriate, covering it with masking tape is an acceptable alternative.

Window furniture

Curtains should ideally be removed before carrying out any work because cleaning, repair or replacement is usually very costly.

Remove curtains by first pulling them apart and then taking them off their track or pole. Next, carefully and neatly place the curtains in a plastic bag and remove them from the room, storing them safely in a dry place.

A pelmet is a piece of cloth or other material that covers the curtain pole or track. Remove it and cover it with a protective sheet, or place it in a bag and store it in a safe dry place.

For curtain poles and tracks, the best protection is to remove the item from the work area. Alternatively, cover the pole or track securely with a suitable material. Remove the pole or track from its brackets then unscrew the brackets from the wall. Place any small parts in a container to prevent them from being lost. All items should then be taken from the room and stored in a safe place.

There are various types of blind that you will need to be aware of when you are working, such as:

- roller blind
- vertical blind
- Venetian blind.

Before removing a blind, make sure it is retracted or rolled up. Next, remove the blind from its bracket and then unscrew the brackets from the wall. Place any small parts in a container and remove all parts of the blind from the work area.

Wall and ceiling mounted fixtures

It is possible to work around shelving, but it is much easier to remove it, which also helps protect the shelving.

Wooden shelves can be removed easily. Place them in a box or wrap them in protective material and move them out of the way. Wrap glass shelving in newspaper, bubble wrap or other similar material to avoid breakage. Shelves are attached to walls with brackets, which are screwed on to walls with the aid of Rawlplugs™. Remove these brackets and fixing screws and put them in a safe place.

Light fittings are another type of fitting you may deal with. These can be anything from wall lights to ceiling lights but may also include larger and heavier items such as chandeliers.

Only a qualified electrician should remove light fittings, although a decorator can remove light shades once the electricity has been turned off at the mains. The fuse must be removed from the mains fuse box or a warning notice put in place to prevent the power from being accidentally reconnected.

Once the fittings have been removed, wrap them and store them in a box or crate and in a safe location. Bag shades and secure them with tape. If chandeliers cannot be removed, cover them with light polythene sheeting and tape them securely.

You may also come across various types of covers and grilles used in ventilation, heating and air conditioning systems.

Made from plastic, metal and, in some instances, fibrous plaster, these can be found in various positions on walls throughout a building, providing cover for inlets and outlets. Unscrew these to remove them. You can then store them in a safe place. If removal of a cover or grille is inappropriate or impossible, cover it with masking tape.

You may also work in domestic properties that have ornaments, pictures and small valuable items hanging on walls. Wrap these in newspaper, bubble wrap or another suitable material and pack them into containers such as crates or boxes. These should then be stored within the premises in a safe and dry place in order to protect them from damage, loss or theft.

Furniture

This can be anything from a small coffee table to a dining table or a three-piece suite. Furniture also includes electrical equipment such as televisions, DVD players and stereos.

If possible, furniture should be removed from the work area to another room or a suitable temporary storage location.

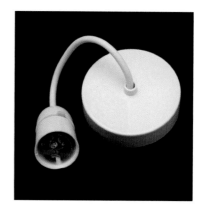

Figure 9.7 A typical light fitting

Remember

When removing items such as curtains, blinds and shelving, where there is more than one of each, it is a good idea to keep them separate and find a method of remembering which item went where. This will prevent mix-ups and save time when the job is finished

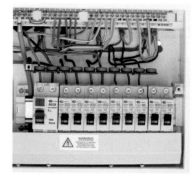

Figure 9.8 Mains fuse box

Remember

A decorator should never attempt to remove any kind of electrical fitting. If you are working on site, ask a qualified electrician to do this. If you are working in a client's house, ask the client to arrange for the fitting to be removed

Figure 9.9 A typical ventilation grille

Did you know?

Electricity on site should be reduced to 110 volts. This voltage reduces the risk of fatalities and serious injuries, but can still give a shock

Remember

Heavy items should be moved with care and appropriate manual handling techniques must be used

Did you know?

If electrical equipment is being removed from the work area, pay particular attention to the choice of storage location. There is always a risk of theft with such expensive equipment

Figure 9.10 Panel radiator

Where removal is not possible, furniture should be stored in a way that maximises the work space (for example, moved to the middle of the room) and covered with suitable sheeting material depending on the type of work being carried out.

Carpets

Decorators are not usually qualified to remove or refit carpets. If necessary, removal and refitting should be arranged by the client.

Where carpets have not been removed, use a combination of dust sheets, polythene sheeting and masking tape to protect them.

Radiators

When working on new buildings, a decorator is able to carry out decorating tasks before radiators are fitted. Other situations may require the removal of radiators in order for certain work to be completed. If you have been properly instructed in how to do so, you may remove a radiator from a wall yourself. The following sequence should be followed:

- Protect the area from leaks and damage.
- Turn off the water supply.
- Undo the radiator connections and drain the radiator.
- Remove the radiator from its brackets and store safely.
- After decoration is complete, place and attach the radiator on to its brackets.
- Reconnect the pipe work to the radiator.
- Open the bleed valve.
- Turn the water supply back on.
- Close the bleed valve.
- Check for leaks and leave the area clean and tidy.

The three main types of radiator are: panel, column and radiant panel.

External items

When carrying out decorating tasks outside, it can be easy to forget about site preparation, but external items need protecting for the same reasons as internal items. External items that require protection include paths and patio areas, garden furniture, plant pots, lawns and flower beds and alarm boxes. As with internal items, removal is the best form of protection, but where this is not possible, covering with an appropriate material is acceptable.

Arthur has been asked to strip the paint from and repaint the cast iron guttering and pipework at the rear of a client's property. Before Arthur begins the work, he looks around the part of the garden nearest the house. He can see patio furniture, a bicycle leant against the house and clothes on a washing line attached to one of the external walls. There are also pot plants and shrubs on the patio near the house.

- Before Arthur begins the paint job, what items and areas do you think he will need to protect?
- What is the best way to protect each of these items and areas?
- What safety precautions will Arthur have to consider?

Think about things such as the equipment and tools Arthur will use and the fact that he will be working at height.

Appropriate use for masking tape

Masking paper and tapes are also used in the protection of items. Masking paper is a smooth brown paper and is used to protect floors, furniture and also windows. It comes on a roll in various widths. Masking paper can be held in place with masking tape but it is quite often self-adhesive.

Masking tape is often used to block off areas such as light switches, door handles and woodwork. Low-tack masking tape is used with most of these items because it is easy to remove during 'de-masking', when you remove all masking materials after painting. This sort of tape is available in a variety of widths to suit different needs, the most common being 25 mm and 50 mm.

There are several different types of masking tape, all of which are used in the same way when working on protecting surfaces:

- **Exterior masking tape** is a heavy-duty type of tape that is waterproof, strong and ultra-violet (UV) resistant and has the ability to adhere very well to surfaces, even rough surfaces. These tapes are usually used to fix protective sheeting to frames when 'tenting in'.
- **Interior masking tape** is a low-tack tape, ideal for protecting fixtures and fittings. It is also used to keep dust sheets in place when protecting carpets and furniture. The advantage of this tape is that you can press it down firmly when using and not have to worry about pulling any coating off surfaces.
- **Crepe masking tape** is usually tan in colour and is made from a solvent- and moisture-resistant material. It comes in either a crinkled or puckered texture, which allows it to stretch or elongate and makes it ideal to mask irregular or curved surfaces.
- **7-day masking tape** gets its name because it can be left in place when masking for up to seven days without damaging the surfaces that have been masked. This tape is usually used on more demanding surfaces such as glazes and acrylic lacquers.

Turn off the electricity and water supplies to wall heaters and radiators. This is as much to prevent harm to you as it is to protect the work area

Masking paper comes in different widths – 150 mm, 225 mm, 300 mm and 450 mm – and masking tape comes in 25 mm, 50 mm and 75 mm widths

Polythene bags such as shopping bags are useful for protecting light fittings, wall lamps and so on when secured with masking tape.

Larger items such as doors, furniture and machinery are usually masked with polythene sheets and dust sheets secured with masking tape. Rolls of polythene secured with tape are good for wrapping tubular items.

a–b	Protect doors and windows with polythene or dust sheets and secure with making tape.
c–g	Protect furniture and machinery with polythene or dust sheets and secure with masking tape.
h–i	Mask electrical sockets and light switches with masking tape.
j	Wrap light fixtures in polythene bags and secure with masking tape.

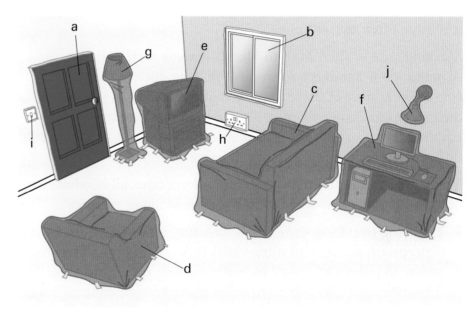

Figure 9.11 Masking larger items

Appropriate uses for dust sheets, tarpaulin and corrugated sheeting

Sheet materials such as dust sheets, tarpaulin and corrugated sheeting are the most commonly used and useful protective materials. Sheeting can protect against paint and paste splashes, spillages and also small particles created when sanding or scraping.

Dust sheets and drop sheets

Dust sheets of the highest quality should be used where possible because cheap alternatives do not always provide adequate protection. There are two basic types of dust sheet, each with very different characteristics: cotton twill and polythene.

Drop sheets are similar to dust sheets and are available in both plastic and cloth material. They have similar uses to normal dust sheets and are usually used as protection against paint, dust, dirt and rain. They are therefore ideal for using outdoors.

To prolong the life and use of dust sheets, you should always take care of them. To maintain your dust sheets, thoroughly shake them after use to remove any dust or debris, then fold them up correctly so they are neat and tidy. Store them in a dry area and, if possible, on a shelf, so they keep their shape and stay clean.

Cotton twill dust sheets

The best-quality dust sheets are cotton twill sheets, which should be double folded to increase thickness. Cotton twill dust sheets are generally used to protect flooring and furniture and come in a variety of sizes, the most common being 4 m × 6 m. There are also special width and length dust sheets for use on staircases.

Advantages:

- present a professional image (when clean)
- when laid, they remain in place well and are not easily disturbed when walked on
- are available in different weights and sizes

Disadvantages:

- expensive to purchase and clean
- heavy paint spillage can soak through the sheet
- can absorb chemicals such as paint stripper
- possible fire risk

Polythene dust sheets

Polythene dust sheets can be used in the same way as cotton twill sheets, but they are waterproof and can be thrown away after use.

Advantages:

- inexpensive to purchase
- heavy paint spills do not soak through the sheet
- do not absorb chemicals such as paint strippers

Disadvantages:

- do not present such a professional image as cotton dust sheets
- when laid they do not remain in place well and are easily disturbed

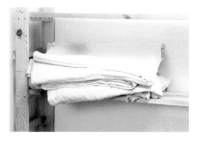

Figure 9.12 Dust sheets

Did you know?

If you use well-maintained dust sheets at the start of a job, you will look more professional to the client. This can have a very positive impact on your business reputation

Remember

It is important to select the type of sheet that is most suitable for the task at hand

Tarpaulin

Tarpaulin sheets are made of different types of material, including:

- rubber-coated cotton
- heavy cotton canvas (usually very expensive)
- **PVC**-coated nylon
- nylon scrim (coated with a polyester resin).

The most common size of tarpaulin sheet is 6 m × 4 m, although larger sizes can be made to order. Because tarpaulin is protective against moisture, it is best to use it when washing down surfaces or when steam-stripping wallpaper.

Tarpaulin sheeting is also used on and around scaffolding in order to give workers and the work area protection from bad weather conditions. It also offers protection to equipment and surfaces if there is a lot of movement around them.

Corrugated sheeting

Some work is aggressive and/or extensive (for example, paint stripping to restore ceiling plaster), in which case the sheeting materials discussed above would not provide enough protection.

Corrugated PVC and cardboard can be purchased in sheet form and laid over the floor and jointed with 50 mm masking tape, offering more appropriate protection. Although this type of protection may be expensive to install, it helps to avoid corrective work and undamaged sheets can be reused.

Other materials used for protection

A decorator can use all manner of ordinary items in site preparation. Plastic carrier bags or bin liners are excellent for protecting light fittings, wall lights, chandeliers and so on. The item is simply inserted into the bag, which can then be tied up and secured with masking tape – cheap and simple but very effective.

Cardboard boxes can be used to store smaller items such as pictures and ornaments. A small box or a bag can also be used to hold screws and nails that are collected when removing items and preparing the area (for example, picture hooks, shelves, ventilation grilles). This will ensure that nothing is lost or damaged.

Key term

PVC – polyvinyl chloride (a tough plastic)

Remember

Take care when handling items during site preparation – you will be responsible for any breakages you cause! It may be prudent to ask the client to remove valuables prior to beginning work

K2. Preparing materials for application, and applying water-based and solvent-based coatings by brush and roller

Paint is used to give protection and colour to walls, ceilings and other surfaces. Made up of pigment (the colour) and an oil- or water-based binder, paint can be applied easily and quickly to give a basic addition of colour or, with special tools and techniques, paint can also give very creative and striking effects and finishes.

Find out

What are the pros and cons (advantages and disadvantages) of the different fillings available?

Brushes and rollers

Paintbrushes

A brush's bristles, also known as the filling, can be either natural or synthetic or a combination of these. The filling is attached to the handle of the brush via the stock and secured with the use of an adhesive.

The ferrule is the metal part of the brush and is positioned between the handle and the filling (bristles), and is usually made from copper- or nickel-plated polished steel. This can be fixed to the stock (term used for the fixing of all components of the brush) by either riveting it to the handle or by seaming the joint to the stock with a special bonding material. The setting is the fixing or gluing of all the bristles at the root, which is then attached (when set) to the shaped ferrule, which then makes up part of the structure of the brush.

Figure 9.13 Flat brush

Flat brush

A flat brush is the type of brush used for the majority of paint and varnish work and is available in a wide variety of sizes and filling types. The 1-inch/25 mm flat brush is also known as a sash brush as it is normally used for painting sashes and frames. Larger flat brushes, including the 4-inch/100 mm size, are used mainly for painting walls and ceilings. The handle is usually made from beech or birch, although cheaper varieties with plastic handles are available.

Figure 9.14 Radiator brush

Radiator brush and crevice brush

A radiator brush is used to apply paint behind radiators and pipes. It has a long flexible handle and is ideal for painting awkward and hard-to-reach areas. Crevice brushes are much the same as radiator brushes but are angled to allow access to the most awkward areas.

Figure 9.15 Crevice brush

Figure 9.16 Lining brush

Figure 9.17 Stencil brush

Figure 9.18 Masonry brush

Figure 9.19 Fitches

Lining brush

A lining brush, known as a lining fitch, is used together with a straight edge to produce straight lines. This type of brush is very flat and thin.

Stencil brush

A stencil brush is a short, stumpy brush used for applying paint to stencils or around templates.

Masonry brush

Masonry brushes are used to apply paint to surfaces such as stonework, brick, concrete and **rendering**. They are cheap to buy and very **durable**.

Fitch

A fitch is ideal for painting areas difficult to reach with a standard paintbrush and also for more detailed work. Fitches are available in either a flat or round style.

Rollers

A roller can quickly and effectively coat large, flat surface areas with paint. Specially shaped rollers are also available for painting corners and unusually shaped surfaces, although sometimes it can be easier simply to use a brush.

The part of the roller that holds the paint is the sleeve – a plastic or cardboard tube covered with fabric. The type of sleeve, and thus the type of fabric, chosen depends on the kind of coating to be applied and the structure of the surface. The sleeve slides onto the frame of the roller. The frame will be either a cage type or a stick type.

Rollers are available in many sizes and can have single or double arms. A double arm roller is available for roller sleeves of 300 mm and above.

Figure 9.20 Roller sleeves

Figure 9.21 Roller frame (single arm cage type)

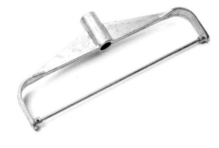

Figure 9.22 Double arm roller

All rollers must be cleaned thoroughly after use. Always hang them up to dry because if you leave them resting wet on a surface, the fabric will get damaged, which will seriously affect the finish of future paint applications.

Radiator roller

Radiator rollers are also known as mini rollers and are available in sizes of up to 150 mm. As the name suggests, they are ideal for use on radiators and small surface areas where the use of a standard roller would be impractical.

Specialised rollers

There are a number of types of roller designed for specific tasks such as painting pipe work or producing decorative and textured effects. One such roller is the Duet®, which is made from uneven pieces of chamois leather attached to a spindle.

Synthetic filament application tools

The filling for brushes can be made from natural pure bristle, such as hog hair, or synthetic bristles made from nylon or polyester. The synthetic types of brush are hard wearing and are not affected by ordinary solvents and many other chemicals. They can be used equally well in both water-based and solvent-based coatings.

For latex and other water-based paints, the synthetic filament brush is ideal. This is because the filaments (filling) do not absorb the water from the paint and cause the filling to become soft and limp. Because they are more water resistant, they hold their shape and perform like high-quality bristle brushes.

Other types of painting tools and equipment

Paint stirrer

Quite simply, this is used to stir paint as well as other decorating materials such as varnish and paste. Available in various lengths, paint stirrers consist of a blade with a series of holes, through which the paint passes as it is stirred. Stirring in this way enables the paint or other liquid to be mixed more thoroughly than if mixed with a stirrer without holes, such as a stick.

Paint kettle (work pot)

Made from either plastic or metal, a paint kettle (often known as a work pot) is a convenient way of holding manageable amounts of paint while working from stepladders or other platforms. Always ensure that your paint kettle is thoroughly cleaned out

Find out

What are the differences between the two types of roller frame (cage and stick)?

Figure 9.23 Radiator roller

Find out

What types of roller fabric are available? What type of decorative or textured effects does each type produce?

Figure 9.24 Duet® roller

Remember

Because synthetic filaments are factory-made, they are available in many different qualities and can be bought for a variety of costs

Figure 9.25 Paint stirrer

Figure 9.26 Paint kettle (work pot)

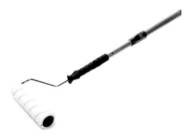

Figure 9.27 Extension pole

Figure 9.28 Scuttle

Did you know?

Water-based paints are now widely used on both internal and external surfaces that were traditionally the strict domain of solvent-based paint systems

---

Safety tip

Solvents used in solvent-based paints are usually toxic and highly flammable so take proper precautions when using them

---

after use in order to avoid contamination of paints and to prolong the life of the kettle.

Extension pole

Extension poles are attached to roller handles in order to give additional reach, thus reducing the need for working on stepladders when painting areas such as ceilings or high walls.

Scuttle

A scuttle is used to hold paint when using a roller from a ladder. Some scuttles have attachments that allow them to be hung on the ladder's rungs.

Surface coatings

Surface coatings are applied in order to:

- **Protect** – steel can be prevented from corroding due to rust and wood can be prevented from rotting due to moisture and insect attack.
- **Decorate** – the appearance of a surface can be improved or given a special effect (for example, marbling, wood graining).
- **Sanitise** – a surface can be made more hygienic with the application of a surface coating, preventing penetration and accumulation of germs and dirt and also allowing easier cleaning.
- **Identify** – different colours or types of surface coating can be used to distinguish areas or components (for example, pipework identified using the British Standards Institution's colour coding system).

Surface coatings generally fall into one of the following categories:

- paint
- varnish
- wood stain
- sealers and preparatory coatings.

Paint

Paint is either water-based or solvent-based. The main liquid part of water-based paint is water. In solvent-based paint, a chemical has been used instead of water to dissolve the other components of the paint. When paint is applied to a surface, the water or the solvent (depending on the type of paint) evaporates into the air, leaving the other components behind on the surface.

Until recently, solvent-based paints were the number one wall coating choice for plaster, masonry and other surfaces, but changes in safety and environmental legislation have forced manufacturers to develop water-based products as safer alternatives to solvent-based paints.

Reasons for painting include preservation, sanitation, identification and decoration, but none of these is possible if the paint has not been produced or applied properly. Paint has to have basic qualities if it is to be used for these tasks. It should be:

- appliable – easily brushed, rolled or sprayed
- dry – in a reasonable length of time
- adaptable to physical changes to the surface, such as weather conditions
- able to maintain its function – for an acceptable time.

Paint should also have the right consistency for application – this refers to the thinness or thickness of the paint.

Paints such as non-drip gloss are classed as thick paints and are known as **thixotropic** paint. Thixotropic agents give paint gel-like properties. **Most thixotropic paints should not be mixed!** The paint turns into a liquid when mixed due to friction, which makes it easy to apply. Once laid off correctly, the paint will turn back into a gel, reducing the possibility of runs or drips.

Paint should be flexible too, as certain surfaces have a small amount of movement: for example, metal and timber naturally contract and expand throughout their life. Atmospheric conditions, such as humidity and different temperatures, affect the surfaces of different items, so paint needs to be able to stretch and shrink to the same degree. This property is called elasticity.

Opacity and adhesion are also important properties of a coating or paint. Opacity refers to the covering power of the paint. If the opacity is not correct, the coating or paint will be too transparent and will not block out the surface it is being applied to. If a coating or paint does not have the correct adhesion, or 'stickability', it will not stick to the surface.

The components of paint

Paint is a liquid material that changes into a solid material when it dries, forming a decorative and protective film on a surface. You could say that the liquid part of paint is only temporary and is a way of getting the other components onto the surface.

Key term

Thixotropic – the property of some gels of becoming liquid when stirred or shaken

Opacity – the degree to which a substance is opaque, or not see-through

Unit 1009

Know how to apply paint systems by brush and roller 1

167

Paint consists of three components:

1 **Thinner** – this is either the water or solvent part of the paint that dissolves the other components and makes them suitable for surface application. When paint is applied to a surface, the thinner evaporates totally as it dries.

2 **Binder** – this is a resin and forms the film of the paint. The binder also determines the performance of the paint (how long it lasts) and the degree of gloss (shine).

3 **Pigment** – the colour. Pigment is also responsible for the paint's opaqueness (the ability to cover the underlying surface). Some pigments, in paints such as primers, also influence the performance of the paint; for example, rust-inhibiting pigments prevent the formation of rust.

Varnish

Varnish is a transparent finish that is applied to wood. It comes in matt, satin and gloss varieties and provides a tough water- and heat-resistant protective coating. The components of varnish are as follows:

- **Drying oil** – this is a substance such as linseed oil, tung oil or walnut oil, which dries to form a hardened solid film.

- **Resin** – yellow-brown resins such as amber, copal or rosin are used in many varnishes.

- **Thinner or solvent** – white spirit or paint thinner is commonly used as the thinner or solvent.

Wood stain

Wood stain is a type of dye, which, when applied to timber, soaks deep into the fibres and emphasises the grain of the wood. Available in a variety of colours and suited to either indoor or outdoor purposes, wood stain can transform bare timber surfaces into beautiful shades of natural wood. Quite often, wood stain does not offer any protection to a surface; it simply colours it. Always check the type of stain you are using and seal the wood with a varnish or polish after staining if necessary.

Sealers and preparatory coatings

Sealers and preparatory coatings are substances that are applied to a surface in order to prepare it to receive subsequent surface coatings. Sealers, such as knotting solution, act by sealing in the surface material, thus preventing anything from leaking out of or into the surface. Preparatory coatings are special substances that protect and preserve the surface from things such as water, mould, rust or alkali surface coatings. Applying a suitable and

Remember

Resin can be either natural (produced by plants and trees) or artificial, called 'alkyd'

Remember

Because varnish is transparent, careful preparation of the wood surface is very important. Any faults or defects will be clearly visible

Remember

All coatings have the recommended application methods written in their manufacturer's technical information, which is printed on the container. If not, you can request it from the manufacturer, who will supply you with a data sheet appropriate sealer or preparatory coating to your surface before decorating it will preserve the surface and ensure a high-quality, long-lasting finish.

Brush application

Applying paint with a brush is not as popular as it used to be and is now often replaced with roller application. In order to achieve a high-quality finish with a brush, the following three actions should be followed:

1 Working in the brush and getting a dip
2 Cutting in
3 Laying off.

Working in the brush and getting a dip

Working in the brush means dipping the brush into the paint and then gently rubbing the brush against the inside of the pot until all the bristles are evenly coated with paint. If you were to simply dip the brush into the paint and then start painting, you would only have paint on the outer bristles of the brush.

After you have worked in the brush, you can scrape the brush against the top of the work pot in order to get it back into shape.

Getting a dip means applying paint to the brush, ready to begin painting. Get a dip by dipping the brush into the paint and then tapping alternate sides of the brush onto a dry area of the inside of the work pot. This action locks the paint into the bristles, stopping it from dripping or spilling during the transfer from work pot to surface.

Cutting in

Cutting in is the action of applying paint to one surface while keeping paint off an adjoining surface; for example, when painting a wall, keeping paint off the ceiling, or when painting the putty in a window, keeping paint off the glass.

Cutting in is normally done first so that the paint is applied in sections small enough to handle (that is, just enough to keep the edge of the applied paint wet). A dip of paint can then be applied in a vertical (up and down) motion. The paint can then be crossed, which means moving the paint in a sideways motion with the brush in order to spread it evenly.

Figure 9.29 Working in a brush ensures that all of the bristles are coated with paint

Figure 9.30 Getting a dip will ensure that paint stays on the brush until you apply it to the surface

Figure 9.31 Cutting in gives a clean and straight line

Remember

Laying off will need lots of practice to perfect

Laying off

Laying off is done at the end of the paint application process and prevents misses and runs and ensures that the paint is evenly spread. It is an action that the painter must perform in order to achieve the best possible finish. As the brush is brought down the surface, a small 'roll' of paint forms in front of the bristles. If the brush is not lifted off the surface by moving it back in the opposite direction, a run or sag will form. This is called laying off.

Laying off

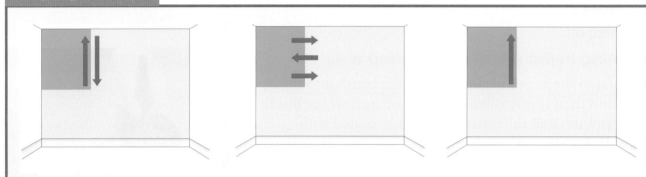

Step 1: Move the brush in a vertical motion (up and down)

Step 2: Move the brush in a horizontal motion (side to side)

Step 3: Move the brush upwards in a vertical motion (up and down motion should only be attempted by an experienced painter)

Figure 9.32 Laying off emulsion paint should be done with an arcing motion

Laying off emulsion paint requires a slightly different brush movement. The brush should be moved across the surface in an arcing motion so that it doesn't run or sag (Figure 9.35).

Roller application

Rollers come in various shapes and sizes to suit different surfaces and requirements. Table 9.1 shows examples of different roller types available, along with their purpose.

Did you know?

You should apply paint in a methodical manner. If painting a wall, start at the top and cut into any dissimilar surfaces first

Roller type	Purpose
Large	Covering large surface areas
Small	Covering small surface areas
Curved	Covering curved or rounded surfaces, such as pipes
Small and thin with a long handle	Covering surfaces behind radiators and other difficult-to-reach areas
Long pile	Creating rough, textured paint finishes
Short pile	Creating smooth, untextured paint finishes

Table 9.1 Roller types and their purposes

Whichever type of roller you use, you will need a container in which to hold the paint. A roller tray or a scuttle has a deep end that holds the paint, and a shallow, rough area where you can work the roller in preparation for applying the paint to the surface.

The roller should be dipped into the paint and then repeatedly rolled against the rough part of the container. The rolling action removes excess paint from the roller, ensuring that the right amount of paint is applied to the surface.

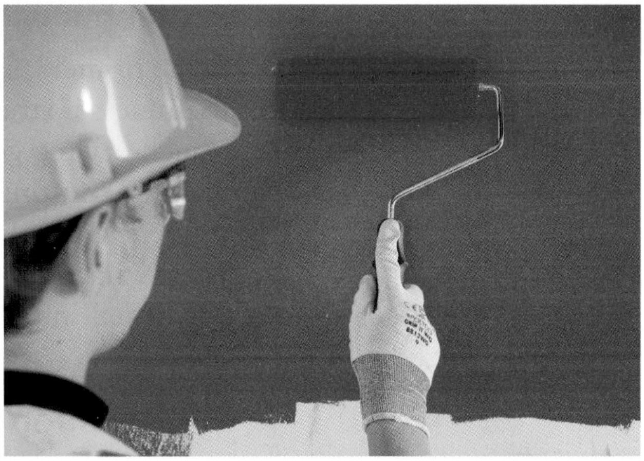

When painting a surface using a roller, use a 'W' motion (Figure 9.33). Laying off with a roller should be done in a vertical movement, which, if done well, will ensure that no lines are left on the surface.

Figure 9.33 Apply paint with a roller using a 'W' motion

Stages of surface coating preparation

You may think that there is not much to opening a tin of paint and **decanting** it into a work pot. However, if you follow a few golden rules at the very beginning of a painting job, you will find that the rest of the job is much easier.

- It is always better to work from a work pot and not the stock pot. This is because a full stock pot will be heavy and difficult to manage. In addition, if a stock pot is knocked over, you will lose a lot of paint.
- Gently dust the stock pot before you open it. This will greatly reduce the amount of dust and debris that gets into the paint.
- Most paints require a thorough stir before use, but always check the manufacturer's instructions first, just in case they advise different treatment of the paint.
- Before you decant, you may need to adjust the viscosity, or thickness, of the coating. This is normally carried out when you use spray equipment to apply the coating to a surface.
- Decant paint *slowly* from the back of the stock pot into a work pot. By pouring from the back of the tin, the front is kept clean, which will help it to be quickly identified when it is on a shelf.
- Only pour enough paint into the work pot to work from (usually to the height of the bristles on a paint brush).
- When decanting the paint, keep a paint brush or cloth handy to wipe up any spills from the stock pot.

> **Key term**
>
> **Decanting** – pouring liquid from one container to another (in this case, from the stock pot into the work pot)

Figure 9.34 Remember the golden rules when decanting paint

Did you know?

Some primers require thinning to help the penetration of the coating to the surface that requires sealing. For example, for new timber structures, thinning the primer means that the coating soaks into the surface and speeds up the application system

Remember

Always remember to use the manufacturer's recommendations when thinning any paint

Problems with straining primers

Some primers, such as aluminium wood primer, will lose their usefulness if strained. This is because the properties of the coating (quick-drying, good opacity, heat reflecting, spreading capacity and self-knotting) can be separated from the paint in some primers. With aluminium wood primer, most of the aluminium flakes (pigment) in the paint, which give the paint its name, will be left in the strainer and therefore the primer will become useless.

Reasons for thinning paints prior to application

At times, some paints will need to be thinned to aid the flow of application and to penetrate and seal surfaces such as timber structures and new plaster and plasterboard surfaces. Some paints need thinning because they have been used previously and exposed to the atmosphere. This can create a thicker consistency to the paint and the paint may have lost some of the thinner or solvent through evaporation, making it harder to apply.

By adding a suitable paint thinner to the paint, you will be able to apply the coating more easily and still complete the job professionally.

Working life

Daniel has just been placed on a site after completing his second year of training. A local decorating firm gives Daniel a placement as part of his training. Daniel is asked to apply a suitable paint system to all the new plaster walls in a property and apply gloss to the exterior woodwork and garage door of the property. He is asked to gloss the outside woodwork and garage door before he starts the plastered walls. Daniel starts to prepare the woodwork and garage doors by lightly sanding them down and dusting them off and then asks the charge-hand for some undercoat to apply to the outside substrates. However, the charge-hand tells him to apply the gloss to the substrates as it is about to rain and they need to complete this job.

- Should Daniel follow this instruction? You will need to think about what will happen if Daniel applies gloss straight onto the primed woodwork, and the defects that could occur if gloss was applied directly to the external woodwork.
- If it is going to rain, what should have been done first that day?
- What would have been a suitable paint system for both the internal and external work for this job?

Volatile organic compounds (VOCs)

Volatile organic compounds (VOCs) are materials that evaporate readily into the atmosphere and affect the ozone. They can create smog and can be caused by decorative materials.

Although the VOCs in decorative materials account for less than 1% of the total amount emitted in the UK (source: BCF British Coatings Federation Ltd), new regulations were introduced in 2010 which require lower VOC levels in all materials produced in the UK. This includes solvent- and water-based coatings, thinners and cleaning agents.

The British coatings industry has adopted a VOC labelling scheme to inform users about the levels of organic solvents and other volatile materials present. All companies are now required to add the VOC information to their products to warn about the pollution that the products contribute to the atmosphere.

There are five bands of VOCs.

Minimal	VOC content 0% to 0.29%, e.g. acrylic primer/undercoat and masonry paints
Low	VOC content 0.3% to 7.99%, e.g. water-based coatings (matt/silk emulsions, acrylic eggshell)
Medium	VOC content 8% to 24.99%, e.g. acrylic glosses
High	VOC content 25% to 50%, e.g. non-drip gloss, one-coat gloss, solvent-based eggshell, satinwood, wood primer, alkali-resisting primer, all-purpose primer, heavy-duty floor paints
Very high	VOC content more than 50%, e.g. stabilising primers

Table 9.2 VOC bands

Causes and remedies of post-application defects in surface coatings

You can cause defects even after you have applied coatings if you have not correctly followed some basic methods. We looked at defects in some depth in Unit 1008. Refer back to this unit for information on some of these defects, in particular cissing and runs and sags (pages 142–43).

Blistering occurs if coatings are applied under direct sunlight or in damp conditions. To avoid this, make sure there is no moisture in the area you are painting before applying any coatings. If blistering occurs, remove any unstable paint film and let the area dry thoroughly, then repeat the application, making sure each coating fully hardens before further coatings are applied.

Functional skills

When carrying out tasks you are practising the functional skills required to read different texts and take appropriate action, e.g. respond to advice/instructions. This may also involve giving oral explanations and is practice for speaking and listening (**FE** 1.1.1 – 1.1.4)

Did you know?

Some of the main causes of VOCs other than decorative materials are:

- aircraft exhausts
- vehicle exhausts
- cleaning agents
- fabric softeners

Did you know?

Some products and materials that a decorator will use are exempt from the new legislation because it only refers to coatings. The most common exempt products are colourings for tinting, sugar soaps, brush cleaners, fillers and sealants/caulks

Remember

If the surface has been oily or greasy, then key the surface as well as cleaning it to allow the coating to adhere correctly.

Only thin surface coatings if necessary, and use the correct thinners as recommended by the manufacturer.

Did you know?

The Munsell System is used because it is a way to describe a colour without actually using a name. Colours can look different to different people and using a name can lead to mistakes and confusion

Brush marks occur when the coating has been poorly applied. This can be caused by under-thinning of paints or by using a poor-quality brush. To avoid this make sure the coating is thinned to the correct consistency and that you use a good-quality brush. When applying the coating, make sure that it has been fully brushed out in all directions, then crossed and finally laid off correctly. To remedy this defect, wait until the coating is fully dried, then prepare the surface again and repeat the application.

Flashing or **sheariness** is a defect caused by faulty application or by the coating setting too quickly due the surface being porous. It causes patches of uneven sheen on the surface. To remedy this make sure the surface has been sealed correctly and use a large brush or roller to cover the area quickly.

Wrinkling occurs if you apply too much coating to a surface or apply it on top of a coating that has not dried correctly. It is also caused by drying during high temperatures. Always make sure the previous coating has had the required drying time before applying another coat and apply the coating in the correct atmospheric conditions.

Grinning is when the previous colour shows through a coating that has just been applied. This can be caused by the base colour being too dark or the new coating being thinned too much or applied badly. To remedy, apply a correctly thinned coating to the surface and make sure the correct base colour has been used.

Colour organisation systems and terms

The BS 4800 Paint Colours for Building Purposes and the Munsell Colour System are used in the industry to enable the selection of different colours needed for various jobs.

The Munsell System is an international system which gives a definite description of a colour by using the properties of hue, value and chroma. This system helped prepare the BS 4800 system.

Hue describes the basic colour with a letter, for example (Y) represents yellow, (B) represents blue. The following codes represent the ten principal hues that the Munsell System uses. They are split into ten subdivisions, creating a full circle of 100 different hues:

- (Y) Yellow
- (YR) Yellow-Red
- (R) Red
- (RP) Red-Purple
- (P) Purple
- (PB) Purple-Blue
- (B) Blue
- (BG) Blue-Green
- (G) Green
- (GY) Green-Yellow.

The value represents the lightness (whites) or darkness (blacks) of a colour and is split into 11 numbers from 0 to 10. This number is written to the right of the hue. The number 0 represents black and the number 10 represents white. The numbers in between (1–9) represent the scale of greys – that is, 1 is dark grey and 9 is light grey. The code 5Y8 represents part of the code for pure yellow because the tone of yellow is equivalent to 8 on the value scale.

The chroma stands for the greyness of a colour and is also represented by a number, 0 being neutral grey to 14 which is pure grey. This number is written after the value scale and is separated by a forward slash, for example 5Y8/14 (this is the code that represents pure yellow).

Colour wheel

A colour wheel is a radial diagram of colours in which primary, secondary and sometimes tertiary colours are displayed. See pages 176–177. Colour is a powerful visual force, and the colour wheel is a tool for understanding how colours relate to each other. Colour wheels help many professionals such as artists and decorators with their work, by helping them to mix and think about colours.

A system had to be created to help us make sense of colour, to understand it and put it into some kind of order. This system became known as the 'natural order' of colour or, more commonly, as the colour wheel.

Where's there's light, there's colour, and white light contains all visible colours. These form an infinite spectrum that appears in a sequence from red to violet, just like the rainbow. The colour wheel represents this infinite spectrum through 12 basic hues (colours). These 12 basic hues consist of 3 groups: primary, secondary and tertiary colours.

The three primary colours are red, blue and yellow. Primary colours cannot be made from other colours because they are pure colours, but by mixing these three colours you can create all the colours of the rainbow.

Did you know?

You can create your own 'rainbow' by facing 180° from the sun and spraying mist from a garden hose in front of you in a circular motion

The three secondary colours are green, orange and violet. These are created by mixing two primary colours together: each secondary colour is made from the two primary colours closest to it on the colour wheel. For example, to create green, you would mix yellow and blue together. To create a tertiary color, you have to mix a primary colour with a secondary colour.

The 12 basic hues are red, red-orange, orange, yellow-orange, yellow, yellow-green, green, blue-green, blue, blue-violet, violet, red-violet. This circle allows the user to visualise the sequence of colour balance and harmony.

On the main part of the colour wheel, each individual hue is at a level of full saturation or brightness. There is no black (shade) or white (tint) added to it, but when a black or white is added to a hue, the colour has lightness or darkness, called 'value'. To show value, the colour wheel has more rings: two outer rings, which represent the dark shades, and two inner rings, which represent the light tints (Figure 9.38).

As you can see, no one colour stands alone on the colour wheel: a segment of colour is always seen in the context of other colours.

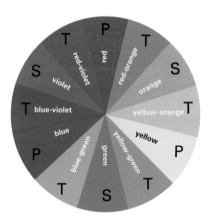

Figure 9.35 The colour wheel

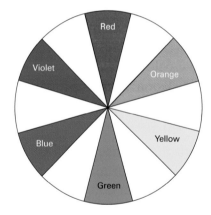

Figure 9.36 Primary and secondary colours

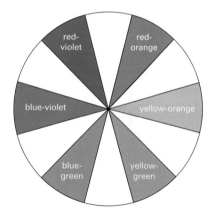

Figure 9.37 Tertiary colours

Creating moods with colour

By using different colours, you can 'create a mood' within your colour scheme or make a room feel 'cosier' or 'lighter'. Knowing the colour wheel can help you if are asked by clients to design a colour scheme for their home or business.

On one side of the colour wheel the colours, which range from red through orange to yellow, are classed as 'warm' or 'hot'.

When used in a colour scheme, these warm colours tend to come towards you, or feel closer to you.

On the opposite side of the wheel you have the 'cool' or 'cold' colours of the spectrum, ranging from light blue through green to yellow. These cool colours tend to recede from you, or feel distant to you when used in painting schemes.

You can also mix in and use a small amount of a warm colour – red, for example – to 'warm up' a cool colour, or a little of a cool colour – such as blue – to 'cool down' a warm colour.

Colours have meaning and express moods and emotions in almost everything in our lives. Some colours raise or lower our feelings or expectations; other colours convey a universal meaning, such as yellow and red being used as warnings or cautions.

To create a tint, add white to a colour, which will be lighter in value than the pure hue. By adding black to a colour, you create a shade of that hue, which will be darker in value than the pure hue. To show value, the colour wheel has more rings, which represent shades and tints. (See Figure 9.38.)

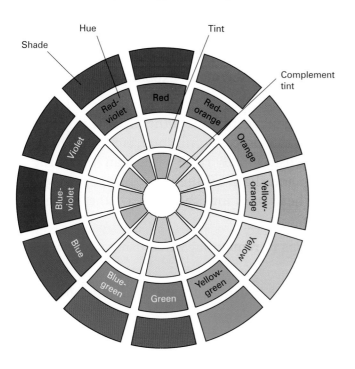

Figure 9.38 Colour wheel with outer and inner rings

K3. Cleaning, maintaining and storing brushes and rollers

You must always clean, maintain and store all paint brushes and rollers correctly after use.

Avoid leaving brushes and rollers in water or solvents at the end of each job. The ferrules can become rusty, the filling can become misshapen and sometimes paint hardens in the stock. Even after removing the water or solvent from the brush prior to applying coatings, you will have to deal with drips falling from your brush. This can be avoided if you take care of your brushes and rollers correctly.

Differences in cleaning procedures for natural bristle and synthetic filament brushes

When cleaning coatings from natural bristle brushes and synthetic filament brushes, take your time and be patient. Remove as much coating from the brush as possible, making sure not to pull on natural bristles as they will become dislodged and fall out.

Rinse the brush in white spirit or brush cleaner if you have used oil-based coatings and in lukewarm water if you have been using water-based coatings. Do not use hot water on natural bristle brushes as this will cause the ferrule to expand and the bristles to drop out.

When the coating has gone, gently wash the brush out with mild soap and rinse; repeat this process until there is no trace of colour coming out of your brush. Finally rinse with clean lukewarm water to remove soap and shake off the water before gently easing the bristles or brush head back into shape. Leave the brush to dry at room temperature.

There are some key tips to remember when using and cleaning brushes:

- It's best to use separate brushes for oil-based and water-based coatings and for varnishing.
- Don't let acrylic paints dry on a brush as they are water resistant when dry.
- You can wrap tissue paper tightly around natural bristle brushes when drying them out and they will hold their shape better.
- Misshapen synthetic brushes can be reshaped by soaking them in hot water and moulding them back into shape.

Cleaning procedures for roller sleeve types

After using rollers, clean them immediately to maintain their quality and durability.

Rollers used for water-based coatings

The most common types of roller used with water-based coatings are sheepskin or lambswool rollers and short/medium/long-pile rollers.

Roll out as much of the coating from the roller as possible, either on parts of the surface that need touching up or onto a rag or cardboard if any is available. Scrape excess paint back into your work pot with a scraper or putty knife. When you have removed as much paint as possible, wash off the remaining paint with clean water, making sure you squeeze as much coating out of the roller as you can.

Once all the coating has been removed and clear water is running through the roller head, either spin the roller head into a container to remove the excess water or hang it up to drip dry.

Rollers used for solvent-based coatings

For solvent-based coatings foam, woven fabric and mohair rollers are the most suitable. Foam-based rollers are often disposed of after use.

Follow the same procedures as for cleaning water-based rollers. Use clean white spirit instead of water to remove the coating. Steep the roller head in the white spirit for a short period to remove as much coating from it as possible. Roll out the roller head against the roller bucket or tray, repeating this method until clear white spirit is coming from the roller. Finally clean the roller with detergent and warm water to remove all white spirit as it could cause the roller head to harden.

Storage of brushes and rollers

If you are continually using your brushes and rollers, there are different methods of storing your equipment without constantly cleaning it. You could steep the brushes and rollers in the actual coating (suspension) or steep them in water if you are leaving them for longer periods (but this could damage the bristles on your brushes by misshaping them).

A brush keep is used to store brushes used for solvent-based coatings in a wet state. It works by a solvent being placed in a bottle with an evaporating wick. The fumes from the evaporating

> **Remember**
>
> Roller heads absorb a lot of coating and therefore this procedure for cleaning them is time-consuming

> **Safety tip**
>
> When cleaning solvent-based rollers, make sure that you are wearing the correct PPE at all times

> **Remember**
>
> After applying coatings, simply clip your wet brush into the brush keep. Due to its unique vapour system, it will keep the brushes both soft and pliable and ready for immediate re-use within hours, days or weeks. This will save time and money and prevent waste

Figure 9.39 Brush keep

solvent replace the air in the brush keep, preventing the brushes from drying out.

In a brush keep, the brushes are not in contact with any fluid and are ready for instant re-use. The life of the brush is also prolonged. You can quickly change the size of the brush you need when applying coatings and keep brushes in the colours you are using.

You can also suspend oil-based brushes in white spirit and water to keep them from drying out and leave water-based brushes in water. However, when you use them again, you may have drops of water or white spirit coming off your brushes and affecting your workmanship, so this method should be avoided if possible.

K4. Storing paint materials

Storage of materials has been covered earlier in Unit 1001 pages 42–43. Refer back to this section for more information.

Correct storage of materials

Most materials used by a decorator should be carefully stored away when not in use to keep them useable and to save money and time for future jobs. The storage area should be dry, frost-free and ventilated for keeping paints, varnishes, cleaning agents and other materials. There should be a racking system in place for materials and tools so that **stock rotation** can take place. This will also prevent things from being stored on damp floors.

Solvent-based coatings have to be stored in a well-ventilated area to stop any build-up of fumes. Water-based coatings should be kept frost-free.

Did you know?

Another method for short-term storage of water-based coating brushes and rollers is to wrap them up tightly in plastic bags so that no air can get to them and dry them out. You can also use this method for oil-based coatings but only for very short periods of time

Key term

Stock rotation – moving older materials to the front of a shelf to make sure that these are used first

Working life

Raisa is a first-year apprentice and has been asked to look after the storage room of a local decorator as part of her training. Kamal has just completed his apprenticeship with the local decorator and has come over to Raisa for a chat about looking after the store room. Kamal has told Raisa not to worry too much about keeping the store room in order as most of the materials are constantly being used. Kamal has said that it is easier just to place items such as burning-off equipment, drums of floor paint, dust sheets, powdered filters and tubes of caulk in an easy-to-reach area, as it will save time when handing out items, and will save her the bother of repeatedly putting items into their correct storage place.

- Do you think that Kamal is right? Would this save Raisa time in the long run?
- Does it make sense to keep materials close at hand so Raisa can hand items out more quickly?
- Will this make a good impression in regard to looking after the store room?
- Is Kamal thinking about safety or stock rotation when giving advice to Raisa?
- How should the store room be looked after, and where should these materials be kept?

FAQ

What is a paint system?

A paint system is a term used to describe what coatings need to be applied to a substrate and in what order they need to be applied to coat the surface or substrate correctly. If you are required to finish new softwood furnishings such as skirting boards, architrave, doors and windows with white gloss, you would need to apply the correct system.

The first stage in the system would be to apply knotting to any bare knots and then apply a suitable white primer followed by a white undercoat, then finished with a white gloss.

How do I know what a substrate is?

A substrate is a term used for a surface such as brick, plaster, timber, steel or cement – as well as natural stone, masonry surfaces and ceramic or porcelain tiles – that needs coatings applied to it either for protection or decoration.

Do I have to mix all paints prior to using them?

No. Thixotropic paints (for example, non-drip gloss) should not be mixed as these coatings have been specially made for their non-drip properties. If you mix them you will reduce their usefulness and purpose. It is always recommended that you follow the manufacturer's information regarding using coatings so that you use them correctly.

Check it out

1 Prepare a method statement describing the steps that need to be followed to protect the surfaces in a property during decoration.

2 Explain the best methods that can be used for protecting different floors and surfaces. Use diagrams to help explain the reasons behind your answers.

3 Describe some of the different types of paint that are available and state some of the different uses they have.

4 Explain some of the processes or paint systems used in painting by writing a series of step-by-step instructions for carrying out common painting processes. You may wish to use diagrams as part of your explanation.

5 Explain why surface coatings are used.

6 With the use of a diagram, explain how the colour wheel works and the different shades of colour that can be found on it.

7 Describe the Munsell System and explain what information it gives you and how this can be used in paint choice.

8 Describe some of the basic processes that can be used to clean and store brushes and paint equipment.

Getting ready for assessment

The information contained in this unit, as well as practical assignments that you will carry out in your college or training centre, will help you in preparing for both your end of unit test and the diploma multiple-choice test. It will also aid you in preparing for the work that is required for the synoptic practical assignments.

To complete any work as a painter, you will need to know how to prepare a working area and select the correct tools and equipment for applying coatings. This will be the case for all jobs you work on, and will be an important part of all practical work that you undertake as part of any qualification you study. When applying coatings, you will also need to understand the practical implications of selecting colours, as well as the techniques used to apply paint to surfaces. With all practical work, you will need to protect and store equipment correctly, as this will ensure that the equipment has a longer lifetime.

You will need to be familiar with:

- preparing the work area and protecting surrounding areas, furniture and fittings
- preparing materials for application and applying water-based and solvent-based coatings
- cleaning, maintaining and storing brushes and rollers
- storing paint materials.

For learning outcome 2, you have seen how to identify the correct application tool for surface coatings and seen the stages used to prepare and apply surface coatings. You will need to apply this knowledge to select the correct application tools for working with a range of surface coatings. You will also need to know how to apply surface coatings to a range of areas, such as walls, ceilings, doors and windows. As part of this, you will need to know how to cut in by brush to angles and obstructions to complete work accurately and avoid creating defects on surfaces while you paint. You will always need to be sure that you are working to current health and safety regulations.

As part of the practical work for learning outcome 2, you will need to produce a colour wheel of primary and secondary colours, showing how the colours relate to each other.

Before you carry out any work, think of a plan of action, which will tell you the order you need to do things in. It will also record a rough timescale for the work you need to carry out, in order to make sure that you complete everything you need to do safely. You will need to refer back to this plan at each stage to check that you are not making any mistakes as you work. You will need to make sure that the area you are working on is fully protected and that you are using the correct equipment to apply the correct mix of paint to a surface.

Your speed in carrying out any tasks in a practice setting will also help to prepare you for the time set for the test. However, you must never rush the test! Always make sure you are working safely. Make sure throughout the test that you are wearing the appropriate PPE and using tools correctly.

Good luck!

CHECK YOUR KNOWLEDGE

1 Give one advantage of cotton twill dust sheets.
   a They are inexpensive to purchase.
   b They do not absorb chemicals such as paint stripper.
   c Heavy paint spills do not soak through them.
   d They remain in place when laid.

2 If a floor requires prolonged protection or the work to be carried out will be aggressive, the best form of protection is:
   a tarpaulin
   b polythene dust sheets
   c corrugated PVC or cardboard sheeting
   d newspaper

3 Door furniture is best protected by:
   a masking tape
   b removal and storage
   c plastic bags
   d masking paper

4 When working around electrical fittings, you should:
   a remove them with your tools
   b cover them up with paper
   c have them removed by an electrician
   d be careful of electric shock

5 When protecting a room, any furniture that cannot be removed from the room would normally be stored:
   a along the left-hand wall, covered with a sheet
   b along the right-hand wall, covered with a sheet.
   c in the middle of the room, covered with a sheet
   d in its existing position, covered with a sheet

6 A basic quality of paint is that it should be applicable. What does this term mean?
   a easily brushed
   b easily rolled
   c easily sprayed
   d any of the above

7 Wood stain is a type of:
   a varnish
   b dye
   c primer
   d sealer

8 What is a colour wheel?
   a a radial diagram of colours
   b a description of colours
   c a circle of different colours
   d none of the above

9 How many basic hues are there?
   a 9
   b 3
   c 6
   d 12

10 How could you keep paintbrushes in a wet state?
   a Put them in a brush keep.
   b Store them in a container of water.
   c Store them in a container of white spirit.
   d any of the above

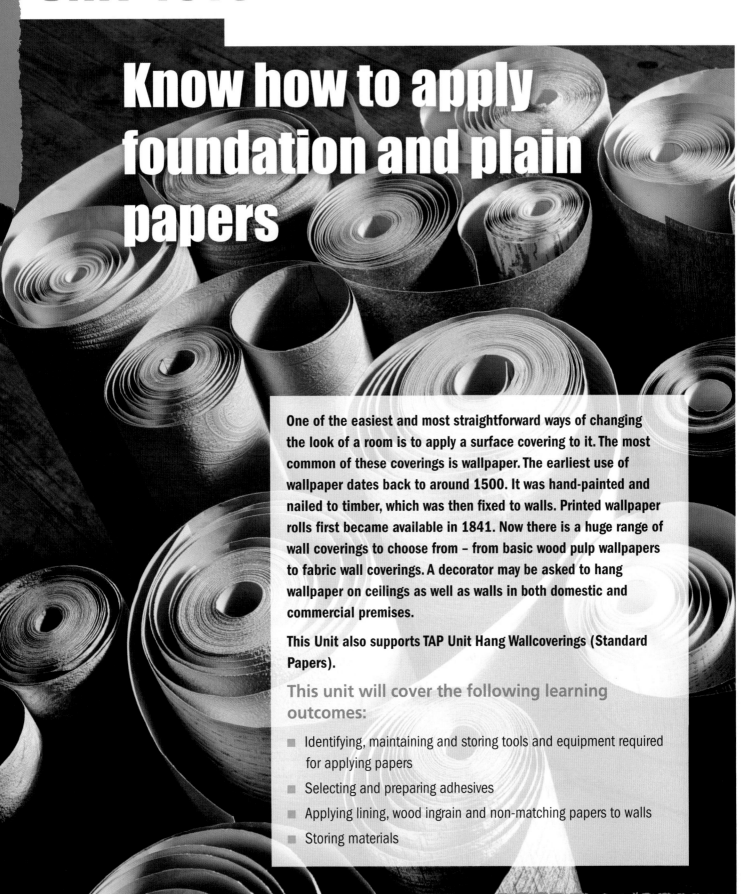

UNIT 1010

Know how to apply foundation and plain papers

One of the easiest and most straightforward ways of changing the look of a room is to apply a surface covering to it. The most common of these coverings is wallpaper. The earliest use of wallpaper dates back to around 1500. It was hand-painted and nailed to timber, which was then fixed to walls. Printed wallpaper rolls first became available in 1841. Now there is a huge range of wall coverings to choose from – from basic wood pulp wallpapers to fabric wall coverings. A decorator may be asked to hang wallpaper on ceilings as well as walls in both domestic and commercial premises.

This Unit also supports TAP Unit Hang Wallcoverings (Standard Papers).

This unit will cover the following learning outcomes:

- Identifying, maintaining and storing tools and equipment required for applying papers
- Selecting and preparing adhesives
- Applying lining, wood ingrain and non-matching papers to walls
- Storing materials

Remember

Working with high-quality tools and equipment that have been stored correctly to preserve their quality will help to build and improve your professional reputation

Figure 10.1 Paste brush

Did you know?

Some types of roller can be used as an alternative to the paste brush in order to apply paste to wall coverings

Figure 10.2 Paper hanging brush

Figure 10.3 Straight edge

K1. Identifying, maintaining and storing tools and equipment required for applying papers

Paper hanging is the technique of applying wallpaper to areas such as walls, ceilings and so on. The term also includes the hanging of **relief materials**, fabrics and vinyl papers.

As with all jobs in painting and decorating, in order to work successfully you have to know how to select, maintain and store the tools you need to complete the job. Many of the points on tool maintenance and storage will be familiar from earlier units.

Tools, equipment and their uses

Brushes

Paste brush

Apart from being used to apply paste to wallpaper, a paste brush can also be used for washing down and sizing. Paste brushes are available in a range of sizes between 100 mm and 175 mm.

Paper hanging brush

The paper hanging brush is also known as a sweep. It is used to remove all air bubbles between the wall covering and the surface to which it is being applied. After use, the brush should be cleaned in soapy water and hung up to dry.

Measuring and levelling tools

Straight edge

Bevel-edged lengths of steel or wood provide straight edges and can also be used for several other activities such as, when used with a trimming knife (see below), producing butt joints and mitres when hanging wall coverings.

Spirit level

A spirit level can be used as a straight edge. It can also be useful when marking horizontal and vertical lines and can aid cutting of coverings before pasting.

Figure 10.4 Spirit level

Folding rule

Folding rules are used for measurements. They are normally 1 metre long when unfolded and made of wood. They can show both metric and imperial units.

Figure 10.5 Folding rule

Plumb bob and line

A plumb bob is a weight to which string or twine is attached in order to produce a completely vertical line. These are still sometimes used instead of straight edges and spirit levels.

Cutting equipment

Scissors and shears

Scissors or shears usually have polished stainless blades and are used for cutting or trimming wall coverings. Make sure that they are kept clean and dry to prevent rusting. Scissors and shears must also be kept sharp or damage to wall coverings will result.

Figure 10.6 Plumb bob and line

Trimming knife

A trimming knife can be used as an alternative to scissors or shears but is most effective when used with a straight edge of some kind, for example a caulking blade or spirit level.

Figure 10.7 Scissors

Casing wheel

Casing wheels can have a serrated (jagged) or plain blade and are used for trimming surplus paper around angles and obstacles such as light fittings and brackets.

Other types of paper hanging tools and equipment

Pasteboard

A pasteboard is a long sturdy table made from wood or heavy-duty plastic that can be folded down for easier transportation. It is used to support coverings during preparation, cutting and pasting. The pasteboard surface should be kept clean at all times.

Figure 10.8 Trimming knife

Figure 10.9 Casing wheel

Wallpaper trough

A wallpaper trough is a container that is filled with water, in which pre-pasted wallpaper is submerged before hanging.

Figure 10.10 Pasteboard

Figure 10.11 Wallpaper trough

Figure 10.12 Caulking blade

Figure 10.13 Seam and angle roller

Figure 10.14 Retractable tape measure

Figure 10.15 Felt roller

Figure 10.16 Rubber roller

Caulking blade

Caulking blades can be used as alternatives to paper hanging brushes with fabrics or vinyl papers, but only on flat surfaces.

Seam and angle roller

A seam and angle roller is used to roll down joints in wall coverings during hanging.

Tape measure

A retractable metal tape measure is an important element of any decorator's toolkit. Available in a variety of lengths, most have both metric (centimetres and metres) and imperial (inches and feet) measurements. It is important to keep a tape measure clean as a dirty tape measure is likely to eventually clog up, making retraction of the tape back into the casing difficult.

Felt and rubber rollers

Felt rollers are either a felt-covered one-piece roller or several felt cylinders in line on a roller cage. They act as another alternative to the paper hanging brush.

Rubber rollers are used to hang very heavy materials, generally when a felt roller or paper hanging brush would not be heavy enough.

Pasting machine

Available as either table-top machines or as free-standing heavy duty pieces of equipment, pasting machines make applying paste to wall coverings easy. Paper is drawn through a paste trough, which coats the backing of the wall covering evenly. Care must be taken when using these machines and you need to be aware that some delicate, decorative and other specialist coverings may be damaged if passed through a pasting machine. Always check the manufacturer's instructions.

Care, maintenance and storage of tools and equipment

As you have learned in previous units, it is always very important to make sure that all your tools and equipment are kept in good condition as this will help keep up the professional standard of your work. Materials should be stored in a secure, dry and well-ventilated area.

After paper hanging, make sure that all your equipment is cleaned and stored away straight away. For example, it is also very important to clean the paste table as you use it, as this will prevent staining of wallcoverings and other defects.

Some decorators use a sponge for both cleaning down the table and wiping any excess paste from ceilings, skirting boards and so on. If you use a sponge, always make sure that it is clean.

Follow the same cleaning rules when working with your bucket and paste brush. If you do not clean the bucket out correctly, a dry paste will stick around the inside of it. The paste brush will need to be washed carefully with soapy water, then rinsed with clean water and left to dry.

Shears and trimming knives must be kept clean with a clean cloth and sharpened when blunt. Some come with snap-off blades. These will need replacing when they become dull as this will drag on wall coverings and tear the paper.

Types of deterioration in tools

If tools and equipment are not stored correctly, there are a number of types of deterioration that could occur:

- **Mildew** – occurs when tools are not stored in a dry storage area and is a growth of mould on the tool.
- **Rust** – occurs on metal tools, making then less sharp. Paste brush fittings can also rust, and rusty tape measures will not emerge easily from their casing.
- **Rot** – wooden tools (such as paste tables) will rot if left in wet conditions

K2. Selecting and preparing adhesives

There are three main types of wallpaper adhesive. They each have a different moisture content – low, medium and high. You will need to choose the right one for the job.

Adhesives are available in:

- ready-mixed tubs, in heavy, medium or light grades
- sachets or boxes of powder or flakes, to which you need to add water.

Adhesives are also available for use with very specific wall coverings.

Did you know?

You cannot expect your work to be of high standard if you use sub-standard equipment, such as rusty shears, tape measures and trimming knives, dirty paste tables, buckets, paperhanging brushes, seam rollers and sponges. Treat all your equipment with great care to help maintain the tools of your trade

Remember

When the task is complete, make sure that both the paste brush and the paper-hanging brush are left hanging in a dry storage area on hooks to help the brushes drip dry

Safety tip

Be careful when replacing blades to prevent any injuries to yourself or others. The same applies to shears; when cleaning them during use, it is easy to cut yourself if you don't do it correctly

Remember

Rusty brushes and seam rollers will transfer rust stains to the paper

Safety tip

Generally, the health hazards associated with adhesives are low. However, fungicides added to pastes can be dangerous if swallowed so care should be taken when using any adhesive that contains these. Always wash your hands thoroughly after use

Did you know?

Most modern adhesives contain a fungicide to prevent mould growth

Figure 10.17 Ready-mixed tub adhesive

Remember

Always check adhesive to see whether it is still fresh

Advantages and disadvantages of adhesives

Ready-mixed adhesive

Ready-mixed tub adhesives have a very low moisture content. They contain a chemical called PVA, which improves the adhesive property of the paste (how well it sticks). Some tub adhesives are very thick and must be diluted before use.

Advantages	Disadvantages
Very good adhesive properties. Ideal for use with vinyl and contract vinyl such as Muraspec®	Expensive
Can be used to size surfaces	Large container
Can be applied directly to wall surfaces to hang certain types of wall covering	
Contains a fungicide to prevent mould growth	
Does not rot and remains useable for a long time	

Table 10.1 Advantages and disadvantages of tub adhesive

Adhesives that are mixed with water

Starch adhesive

Starch adhesive is also known as flour adhesive because wheat flour is its main ingredient. It has a medium moisture content and comes in a powder form. It needs to be mixed with water to produce a paste suitable for lightweight to heavyweight wood-pulp wallpapers.

Advantages	Disadvantages
Good adhesive properties. Suitable for hanging heavy-textured preparatory paper	More expensive than cellulose adhesive
Contains a fungicide so can be used with vinyl papers	May stain the face of the wallpaper
	Difficult to mix
	Adhesive will rot and so is only useable for one to two days

Table 10.2 Advantages and disadvantages of starch adhesive

Cellulose adhesive

Cellulose adhesive has the highest water content of any paste and comes in a powder form that needs to be mixed with cold water before use. It is used with lightweight wallpapers such as lining papers and vinyls.

Advantages	Disadvantages
Inexpensive	Less adhesive than starch paste
Little risk of staining	Can cause paper to over-expand, resulting in wrinkling or mismatch
Easy to apply	If used on wallpaper that is unable to let water pass through it, such as vinyl, the water content in the adhesive may be prevented from drying out through the paper, leading to damage
Easy to mix	
Does not rot and can remain useable for a long time	
Contains a fungicide to prevent mould growth	

Table 10.3 Advantages and disadvantages of cellulose adhesive

Adhesives designed for specific wall coverings

- **Border adhesive** is ideal for applying vinyl on vinyl, for example when applying a border paper on top of another paper. It has strong adhesive properties.
- **Lincrusta®** glue is a very strong adhesive with good bonding properties.
- **Overlap adhesive** is designed for bonding vinyl to vinyl. It can be used on vinyl to bond overlaps on internal/external angles and to apply border paper over vinyl.

Factors that may affect the consistency of adhesives

Before hanging surface coverings, always read the manufacturer's instructions. These will contain all the information required to hang the wallpaper correctly, including soaking time, recommended paste and surface preparation required.

Wallpaper adhesives come in dry powder or flake forms and ready-mixed forms. If using dry powder, make sure that you have the correct amount of water while mixing the paste. A good tip is to remember that you can always add but not take away.

Safety tip

Take care when mixing dry flakes or powder pastes so you do not inhale any particles, as these can cause breathing problems or choking. If any adhesives get in your eye, wash the eye out carefully

Safety tip

Make sure that you read the manufacturer's information carefully prior to using any form of adhesive

Working life

Alex has just started his apprenticeship and is working with his mentor Dylan. Alex is applying wallpaper to a work bay and he has set up the tools, equipment and material. Dylan has measured the room and worked out the area for the wallpaper and has asked Alex to set the table up and to mix the paste to paste the wallpaper.

Alex fills the bucket with the required amount of water and empties the contents of the dry flake paste into the water and uses his hand to mix the paste. Dylan shouts at Alex to stop and tells him to wash his hands straight away. Alex explains that he has seen other apprentices mixing paste this way and did not know it was wrong. He tells Dylan that he will just wipe his hands dry with a cloth.

- Was Dylan right to stop Alex mixing the paste this way? If so, explain the reasons behind your decision. You will need to think about the health effects of doing this. If other apprentices were using this method, what could have been done about it?

Functional skills

Answering questions allows you to practise the functional skills required to read different texts and take appropriate action, e.g. respond to advice/ instructions. This may also involve giving oral answers to questions from your tutor and is practice for speaking and listening (**FE** 1.1.1 – 1.1.4).

For example, decide how much water is needed (usually three-quarters of a bucket for most papers) and slowly add the paste flakes while continually stirring the water. When the paste starts to thicken, let it stand for a while, then mix again prior to using. Ready-mixed paste usually only needs stirring prior to use but can have water added if you need to make it thinner.

Consistency of paste

You must make sure that you have the right consistency of paste prior to applying it to your wall covering. The type and weight of wallpaper can be a factor when mixing your paste, as well as the surface, room type and temperature. If you do not follow the manufacturer's information regarding the mixing of paste, you may create defects you have to rectify later.

The amount of water added to a dry flake paste will make a difference to the consistency of the paste, so always follow the instructions. If too much water is added, the paste will be thin and weak. This could lead to the wall covering peeling off the surface. It could also stretch due to the weak paste, therefore making it difficult to match up the different pieces.

If you don't add enough water, the paste will not spread correctly, which can lead to dry spots on the paper. This will prevent the paper adhering to the surface correctly, creating dry and lifting edges. Having the right consistency of paste is important if you want to complete a professional wallpapering job.

Defects related to incorrect adhesive consistency or poor handling

The following are some common defects you will encounter if you work with an adhesive with an incorrect consistency.

- **Delamination** – causes the decorative side of the paper to peel away from the backing during the application of the paper to the surface.
- **Blistering** – the appearance of a 'blister' or 'bubble' in a surface covering. It is caused by poor smothering, over-brushing, uneven pasting, use of incorrect adhesive or the lining not adhering properly.
- **Stretching** – horizontal stretching occurs when wallpaper has been adhered to a wall then moved up. Vertical stretching is caused by the weight of the paper after it has been soaked with paste. Stretching can lead to gapped or mismatched seams.

K3. Applying lining, wood ingrain and non-matching papers to walls

Factors to consider when planning

More information can be found about preparing a site in Unit 1008, pages 125-49.

The following golden rules should always be followed when preparing to apply surface coverings:

- Read the manufacturer's instructions supplied with each roll.
- Check each roll individually to ensure that it is not damaged.
- Check that the batch numbers and shades are identical.
- Open the rolls to check the pattern and printing.
- Identify the pattern, for example **straight match** or **drop match** pattern.
- Check which way the paper should be applied. Some patterns are not easy to identify. If you are unsure, contact the client or the manufacturer.

Starting and finishing points

When papering, it is advisable to have a starting and finishing point to aid with the application process. This avoids mistakes later on.

To mark your line on the wall, measure the wall and decide where to hang your plumb line from. Allow the plumb line to swing freely from your starting point at the top of the wall and then, when the line has stopped, mark a pencil line down the wall behind the string.

Papering walls and ceilings

Papering vertically

Take the first length of wallpaper and offer it up to the plumb line, with the longest fold opened, and then place it on the wall. You should be able to slide the paper accurately towards the plumb line. Smooth the paper down with the brush, working from the centre towards the edges. When all the air is smoothed out, fold down the bottom fold and apply it to the wall as before.

Papering horizontally

When papering horizontally, or when papering a ceiling, always work away from any light source (for example, a window). This is because a light source will create shadows on the surface should an overlap in the paper occur.

> **Key terms**
>
> **Straight match** – a wallpaper design that is repeated horizontally across the paper
>
> **Drop match** – a wallpaper pattern that is repeated but with a large space between matches, as recommended by the manufacturers

Figure 10.18 Hanging paper vertically

Key terms

Concertina fold – a series of small folds that can be easily unfolded during the paper hanging process

Decorator's crutch – a rolled-up length of wallpaper or a piece of wood used to support a concertina fold

Make a chalk line on the ceiling or wall to work from, which should ensure that the first length is straight. Always use a **concertina fold** and, after soaking the paper, offer up the first length to the line that allows for a 20-mm overlap at the wall edge. The concertina folds should be around 350 mm per fold. Apply one fold to the ceiling while supporting the unopened folds with a **decorator's crutch**. Smooth out the first fold. Then open one more fold and repeat the process – do not try to apply more than one fold at a time. When free of air pockets and creases, the paper should be trimmed out to both wall edges.

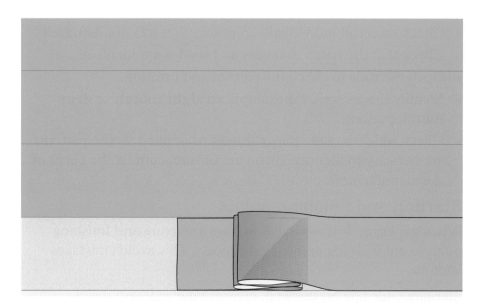

Figure 10.19 Papering horizontally

Remember

Measure twice but only cut once. In other words, double-check your measurements before making the cut

Did you know?

Smooth out wallpaper from the centre to the edge. This pushes any air bubbles to the edge and out from the surface

Remember

Prevent the edges of the wallpaper from curling by making sure you apply enough paste to the edge

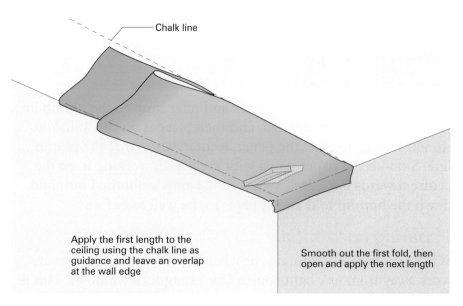

Chalk line

Apply the first length to the ceiling using the chalk line as guidance and leave an overlap at the wall edge

Smooth out the first fold, then open and apply the next length

Figure 10.20 Papering a ceiling

Features and obstacles

With a little practice and the right technique, hanging paper around features such as windows will soon become easy.

Hanging paper around a window

One of the most difficult areas in a room to hang paper is around a window.

First, hang the paper on one side of the window (see 1 in Figure 10.21), making a cut that allows some of the paper to be folded around the reveal (the side of the recess). Next, hang paper above and below the window, ensuring that it is plumb (see 2 and 3). You can now patch the underside of the reveal in the corner (4). Allow approximately 10 mm of paper to overlap (see dotted lines). Repeat this process for the other side of the window. If the window is particularly wide, you may want to mark a plumb line to make sure that the next full length of paper after the window is straight.

Paper hanging a staircase

When applying paper to a staircase, always start with the longest drop (length). After applying this first length, work from either side of it.

Centralising a patterned wallpaper

Figure 10.23 shows a chimney breast and alcoves of a room papered with a patterned wallpaper. The wallpaper has a set pattern and the pattern match is horizontally set – it does not drop. The wallpaper has been centralised – that means that the first length of wallpaper has been placed in the centre of the chimney breast. Notice how this creates a balanced effect.

The chimney breast is a feature of a room and can be the place to start papering if the whole room is to be papered in the same patterned paper. If a room does not have a chimney breast, choose one wall of the room as the feature wall and start paper hanging from the centre of that wall to ensure that the pattern of the paper is centralised.

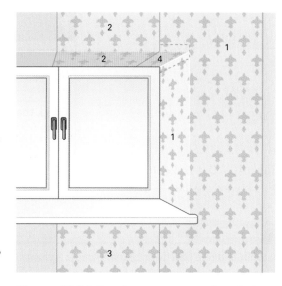

Figure 10.21 Hanging paper around a window

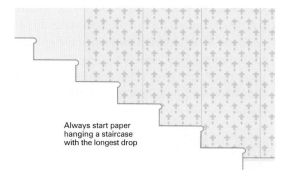

Always start paper hanging a staircase with the longest drop

Figure 10.22 Paper hanging a staircase

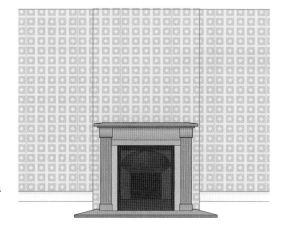

Figure 10.23 Centralising patterned wallpaper on a chimney breast

Do	Don't
Remove lumps from the paste	Leave areas of the covering unpasted
Remove any loose bristles from pasted lengths	Get paste on the pasteboard or the face side of the paper
Check that you are using the right paste for the paper and its application	Mix the paste too thinly
Keep edges parallel (aligned) when folding	Place the paste bucket on the pasteboard
Keep all tools and equipment clean	Have an untidy work area

Table 10.4 Dos and don'ts when folding and pasting

Working life

Emily and Ellie have been asked to paper a client's feature wall in a living room area. After visiting the client's home and discovering that the feature wall need two rolls of wallpaper, they agree to carry out the task as soon as possible.

They prepare the room to carry out the job and check the batch numbers and pattern numbers match on both rolls of wallpaper. Emily measures the drop of the wall and asks Ellie to start cutting lengths ready to paper. Ellie then pastes the paper quickly and gives a strip to Emily to hang. After the first strip is hung, Emily places a spirit level next to the paper to check it is straight but then has trouble matching the next strip. Eventually she has it in place, but has the same trouble throughout. When the job is complete, the paper is lifting at the edge and is pulling apart at the seams. The customer is not happy.

What did Emily and Ellie do wrong? Why had the paper lifted at the edges? Why did the pattern not match? Why did the paper come away at the seams? You will have to think about the way Emily and Ellie were working. What should happen now to rectify the situation?

Calculating quantity of paper

There are two main methods of calculating how much wallpaper you will require: the girthing method and the area method.

Girthing method

Table 10.4 gives some general golden rules you should follow when folding and pasting a surface covering.

Functional skills

Calculating paper for an area will allow you to practise several functional mathematic skills. These include **FM** 1.2.1b relating to interpreting information from sources, such as diagrams, tables, charts and graphs; **FM** 1.2.2 checking accuracy of results and **FM** 1.3.1 judging whether findings answer the original problem.

Use a roll of wallpaper as width guide to measure the number of full lengths required. Mark where each width will appear along the area to be papered then repeat this method until you have gone across the whole area. Then measure the area to see how many full lengths can be cut from a single roll of wallpaper.

Generally, most rolls of wallpaper come in 10 m lengths, so if a room has a ceiling height of approximately 3 metres, you will be able to cut three lengths from one roll of wallpaper.

This method can measure an area quickly. However, any miscalculations will cause you to run out of paper.

Area method

Measure up a room or take dimensions from a drawing. To measure up for a room you will need to measure each wall area separately. Measure the width and height of each wall area then multiply together to get the area which needs papering. This also applies to the ceiling area as well. Calculate the total surface area of the room, including windows and doors. Finally work out the area of the off-takes (things that will not be papered, such as the doors and windows) and subtract this amount from the total surface area. This will give you the surface area that requires papering. Then find out the surface area of the wallpaper roll and divide it into the surface area. This method is time-consuming, but more accurate than the girthing method.

To ensure you get the right quantity of wallpaper, you need to allow for wastage. This is usually 15–20 per cent depending on the type of pattern, shape and height of the room. To be on the safe side, a decorator should work on 20 per cent wastage.

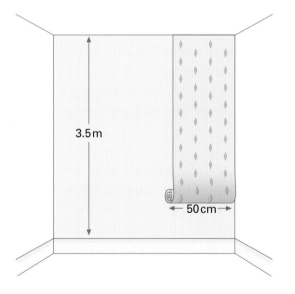

Girthing method – use the width of a roll of wallpaper and measure the height of the wall

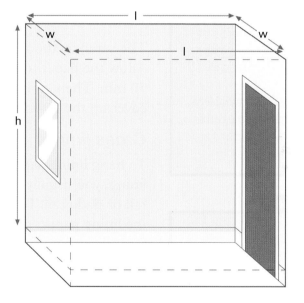

Area method – calculate the total surface area of the room and then subtract the offtakes (e.g. doors and windows)

Figure 10.24 Working out wallpaper quantities

Reasons for marking lines

To hang your first length of wall covering straight, either to a wall area or a ceiling, you must have a straight line to work from. When papering a wall vertically, you will need to use a plumb line or a chalk line with a weight added to the end of it (plumb bob) See page 193.

Key term

Focal point – a place where your eyes will tend to look

If you are hanging a paper with a bold pattern, you need to choose a **focal point** to start from. This is usually a chimney breast or another dominant wall feature in a room.

Internal and external angles

Allow the paper to go around the inside corner by no more than 25 mm. Do not carry on papering around an inside corner or internal angle with an existing length as you will cause the paper to start to run off and not keep straight. It is likely that you will have to cut one length and piece it back together. To do this, measure the space between the edge of the existing length and the internal corner, remembering to add an extra 25 mm to go round the internal angle.

With the remaining paper, measure the distance needed to paper back into the corner. Start again with a plumb bob to mark your straight line, then hang the strip and make sure that you paper into the internal angle, covering up the 25-mm edge. If you are using a patterned paper, you will need to match it up as best you can.

The same method is applied to paper around an external angle. Allow the paper to wrap around the external angle by at least 50 mm. Then, as before, start again with a plumb line and then cover up the 50-mm paper so that your lengths hang straight.

Cross lining

To hang lining paper horizontally, usually referred to as cross lining, you usually start from the top of the wall, or from a picture rail or dado rail. To get your starting line, measure the width of the lining paper (normally 56 mm wide) and then deduct 3 cm from this measurement to mark the wall. (You will also need to measure the width of the wall to get your length of lining paper.)

You need to deduct this measurement (3 cm) in case the ceiling or picture rail is running off. Mark the wall in three or four places with a pencil (56 cm down from the starting point) then, using a long spirit level, draw your starting line on the wall, using the marks as a guide. Use this line to paste your first length of lining paper onto the wall. While smoothing the paper out and applying it to the wall, the extra 3 cm should then be trimmed off.

Did you know?

If you are hanging a non-patterned paper or a plainer design paper, it is best to start in a corner of the room, just in case there are any problems such as walls not being plumb.

Although it is not desirable, a slight mismatch in the corner is not normally noticed and quite often is unavoidable

Remember

If you can, use two separate lengths or strips to paper an internal angle

Ceilings

If papering a ceiling, work away from the window wall and paper across the ceiling to hide any joints. Mark your starting point on the ceiling, parallel with one wall and about 13 mm less than the paper width out from it. Then mark the same point three or four times and use a spirit level to draw your starting line, and then apply paper.

Application sequence for pasting paper

- Stand in front of the pasteboard and place the length of paper on the pasteboard reverse side upwards.
- Move the furthest edge just over the edge of the pasteboard.
- Apply paste down the centre of the cut length.
- Keep applying the paste from the centre to the furthest edge. Do not go from edge to centre because the paste will drop onto the face side of the paper.
- Move the cut length so the nearest edge is just over the edge of the pasteboard and continue to work the paste brush from centre to edge, not from edge to centre.

Importance of aligning pasted edges

When folding the paper, make sure you align the edges of the pasted paper with the next section of pasted paper so that no paste will get onto the board. This is because the wet paste will contaminate the decorative side of the paper and cause staining and damage. If the paper is not aligned, it will become misshapen and will need to be refolded.

Faults and defects caused by careless pasting

Many of the faults that can be caused by careless pasting have been covered earlier. For more information on blistering, delamination and dry edges turn to page 192.

Figure 10.25 A good pasting technique

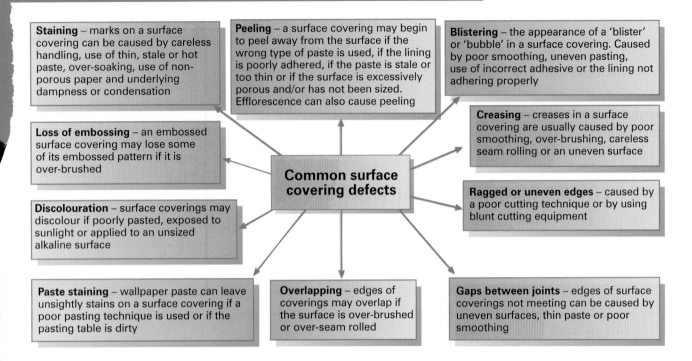

Staining – marks on a surface covering can be caused by careless handling, use of thin, stale or hot paste, over-soaking, use of non-porous paper and underlying dampness or condensation

Peeling – a surface covering may begin to peel away from the surface if the wrong type of paste is used, if the lining is poorly adhered, if the paste is stale or too thin or if the surface is excessively porous and/or has not been sized. Efflorescence can also cause peeling

Blistering – the appearance of a 'blister' or 'bubble' in a surface covering. Caused by poor smoothing, uneven pasting, use of incorrect adhesive or the lining not adhering properly

Loss of embossing – an embossed surface covering may lose some of its embossed pattern if it is over-brushed

Discolouration – surface coverings may discolour if poorly pasted, exposed to sunlight or applied to an unsized alkaline surface

Common surface covering defects

Creasing – creases in a surface covering are usually caused by poor smoothing, over-brushing, careless seam rolling or an uneven surface

Ragged or uneven edges – caused by a poor cutting technique or by using blunt cutting equipment

Paste staining – wallpaper paste can leave unsightly stains on a surface covering if a poor pasting technique is used or if the pasting table is dirty

Overlapping – edges of coverings may overlap if the surface is over-brushed or over-seam rolled

Gaps between joints – edges of surface coverings not meeting can be caused by uneven surfaces, thin paste or poor smoothing

Figure 10.26 Surface covering defects

The following defects can also occur if careful handling or application is not carried out:

- **Tears to wallpaper** – occur when lifting wallpaper to a surface and allowing the paper to drop down rather than sweeping
- **Polished edges** – occur when paste seeps through seams. Remove excess paste immediately with a damp cloth or sponge
- **Corners incorrectly negotiated** – occurs when the starting point is not planned out correctly, meaning you are not applying paper correctly to work round corners. It also occurs if plumbing is carried out inaccurately.

Why lining is used

Lining is used to give a surface even porosity. It is used as a base for finishing papers or as a base for painting. It can mask minor surface defects and is suitable for well-prepared surfaces. It is also used for masking or making good damage to walls and surfaces where filling and sanding has not resolved the defects prior to applying paints.

Lining paper can also be used to hide strong-coloured walls prior to repainting them in a lighter-coloured paint or repapering them with lighter-coloured wallpaper. The use of the right grade of lining paper hides any imperfections on the wall and is ideal as a base for hanging wallcoverings. It is also advisable to hang lining paper on solvent-painted walls to give a more absorbent surface for wallpapers to adhere to.

K4. Storing materials

We have covered the storage of materials earlier. Refer back to Unit 1001 pages 20–21 and 42–43, for more information.

Physical considerations of racks

Remember that areas must be dry and free from damp and frost. Wallpaper rolls and adhesives must be stored on racks and never stood on edge. Do not crush rolls by stacking them too high. Make sure that the racks are not in direct sunlight, as this will cause patterns to fade. Good ventilation is also important; if there is no ventilation in your storage area your wallpaper could deteriorate.

Remember

If wallcoverings are stored and protected correctly, and the storage area is clean, dry, frost-free, covered, ventilated and out of sunlight, they should not deteriorate

FAQ

Nobody seems to have wallpaper in their house anymore – why do I have to learn how to hang it?

It is true that wallpaper isn't as popular as it once was, but as with many fashions and trends, the popularity of wallpaper will probably increase at some point during your career as a painter and decorator. When this happens, you will be glad you know how to hang it!

Why is wallpaper paste sometimes lumpy?

Because it hasn't been mixed up properly! Wallpaper paste should always be smooth. Make sure that you read and follow the instructions on the packaging.

Is it necessary to clean my shears constantly as I paper?

Yes it is important to keep cleaning your shears as you go, as this will remove any paste that has spread onto them. This will help keep the shears sharp for cutting your next piece of wallpaper and prevent any costly mistake, for example tearing the wallpaper.

Check it out

1   Describe what piece of equipment could be used to paste wallpaper instead of a paste brush.

2   Explain the processes that need to be followed to protect tools and equipment during work.

3   Describe when you might use the following types of adhesive: border adhesive; Lincrusta® glue; overlap adhesive.

4   Prepare a method statement explaining how to produce smooth, high-quality paste.

5   Using diagrams, demonstrate and explain the correct methods used to paper surfaces, including walls, ceilings and staircases.

6   Explain what is meant by 'centralising' a wallpaper pattern. Demonstrate with the use of diagrams how this effect is achieved.

7   Explain the two methods that can be used to estimate the correct amounts of paper that will be required for a job.

8   Describe the methods used to make markings on walls for pasting and explain why this is carried out.

9   Explain some of the defects caused by incorrect pasting methods.

10 State the reasons for storing materials on racks, and explain why this method is used.

Getting ready for assessment

The information contained in this unit, as well as continued practical assignments that you will carry out in your college or training centre, will help you in preparing for both your end of unit test and the diploma multiple-choice test. It will also aid you in preparing for the work that is required for the synoptic practical assignments.

Many surfaces you work with will need to be covered with a foundation of plain paper. Because of this, it is very important that you are able to select and use tools and equipment correctly, as well as the adhesives needed to attach papers to walls. Your practical work will require you to use this knowledge to apply lining, wood ingrain and non-matching papers to walls in a range of situations. As with all practical work, you will need to protect and store equipment correctly, as this will ensure that the equipment has a longer lifetime.

You will need to be familiar with:

- identifying, maintaining and storing tools and equipment for applying papers
- selecting and preparing adhesives
- applying lining, wood ingrain and non-matching papers to walls
- storing materials.

For learning outcome 3, you will need to be able to plan the position of paper hangings in a range of situations as well as selecting the tools and equipment needed to complete the work. You will need to be able to calculate quantities of paper accurately using a range of methods, making sure that you have the minimum amount of wastage. Once you have calculated the amount of paper needed, you will then need to measure and mark the lines to hang to, before applying papers accurately and correctly. You will always need to be sure that you are working to current health and safety regulations.

Before you carry out any work, make a plan of action, which will tell you the order you need to do things in. It will also record a rough timescale for the work you need to carry out, so that you complete everything you need to do safely. You will need to refer back to this plan at each stage to make sure that you are not making any mistakes as you work. Applying foundation and plain papers to a range of surface areas is a crucial practical skill for painters and decorators and you will need to follow all the correct procedures to ensure that the final job is completed to the highest possible standard.

Your speed in carrying out any tasks in a practice setting will also help to prepare you for the time set for the test. However, you must never rush the test! Always make sure you are working safely. Make sure throughout the test that you are wearing the appropriate PPE and using tools correctly.

Good luck!

CHECK YOUR KNOWLEDGE

1 Which type of roller is used to roll down joints in wall coverings during hanging?

a seam and angle roller

b felt roller

c check roller

d duet roller

2 Which of these tools can be used along with a trimming knife?

a scissors

b spirit level

c caulking blade

d all of the above

3 To prevent mould growth, modern adhesives contain:

a pesticide

b fungicide

c PVA

d starch

4 Which of these is a disadvantage of cellulose adhesive?

a It can cause paper to over-expand.

b It is tricky to apply.

c There is more risk of staining than with starch adhesive.

d It will rot and so is only useable for one to two days.

5 Which of the following is not a golden rule for preparing to apply wallpaper?

a Read the manufacturer's instructions.

b Check that the batch numbers and shades are identical.

c Keep the rolls wrapped up until just b efore pasting.

d Identify whether the pattern is straight match or drop match.

6 Which of these would be a good place for centralising a wallpaper pattern?

a a window

b a door

c a chimney breast

d the foot of a staircase

7 When mixing a dry powder/flake wallpaper adhesive with water, which item is best used?

a your hand

b a paste brush

c a wooden stick

d a scraper

8 What would happen to wallpaper shears if they were not cleaned properly after use?

a become rusty

b become blunt

c blades could stick together

d all of the above

9 Why should wallpaper coverings be stored out of direct sunlight?

a to prevent the pattern from fading

b so all the rolls are kept together

c to prevent damaged edges

d to keep batch numbers together

10 When applying wallpaper/coverings vertically to areas, what would happen if you did not follow a plumb line?

a nothing

b you would run out of wallpaper

c wallpaper would start to run off and not be straight

d wallpaper would not adhere properly

Know how to produce specialist decorative finishes 1

When carrying out decorating work, you will often be asked to produce more complicated decorative patterns. These specialist decorative finishes need a different set of skills from the more standard decorative finishes we have looked at in earlier units. Special effects such as texture, pattern and the illusion of a different surface can all be created by a skilled decorator using the contents of their toolbox.

This Unit supports NVQ Unit QCF 330 Prepare New Surfaces for Paint Systems in the Workplace and QCF 331 Apply Paint Systems to New Surfaces by Brush and Roller in the Workplace.

This Unit also supports TAP Unit Apply Paint Systems by Brush and Roller.

This unit will cover the following learning outcomes:

- Producing quality finish ground coats for painted decorative work
- Producing broken colour effect using acrylic and oil-based scumbles
- Applying single-colour stencils.

You will need to read through this section and the earlier sections on surface preparation to understand correctly the procedures you need to follow. In doing this you will be practising **FM** 1.2.1–1.2.3 relating to reading and understanding information.

Key term

Scumble – a decorative effect material, a semi-transparent coating containing pigment and linseed oil

Did you know?

As the name suggests, specialist coatings are created to imitate natural products such as marble and wood grain, so it is important that these effects look as natural as possible. If the application method is incorrect, the finished effect will look artificial and therefore will not work

K1. Producing quality finish ground coats for painted decorative work

When working to produce specialist decorative finishes, it is very important to have a good-quality finish on ground coats. Many of the skills you will need to produce high-quality base coats have been covered in earlier units. This section will briefly recap some of the key skills you will need to have.

Preparation processes for decorative work

Surfaces will need to be 'made good'. Most surfaces need to be abraded to give a key for coatings to adhere to. You may also need to fill surfaces to remove dents, otherwise when the **scumble** is applied it will collect in the holes and dents. It will show up as darker areas on the finished effect.

Defects that may occur from low quality of ground coat finish

If the surfaces have not been prepared correctly prior to applying ground coats there is a range of defects that could appear on your finished specialist decorative effect.

- **Bittiness** – occurs if you have not abraded correctly and/or dusted off debris after rubbing down.
- **Ropiness** – occurs if the surface has not been given a full ground coat, making the finished specialist coating look thin and see-through.
- **Uneven colour** – occurs if indentations on the surface have not been filled correctly, meaning the finished coat will not spread out correctly.
- **Sinking** – occurs if spot priming has not been done correctly. The oil in the specialist coating evaporates too quickly if applied onto filler. This makes the coating appear uneven.

How application method may affect quality

It is important to apply the selected specialist coating correctly to avoid any defects occurring such as brush marks, misses, runs, flashing and wet edges. These defects will affect the appearance of the finished work and mean the surface will lose the desired specialist effect if not applied correctly.

Benefits of using a stipple brush and roller

It is important to remove brush marks from your specialist effect so the desired effect will look as natural as possible. Using stipple brushes and rollers will eliminate these and ensure the ground coat has been applied evenly. This will aid with the application of the specialist coating.

Appropriate coating types for decorative work

The most appropriate coatings used for ground coats and base coats when applying decorative specialist effects are neutral coloured vinyl silk emulsions and neutral coloured eggshell paints.

Usually the ground coat is a tone lighter than the lightest part of the desired finish so using neutral colours as base coats will create the desired effect. These coatings are ideal as base coats and can be covered with the desired specialist paint effect colour. Both oil- and water-based paints can be used as ground coats, depending on which system you are using for your specialist decorative effect.

K2. Producing broken colour effect using acrylic and oil-based scumbles

Broken colour effects are effects that produce a multi-coloured finish. To apply broken colour effect, you must have a clean, hard surface with no brush marks, indents or nibs. It is also important to have a good-quality base coat, such as an oil-based or water-based eggshell. You then apply the decorative coat to it.

Overcoats can be opaque or translucent. If a coating is translucent, it means that you can see through it. A clear varnish is translucent. If a coating is opaque, it means that the colour will obliterate, or totally cover, a surface with the colour used.

Materials used to produce broken colour effects

If you use white oil-based coatings for decorative effects, **yellowing** will occur to the effect after a while due to age and lack of light. To avoid this, many decorators use acrylic coatings. However, these types of coatings do not last as long as oil-based coatings.

To aid with the application of oil-based coatings, use white spirit to thin your coating and add **driers** to speed up the drying process.

Figure 18.1 Stippling brushes

> **Key terms**
>
> **Yellowing** – is a defect caused by age and occurs when white oil-based coatings have been used on surfaces and the surface receives little natural light
>
> **Driers** – are a special blend of chemicals that can be added to paints to speed up their drying time. Driers can be added to both oil and alkyd paints and varnishes. They can also be added to old coatings that have been stored away and lost their usual drying times due to age.

Key term

Glycerine – is a liquid chemical material diluted with water, which can be added to acrylic paints to extend their working time. This allows the decorator more time to finish a task

Did you know?

It is possible to buy and use coloured glazes

Remember

Make sure that you have mixed a little more scumble than you need in case you run out before finishing the job. If you run out, you will need to mix more scumble and it may be difficult to repeat the exact shade of colour. This will spoil your finished job

Key term

Lint – tiny, fuzzy fibres of material

During the application of special effects, it may be necessary to reduce or extend the drying times of both oil-based and acrylic scumbles due to time restraints or the size of the task. To do this when using acrylic scumbles, add **glycerine** to the scumble to extend drying time, or wet the surface you are working on with water by using a wet rag or applying a light spray mist to the surface. You can reduce drying time by increasing the room temperature to speed up the drying time. When applying oil-based scumbles, add linseed oil to extend the drying time and add liquid driers to reduce it.

Remember that scumble is a base to which colour is added to create your specific effect. When you apply a scumble, you are actually applying a thin film of colour. This represents the finish you want to imitate for your specialist coating, for example, light oak. You will need to make sure that you have mixed it to the correct viscosity (thickness or thinness of a fluid), otherwise the finished effect will appear thin and colourless.

A glaze is usually a clear coating applied to add shine and can change the colour cast or texture of the specialist surface you have created. It also helps to protect the finished surface.

It is useful to work out how much material you will need for a particular task. Mix enough to finish the job in one go if possible. To achieve this, you may need to have help from someone else and set up a method to complete the task. For example, one person applies the material, such as scumble glaze, to the area; another person follows creating the effect, for example rag rolling. This will allow you to use the material's working time most effectively.

There are two key methods used to produce broken colour effects:

- rag rolling
- sponge stippling (additive and subtractive).

Rag rolling

Rag rolling is created by applying colour to a surface with a brush or roller and then lifting the colour off with the rag, exposing some of the background colour. 'Ragging on' is the name given to the action of applying the colour to a ground coat using a rag or cloth. 'Ragging off' is the name given to the action of lifting off some of the colour to create a different effect. The rag used should be a **lint**-free cloth and bunched up in the hand during paint application.

Chamois leather can be used to create the rag-rolled effect. You should bunch it up and roll it across the surface in different directions to give the effect. You can also use a chamois leather roller (Duet® type), rolled-up paper or plastic bags instead of a rag. These will create softer or sharper effects, depending on how you use them.

Procedure for ragging on

- Mix up a coloured glaze, and pour it into a work pot. To create your specific coloured glaze, either use an oil colourant or acrylic colourant and add it to your clear glaze.
- Bunch up a rag and dip it into the coloured glaze, making sure that the rag is completely saturated (soaked).
- Wring out the rag and roll it into a loose cylinder, twisting it slightly.
- Apply the paint by rolling the rag across small sections of the surface in random directions to create a rag-rolled finish. Overlap each section by a third to prevent stripes, banding or tracking occurring.

Procedure for ragging off

- Apply a coloured glaze to the surface, removing any brush marks with a hog-hair stippler.
- Bunch up a rag and roll it across the surface in different directions, then lift the rag off the surface. Move from top to bottom and make sure that you overlap by one-third to prevent stripes or banding. This method will remove coloured glaze from the surface.
- Clean off the rag and repeat the process, remembering to alter the direction in which you roll the rag across the surface. This will prevent the finished effect from looking uniform.

Figure 18.2 A rag-rolled paint effect can be more interesting than solid colour

Working life

When completing a rag-rolled effect for their customer, Christy is applying the glaze and stippling, and Lydia is using the rag to create the effect. They start arguing about stopping for a break. Christy, who has more experience, insists that they must finish the effect at the end of the wall area but Lydia insists that she is entitled to a break from the task.

Who is right?

- What will happen if the effect is not completed up to the end of the wall?
- Is Lydia entitled to her break?
- What could have been done to avoid this issue?

Did you know?

A natural sponge is the soft and fibrous skeleton of a marine animal

Figure 18.3 Sponging is an easy way to create an interesting broken colour effect

Sponging

Sponging is quite simply creating a broken colour effect by applying and removing paint with a sponge. Either a natural or synthetic sponge can be used.

- Apply a coloured emulsion, acrylic or oil-based eggshell or thinned gloss paint and allow it to dry completely.
- Decant the paint to be sponged into a tray. Load the sponge with colour by dipping it into the paint and squeezing out excess paint.
- Apply the colour to the ground coat by gently dabbing with the sponge, ensuring that you don't overload areas with paint. Remember to dab randomly to avoid set patterns occurring. Use a guard to prevent overlapping on internal corners.
- If desired, build up different layers of colour with the sponge, allowing each coat to dry thoroughly. Different types of sponge can also be used for each colour, giving the finished paint effect the appearance of depth and texture.

Stippling

Stippling is a way of creating a soft, suede-like appearance on a surface. Different colours can also be overlayed in order to create bands of colour. Water-based paints allow the decorator to apply a number of colours in one day, however the colour must be applied swiftly as the drying process will be rapid.

Stippling procedure

Step 1: Following manufacturer's instructions, mix up either an acrylic glaze or oil-based glaze consisting of colour, white spirit (for oil-based), glycerin (for acrylic) and driers. Apply the glaze to the surface with a brush.

Step 2: Use a hog-hair stippler to stipple the glaze, making sure that no brush marks remain. The aim is to achieve a soft, even texture.

Application faults and problems

When applying decorative paint effects, it is very easy to cause application faults. Some of the faults connected with surface coatings have been mentioned above and are covered in Unit 1009. However, there are also some specific issues connected with decorative finishes that can occur:

- **Banding/tracking** – this fault is an uneven pattern effect on the final finish and is caused by not overlapping the scumble by one-third during application when rag rolling on a surface. To prevent this, make sure that you always cross over the last application by one-third of the width of the coating.

- **Slip or skid marks** – this fault is caused by applying too much coating or scumble to the surface when using a roller and applying too much pressure, causing the roller to slide across the surface. To prevent this, simply load the tool up with the correct amount of coating and apply correctly.

- **Loss of wet edge** – this is caused by stopping half-way through the job. The coating then starts to dry where you left off and this will show up in the finished job. To prevent this from happening, make sure that you consider break times and area size carefully before beginning your task.

Problems caused by careless removal of masking material

If you are careless when removing masking tapes from your decorative finish, you can cause more problems and create more work for yourself. Removing the tape carefully will help you to create a professional look for the finished task. If you just pull the tape away from the surface, you can actually remove the finished product, for example a marble or grain effect. This is because the adhesive from the tape will also peel the coating away from the surface. In some cases, it will also remove the ground coat, which will then need repairing.

Tools and equipment

Hair stipplers

These are stiff-bristle brushes used to remove brush marks from applied glazes and to lift off fine dots and flecks of glaze from the surface coating.

Mohair rollers

These short-pile rollers are ideal for use when applying linseed oils, finishing oils and exterior wood oils to surfaces, due to their ability to prevent coatings flicking off and becoming messy.

> **Remember**
>
> Never start a painting job when you know you cannot finish it in the set time, as this will lead to defects and a poor-quality finish
>
> If you damage the ground coat or the top coat, the whole sequence of application will need to be completed again to restore the effect

Figure 18.4 Hair stippler

Figure 18.5 Mohair roller

Figure 18.6 Palette

Figure 18.7 Drag brush

Figure 18.8 A positive stencil

Palettes

These are usually used when carrying out stencilling. They hold small amounts of paint and, when applying the paint to the stencil plate with a stencil brush, you can dab the palette board to remove any excess paint prior to applying the paint to the stencil.

Drag brush

A drag brush is a coarse-bristled brush made from horsehair, fibre or nylon. It is used to produce straight-grained patterns.

K3. Applying single-colour stencils

Stencilling is a way of decorating a surface with a pattern or design using a cut-out template. A client may ask for stencil work because:

- It produces a unique paint effect on a surface. The position and colour of the pattern or design will be unique and tailored to the client's requirements
- It is quick and easy to repeat a pattern or design.

There are two kinds of stencil:

- **positive** – where a pattern is cut out and paint is applied over the openings, reproducing the pattern on the surface beneath (see Figure 18.8)
- **negative** – the opposite of a positive stencil, whereby the background of a pattern is cut out.

Stencils can be made up of more than one part. These are known as multi-plate stencils. For example, a stencil of a flower design may be made up of three plates: the first for the leaves and stem, the second for the first layer of petals and the third for the top layer of petals and flower centre. Multi-plate stencils are particularly useful when a pattern is made up of lots of colours or when it is very complex. When using multi-plate stencils, ensure that you match up the plates or your finished design will not look as it should. Lining up the plates with two pencil lines at right angles is the most effective method.

Planning considerations for stencils

When applying stencils, careful consideration must be taken with the stencil design itself. As you will be pounding, dabbing or stippling the paint onto the design to create the picture, damage can occur such as broken ties or a twisted or buckled stencil. This could mean you have to make the stencil again, costing you time and effort to sort out and complete your task.

There is a range of materials that can be used to produce a stencil:

- **acetate** – a clear, flexible, sturdy sheet material that you can photocopy onto
- **mylar**™ – an inflexible polythene sheet
- **cartridge paper** – a thick paper, just like writing paper, which you can coat with linseed oil or knotting solution to strengthen and make waterproof; this is a cheaper alternative to normal stencil paper, and can be simply produced
- **proprietary paper** – the most common stencil material used.

Positioning the stencil

When planning to use a stencil as a border, a frieze or regularly around a room for decoration, make sure that you have measured and marked up the position for each stencil correctly. If not, the stencil may look a little odd and disjointed once applied. It may meet badly at the corners of a room or become halved when going up to a ceiling on a wall. You will need to work out where you want the stencil to start from and where you want it to finish. If you are repeating your stencil to create a design or theme, remember to space it out correctly.

There are a number of ways in which to position the stencil correctly. Here is the most common way:

1 Mark the area on the surface where the stencil is to go, then measure out the area of the surface.

2 Find the central point of where you want the stencil to go.

3 On your stencil, mark the centre points (registration marks) of the width and length of the design. To create the centre points, cut out a V at each correct measurement on the stencil with your stencil knife, making sure that you follow the procedures for cutting so that you do not harm yourself.

4 Match the stencil centre points to the surface centre points you marked earlier.

The use of chalk lines is a fast way to mark the area and is used in the same way as when applying wallcoverings (see page 194). First, measure and mark where you want the stencil to be placed, then repeat this method along the area until you have at least three marks to work from. Then place one end of the chalk line at the first marking and the other end at the last marking before snapping back to leave the line.

Remember

When cutting out a stencil, always have a stencil mat or glass plate to hand to lay your design onto before cutting out the pattern. This will prevent any damage to the surface you are resting on. Make sure that you position the ties correctly so that you do not risk disfiguring your design

Remember

When creating a stencil, the pattern or design has to be held in place with 'ties'. Without ties, your design will simply fall out of the template so make sure you incorporate ties into your design

Safety tip

Always cut away from yourself or, better still, move the design around as you hold the stencil knife in position to cut out the pattern

Remember

Check that the chalk line is level. Then, when the line is aligned along the marks and the line is taut, pull the chalk line out and let it snap back. This will leave a line on the surface to work from that can be easily removed when the stencil has been applied

Securing methods for stencils

If you are applying a small stencil and can manage to hold it in place, there is no need to stick it. However, if you are using a larger stencil, use a spray adhesive. This allows you to put it in position, then, after stencilling, move it to another area as it will still retain its adhesiveness for a while. Although quick and easy to use, spray adhesive may not stick larger, more complex stencils in place. A low-tack masking tape is more useful if you are applying a larger stencil, for example a border stencil.

Applying the paint for a stencil

1 Mix enough paint colour for the full job.
2 Have a clean stencil brush and palette or tray for your colour or colours, if you are applying more than one.
3 Get a clean sponge and a stencil brush. Or you can use a 1-inch/25-mm sash brush and tape up the bristles to stop them from splaying.

Marking up the wall and stencil

Marked area

Wall

Step 1 Mark area of surface where stencil is to go.

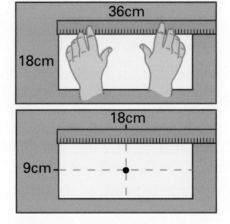

Step 2 Mark the central point of the area.

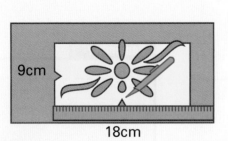

Step 3 Find the central point of the stencil. Cut a V on the stencil's length and width at the correct measurements.

Step 4 Align the centre points on the stencil and surface.

4 Load up the tool you are using with paint from your palette.

5 Dab or stipple onto the palette to remove any excess paint. This will give you an even amount of paint on the brush so that you can apply the paint to the stencil without any defects.

6 Start from the centre of the focal point in the room and then work either side of your first stencil. Apply the paint to the stencil in a stabbing motion, making sure you do not smudge or let paint creep under the stencil.

7 Once the stencil is complete, remove it from the surface carefully to avoid any smudging and tearing of the design. (This is why a low-tack masking tape or spray adhesive is used.)

Another way to apply a stencil design onto a surface is to place your stencil onto an overhead projector then, remembering to pick out your centre marks, project the design onto your surface.

Preventing application faults when stencilling

As with all jobs, you will need to be careful to avoid faults and defects occurring during application of stencils. Some of the key faults you need to be looking to avoid are covered below.

- **Creep** – caused by too much paint applied to the stencil, with the excess creeping under the cut out section, causing the stencil to lose its design.
- **Smudging** – caused by careless removal of stencils.
- **Lifting paint** – caused when masking tape is carelessly removed from a surface.
- **Uneven colour** and **undue texture** – occur when you have not applied paint to the stencil correctly or loaded the stencil brush properly.
- **Bittiness** – caused by dirt or debris being present on the surface prior to stencilling. Correct preparation is needed prior to applying the stencil.
- **Uneven weight of colour over repeats** – occur when applying different colours to a multi-layered design stencil. This can look heavy with colour in one section and not the other. To prevent this apply the colours and try to stipple the same amount of paint to the whole area. You can also try blending in the colours, if necessary.

> **Did you know?**
>
> Using a low-tack masking tape means you can place another stencil on top of the first stencil when adding two or more colours to your design

FAQ

What does the term 'broken colour' mean?

A 'broken colour' paint effect is one that is created by layering paint colours and then breaking them up to reveal the underlying colours. This can be achieved by adding colour (for example, when sponging) or by taking off colour (for example, when ragging off). A broken colour effect can give a surface the appearance of shade and texture.

Why do you need to have enough colour mixed for the whole job? Can you not just mix more later to finish the task?

It is important to have enough colour mixed for the whole job because, if you run out of paint before the job is complete, you will need to mix more. There is a chance that the new mixed colour could be a different shade. If it is, this will spoil your finished job.

What would happen if you removed masking tape carelessly from a finished effect?

You could damage the finished effect. You could pull the top coating away from the surface and expose the ground coat. You could also remove the coats from the surface altogether, exposing the substrate. In either case, you will then have to start the whole process again, which will cost both time and money.

When stencilling in a room, can I just start anywhere I please?

It is important to have a starting point in any room when you come to stencil as it is important that your pattern looks symmetrical and actually finishes whole. If you just start anywhere on a wall or area, you could end up running out of area and need to have half a stencil.

Check it out

1   Draw up a method statement detailing the actions needed to prepare a surface for a specialist decorative finish.

2   Explain how a poor application method will lead to a poor-quality finish.

3   Explain what a broken colour effect is and draw up a method statement detailing how to create the effect when painting.

4   State what two types of material could be used instead of a rag to lift off colour during rag rolling.

5   Explain the difference between a glaze and a scumble and describe where each might be used and why.

6   Explain why a painter may wish to reduce the drying time of paint on a job. Then, describe some of the methods that can be used to reduce drying time.

7   Explain why viscosity is important when working with scumble.

8   Describe the two types of stencil and explain how they work.

9   Describe three faults that can occur when applying stencils and explain how they can be avoided.

Getting ready for assessment

The information contained in this unit, as well as continued practical assignments that you will carry out in your college or training centre, will help you in preparing for both your end of unit test and the diploma multiple-choice test. It will also aid you in preparing for the work that is required for the synoptic practical assignments.

A large number of the decorating jobs you carry out will require some final special decorative work. Many of your future clients will wish to have a final surface coating that adds a high level of decoration to the final job. As such, it is very important that you know all the basic skills needed to create the most common effects, and are confident with the methods used. Your practical work will require you to use this knowledge to apply both broken colour effects and single-colour stencils accurately and correctly. You will have to be confident in your practical skills in order to avoid creating defects when applying paint and effects.

You will need to be familiar with:
- producing high-quality finish ground coats for painted decorative work
- producing broken colour effect using acrylic and oil-based scumbles
- applying single-colour stencils.

For learning outcome 2, you need to be able to check the factors relating to the suitability of the ground coat, and rectify any defects you may discover. You will then need to set out areas for work, making sure that you are protecting any surfaces correctly. You will need to know how to prepare and apply a range of materials, such as different types of glazes and colourants, using correct tools. Your final broken colour effect should be uniform. After completion of work, you must be able to remove all protection used carefully and clean and maintain tools after use. At all times, you will need to make sure that you are working to current health and safety regulations.

Before you carry out any work, think of a plan of action that will tell you the order you need to do things in. It will also record a rough timescale for the work you need to carry out, in order to make sure that you complete everything you need to do safely. You will need to refer back to this plan at each stage to make sure that you are not making any mistakes as you work. This is particularly important when applying decorative paint effects as these are intended to be the 'showpiece' of the final job. If you do not plan correctly when working on these, you will reduce the final quality of the job and this will reflect badly on your skills.

Your speed in carrying out any tasks in a practice setting will also help to prepare you for the time set for the test. However, you must never rush the test! Always make sure you are working safely. Make sure throughout the test that you are wearing the appropriate PPE and using tools correctly.

Good luck!

CHECK YOUR KNOWLEDGE

Unit 1018 Know how to produce specialist decorative finishes 1

1 A rag-rolled effect can be produced using:
  a a lint-free rag
  b a chamois leather roller
  c a plastic bag
  d any of the above

2 To produce a stippled effect you would use:
  a a horsehair stippler
  b a mohair stippler
  c a hog-hair stippler
  d a mottler

3 A stencil made up of more than one part is called a:
  a positive stencil
  b negative stencil
  c multi-plate stencil
  d tie

4 Why do you need to clean stipple brushes after use?
  a to keep their shape
  b to prolong their life span
  c to avoid damage
  d all of the above

5 What does the term 'creep' mean?
  a paint lifting from a stencil
  b paint spreading underneath a stencil
  c not enough paint applied to a stencil
  d none of the above

6 Where should stencils start from when applied to walls?
  a anywhere you want
  b from a corner of a room
  c from a window wall
  d from the centre of the focal point

7 Why is it important to have a ground coat when applying decorative effects?
  a to keep the colour right
  b to enhance the effect
  c to help cover the substrate
  d it's not important

8 What is the main reason for stippling surfaces after applying glaze?
  a to remove brush marks
  b to add effect
  c to see the ground coat
  d none of the above

9 If you were using a drag brush, what would you be doing?
  a painting a ceiling
  b producing straight-grained patterns
  c removing paint
  d stencilling

10 What type of brush is best suited to applying ground/base coats?
  a standard paint brush
  b flogging brush
  c badger-hair softener
  d graining brush

Glossary of key terms

Access – entrance, a way in

Advocacy – actively supporting or arguing for

Alkaline – having a pH greater than 7 (an acid has a pH of less than 7)

Bitumen – also known as pitch or tar, bitumen is a black sticky substance that turns into a liquid when it is heated. It is used on flat roofs to provide a waterproof seal

Bituminous paints – coatings used to protect both steelwork and timber from moisture and corrosive atmospheres, usually used on roof work. They are also known as 'coal tar' and are highly water resistant, therefore applied on rainwater pipes and guttering, railings, storage tanks, concrete posts, fencing, roofs and also used on car and caravan vehicle chassis work

Carded scaffolder – someone who holds a recognised certificate showing competence in scaffold erection

Circumference – the perimeter of a circle, the distance all the way around the outside

Combustibles – substances that burn or can be burnt

Combustion – burning or catching fire

Concertina fold – a series of small folds that can be easily unfolded during the paper hanging process

Contamination – when harmful chemicals or substances pollute something (e.g. water)

Corroded – destroyed or damaged by chemical reaction

Corrosive – a substance that can damage things it comes into contact with (e.g. material, skin)

Crawling board – a board or platform (placed on roof joists), which spreads the weight of the worker, allowing the work to be carried out safely

Datum point – Any fixed reference point at a known height, from which calculations or measurements can be taken

Decanting – pouring liquid from one container to another (that is, from the stock pot into the work pot)

Decorator's crutch – a rolled-up length of wallpaper or a piece of wood used to support a concertina fold

Dermatitis – a skin condition where the affected area is red, itchy and sore

Driers – are a special blend of chemicals that can be added to paints to speed up their drying time. Driers can be added to both oil and alkyd paints and varnishes. They can also be added to old coatings that have been stored away and lost their usual drying times due to age

Drop match – a wallpaper pattern that is repeated, but with a space between matches, as recommended by the manufacturers

Durable – long-lasting

Egress – exit, a way out

Employee – the worker

Employer – the person or company you work for

Enforcing authorities – organisations or people who have the authority to enforce certain laws or Acts, as well as providing guidance or advice

Estimate – to assess something, such as a job to be done, and to state a likely price for it

Fall-arrest system – this means that in the event of a slip or fall, the worker will only fall a few feet at most

Fax – short for facsimile, which is a kind of photocopy that can be sent by dialling a phone number on a fax machine

Feathered edge – when you apply filler to a defect and then abrade it out to make the filler blend in flush with the surface, and therefore look flat and smooth

Felt – a bitumen-based waterproof membrane

Firring pieces – tapered strips of timber

First fixing – refers to work that is carried out before the plastering of a new structure

Flammable – something that is easily lit and burns rapidly

Flush – when one surface is level and even with another surface

Focal point – a place where your eyes will tend to look

Forensics – a branch of science that looks at how things happen

Gauging – measuring the amount of each of the components required to complete the mortar using a specific ratio, such as 1:4

Glycerine – is a liquid chemical material diluted with water, which can be added to acrylic paints to extend their working time. This allows the decorator more time to finish a task

Hazardous – something or a situation that is dangerous or unsafe

Health surveillance – where a company will assess the risks of tasks that are to be done and see if these tasks will create risks to health

Humidity – dampness or moisture in the air

Hydraulic – powered by a liquid, e.g. oil

Hypotenuse – the longest side of a right-angled triangle

In proportion – the correct size in relation to something else

Induction – a formal introduction you will receive when you start any new job, where you will be shown around, shown where the toilets and canteen etc. are, and told what to do if there is a fire

Inspector – someone who is appointed or employed to inspect/examine something in order to judge its quality or compliance with any laws

Inverted – tipped and turned upside down

Key – how the surface should be prepared to receive coatings. This means that you 'scratch' the surface so that coatings can adhere to them. By 'keying' you have made it possible for the new coating in the system to grip the surface and therefore not flake off at a later date and cause defects

Kinetic lifting – a way of lifting objects that reduces the risk of injury to the lifter

Lanyard – a rope that is used to support a weight

Legislation – a law or set of laws passed by Parliament, often called an Act

Leptospirosis – an infectious disease that affects humans and animals. The human form is commonly called Weil's disease. The disease can cause fever, muscle pain and jaundice. In severe cases it can affect the liver and kidneys. Leptospirosis is a germ that is spread by the urine of the infected person. It can often be caught from contaminated soil or water that has been urinated on

Lint – tiny, fuzzy fibres of material

Load-bearing – something that carries a load such as a wall that supports the structure above

Non-proprietary – applied to previously coated surfaces

Obligation – something you have a duty or a responsibility to do

Omission – something that has not been done or has been missed out

Opacity – the degree to which a substance is opaque, or see-through

Open joints – gaps in timber structures

Penalty clause – a condition written into the contract that states the work must be completed to the required quality by a certain date. If the job over-runs, the contractor will not be paid the full amount for each day the job runs over

Permeable – allowing things to pass through it

Perpendicular – at right angles to

Pitch – the angle or slope of the roof

Pneumatic – powered by compressed air

Porous – a surface that contains tiny holes through which liquids and gasses can pass

PPE – personal protective equipment, such as gloves, a safety harness or goggles

Proactive – acting in advance, before something happens (such as an accident)

Proprietary – applied to new bare surfaces

Prosecution – accusing someone of committing a crime, which usually results in the accused being taken to court and, if found guilty, being punished

PVC – polyvinyl chloride (a tough plastic)

Radius – the distance from the centre of a circle to its outside edge

Ratio – one value divided by the other

RCD – residual current device, a device that will shut the power down on a piece of electrical equipment if it detects a change in the current, thus preventing electrocution

Reactive – acting after something happens, in response to it

Regularised joists – joists that are all the same depth

Relief material – a material with a pattern that stands out from the background

Rendering – stone or brickwork coated with plaster

Resin (also known as sap) – a very sticky substance that comes from trees/timber and becomes very hard when exposed to the air

Risk assessment – this means measuring the dangers of an activity against the likelihood of accidents taking place

Rust – a red or yellowish-brown coating of iron oxide

Saponification – a chemical reaction that makes soap and so foams up as a result

Scoring – cutting the paper in an arching method. This is where you drag a scraper through the paper in long curved strokes. This makes the wetting-in process and water penetration easier, helps soak the paper quickly and makes the wallpaper quicker to remove by avoiding lots of small strips of paper coming off

Scumble – a decorative effect material, a semi-transparent coating containing pigment and linseed oil

Second fixing – the joinery work carried out after the plastering of a new structure

Shelf life – how long something will remain fit for its purpose

Significant figure – a prescribed decimal place that determines the amount of rounding off to be done

Skinning – formation of a skin on the product when the top layer dries out

Slate – is a natural stone composed of clay or volcanic ash that can be machined into sheets and used to cover a roof

Spot primed – the application of primer (base coat) to small areas of metal, timber or plaster to seal them. On metals this prevents rust or corrosion from returning

Stiles – the side pieces of a stepladder into which the steps are set

Stock rotation – moving older materials to the front of a shelf to make sure that these are used first.

Straight match – a wallpaper design that is repeated horizontally across the paper

Subcontractors – workers who have been hired by the main contractor to carry out works, usually specialist works, e.g. a general builder may hire a plumber as a subcontractor as none of their staff can do plumbing work

Substructure – all of the structure below ground and up to and including the damp proof course (DPC)

Superstructure – the main building above the ground

Supplier – a company that supplies goods, materials or services

Symptom – a sign of illness or disease (e.g. difficulty breathing, a sore hand or a lump under the skin)

Tack rag – a small muslin cloth coated with an oil and sticky to the touch, used to remove dust and small debris from surfaces prior to painting

Thixotropic – the property of some gels of becoming liquid when stirred or shaken

Tie-rods – metal rods underneath the rungs of a ladder that give extra support to the rungs

Toxic – poisonous

Vibration white finger – a condition that can be caused by using vibrating machinery (usually for very long periods of time). The blood supply to the fingers is reduced which causes pain, tingling and sometimes spasms (shaking)

Volatile – a substance that is quick to evaporate (turn into a gas)

Yellowing – is a defect caused by age and occurs when white oil-based coatings have been used on surfaces and the surface receives little natural light

Index

Index

Index

1